Death is everywhere in these mountains.
It lurks behind every gust of wind.
It hides under every crack in the snow.
Dozens of people have died
here in the mountains of Asia.
Yet climbers keep coming back.
They come from around the world
to take on peaks such as K2 and Everest.

Climbers on Everest.

Climbing small mountains is hard enough.
You need strong ropes, special boots
and lots of courage.
But climbing the world's highest mountains
is even tougher.
The higher you go, the thinner the air gets.
By the time you reach 6,500 metres
your body can hardly work.
There is barely enough oxygen in the air
to keep you alive.

Most climbers carry small tanks of oxygen.
But these tanks don't hold much.
So parts of the climb
must be done on your own.
As your brain becomes starved of oxygen,
you may find yourself
getting dizzy and confused.
Your nose might start to bleed.
You may feel very sick.
This altitude sickness is no joke.
In 1993, a climber on K2 died from it.

Climbers have to use oxygen in the world's
highest mountains.

Others, too, have struggled in the thin air.
One was a well-known climber
who had worked his way
up many tall mountains.
In 1980, he led a group up Mount Everest.
At 9,700 metres, it is the highest peak
in the world.
The climb was a success.
But it wasn't easy.
'I felt the lack of oxygen very much,'
he wrote.

His group also had to deal with bad weather.
That is a common problem on these mountains.
Temperatures often drop far below zero.
At one time it was 40 degrees below zero
inside the group's tent.

Sometimes things warm up a bit.
Even so, blizzards can move in quickly.
K2, the world's second highest mountain,
is famous for its storms.
They can last for days.
They can bury climbers
in several feet of snow.
In 1986, five people died
when they were trapped
in this kind of storm on K2.

Blizzards can move in quickly.

Each snowfall brings yet another hazard.
The weight of new snow
can cause an avalanche.

If you're caught in an avalanche on Everest
or one of the other big mountains,
there's not much you can do.
Just the thought
of being caught in an avalanche
makes climbers shiver with fear.

Scott Fischer, an American climber,
almost died that way.
In 1992, he and another climber
were climbing K2.
Suddenly, huge chunks of snow
crashed down on them.

Fischer was swept down the mountain.
The other climber, who was roped to him,
also began to fall.
Luckily, he managed to dig his ice axe
into the ground.
The two men came to a stop
at the edge of a 1,350-metre cliff.

Winds also pose a threat.
They may whip past at 100 miles per hour.
In 1995, British climber Alison Hargreaves
was killed by these winds.
Hargreaves was one of the best climbers
in the world.
She was the first woman ever
to reach the top of Mount Everest
alone and without an oxygen tank.
Only one other person
had ever done this before.

Alison Hargreaves.

On 13 August 1995, Hargreaves was on K2.
Winds were high.
Late that day, she and five other climbers
struggled to the top of the mountain.
They started back down again.
But the winds grew worse,
slowing the group's progress.

All night, fierce gusts swirled
around the mountain.
Hargreaves and the others kept going.
They tried to get back to their campsite.
But they never made it.
It seems that some time during the night,
they were swept off their feet.
They were blown to their deaths.
The body of Hargreaves was later found
in an icy nook not far from the camp.

Then there is the danger
of falling into a crevasse.
A crevasse is a narrow crack in the ice.
It may be hundreds of metres deep.
If there is a little fresh snow covering it,
you may not see it until it is too late.

Crevasses are dangerous for climbers.

Scott Fischer once fell into a crevasse.
He didn't fall far,
but his body became jammed in the crack.
He was locked between two walls of ice.
When another climber pulled him out,
Fischer found that his right arm
had been twisted out of its socket.

The list of dangers goes on and on.
Mountain climbers can be blinded
by the glare of sunlight
reflecting off the snow.
That happened to Peggy Luce.
The year was 1988.
Luce was trying to become
the second American woman ever
to reach the top of Mount Everest.

A climber on K2 protects her eyes.

Her goggles became foggy on the way up.
She took them off and kept climbing.
Luce made it to the top.
But as she came back down,
she had trouble seeing.
She realised she was suffering
from snow blindness.
People usually recover from this,
but it takes a while.

Luce knew she had to keep going.
She had to get out of the sun
and rest her eyes.
She stumbled on down the mountain.
At one point, she bent over
to see where she was putting her foot.
She lost her balance.
She began to roll down the mountain.

An ice axe can save your life.

Luckily, she dug her ice axe into the snow,
stopping her fall.
Luce made it to safety.
But the next day,
her eyes were swollen shut.

Sometimes climbers simply run out of energy.
Then they might collapse in the snow
and wait for death to come.
Perhaps that's what happened
to a German woman
who died on Mount Everest in the 1970s.
She was later found frozen
in a sitting position
with her head on her knees.
One climber said she had made it to the top
but she couldn't get down.

People will always risk their lives climbing the highest peaks.

Given all the hardships,
why do people choose this sport?
What makes them run such terrible risks?
Many climbers have tried to explain it.
One said he wanted
to conquer the highest peaks.
Another said that to succeed
when chances are limited
is what mountaineering is all about.
But perhaps Alison Hargreaves
explained it best.
Hargreaves knew that some day
she might die on a mountain.
But as she put it

One day as a tiger
is better than a thousand as a sheep.

She sank to her knees. Drum[...]
shoving her over so he could kneel w[...]

"Praying for Joan, right?"

She ignored him, the warmth of his arm, and [...]
him, something earthy. *Probably rotting topiar[...]*
thought uncharitably. She locked her fingers and prop[...]
her elbows on the rail

"This is uncomfortable," he said, shifting and bumping
her side. "What happened to the comfy cushions?"

"They were probably stolen by Joan's gargoyle." She
forced herself to think only of Joan's e-mail messages.

Suddenly, V. F. Drummond and his far-too tempting presence disappeared. She closed her eyes.

She heard a drumming, like boots on the march. The
sound magnified, then softened and melted away on the
draft that flirted with her hair.

Sandals—not boots. A shuffle, not a march.

"I can't pray," she said and tried to rise.

Vic Drummond settled a heavy hand on her shoulder. "So
don't pray. Just meditate."

The wooden kneeler bit into her knees, but it was his hand
that made meditation impossible. It was not meant to distract, just hold her in place, but it trifled with her insides. Her
musings became thoughts best left at the church door.

After a few moments of uneasy silence between them, she
relaxed. *These weird sensations are just hunger.* She longed
for a perfectly grilled burger and maybe a milkshake, extra
thick.

A languid feeling stole over her. She might liken it to
those moments just before waking fully in the early morning, when she wanted to get up and start the day, but her
body seemed content to remain where it was.

Her mind drifted. To last week. Last summer. Last year.

Rose tried to focus her thoughts on the plaque before her
with its sobering list of names. Images of Joan intruded.
Joan in all the stages of her life.

Joan. Joan. Joan.

Rose leaped to her feet and hurried down the nave. This

…ry to prevent her

… ran in front of the
… ing for a break in the
…eading into the heart of

…ed, but without any sarcasm
…ded as if he genuinely wanted

… image out of my head." They
darted b……… and walked up the road toward the
tea shop.

"My father had …ized photo in his office. It was of Joan. I've looked at that photograph for as long as I can remember and I guess that's why it suddenly popped into my head. Have you ever had a sore in your mouth? Your tongue keeps going to it?"

He nodded.

"Well, while I was trying to pray, I couldn't shake this image." She sketched the size of the photograph with her hands, estimating for him the dimensions. "I suppose at one time, it might have served as an example of my dad's work. Of how an enlargement, boldly done, oversized, could offer impact in a room. It was a black and white shot. She wore one of those frilly, Easter dresses." Rose felt a thickness in her throat. "She's clutching one of dad's cameras to her chest, the way other children clutch a beloved doll. The camera was far too large for such a small child."

"Were you jealous of her?" Vic asked.

Rose avoided Vic's gaze and the tea shop, walking past it to an arched stone bridge that crossed a broader section of the brook that wound its way out of sight and past the impossibly quaint cottages where V. F. Drummond camped.

"That's a complicated question," she finally said.

"So, give me a complicated answer."

Flower petals drifted slowly past her under the bridge. Rose pulled out her camera and caught the petals floating on the clear, rippling water.

"Joan wouldn't waste time taking photographs of flower petals. She's far more taken with the work of man. I think our skills are equal. We just choose to do different things with them."

"Does your father still have the picture of Joan in his office?"

"He did until he died six years ago. Joan hung it in her apartment." Drummond had exposed the sore in her mouth. How often had she probed that wound?

"I worked in our studio after school and on summer vacations. The photograph over his desk never changed. He bragged about her to customers and friends." Rose focused on the rough stone and caught the lichens in their dozens of earthy shades.

"After all," she said, trying to change her voice to a lighter tone. "Joan is a photojournalist. She's been to Paris. London."

"Got potted in the Pueblo."

Rose laughed despite herself. "I remember one client who came for her yearly family photos and was shocked to discover I was one of dad's daughters since he only talked about Joan."

"That must have hurt."

His words made her realize she'd revealed more than she'd intended. "Hey . . . enough of all that. I'm usually a very happy person."

"What you need is sustenance."

"Is that all you think about? Food."

"More often I think of sex."

"You and every other man I've ever met." She offered him a rueful smile. On the other side of the bridge lay a meadow with a footpath through it. She wondered where the path led.

Vic stepped in front of her.

"You know. That's a really annoying habit. Blocking my way."

"Then stop walking." He crossed his arms over his chest. "And I think you're jealous of your sister."

Rose did as he directed. Tourists flowed around them,

parting and closing ranks when past. It irked her that he'd come so close to the truth. "I'm jealous of Joan's freedom, that's all."

"In what way is she freer than you?"

Rose waved her hand at the Norman church. "She's here isn't she? I'm there. I'm always *there*. And that's not the spoil-sport whining."

Joan rarely set foot in their shop. She made promises to help out at the busy times, but usually found her side projects interfered.

Vic nodded. "Maybe you should talk to my friend Trevor. He's with the Warwickshire Constabulary. He might have a few suggestions. I'll ring him now if you like."

"Thank you, I'd really appreciate that."

He licked his thumb, and swiped at something on her cheek. "Your face is dirty," he said.

Great. Not good-looking and dirty, too.

8

ROSE SLATHERED MUSTARD ON her second ham sandwich and thought about making another trip to the library to check her e-mail. How many times a day could she check and not be labeled a lunatic?

Rose toyed with Joan's file folders. Just how long should she stay and look for her sister? What made sense?

She called Max. He hadn't heard from Joan, but promised to make a round of calls to Joan's best friends in case she'd contacted them.

Despite the home equity loan she'd need to take out to cover the phone bills, Rose methodically called each of Joan's English contacts, asking them the same question: When had they last seen or heard from Joan?

Seven of the priests who'd dealt with Joan on the book project had not seen her since the dates she'd photographed some particular treasure in their churches. Three had not met her and could not say when she'd been at their church.

Rose stared down at her cell phone. She keyed in the

quick dial for Joan's cell phone and hit the call button. As it had the dozens of times Rose had tried the number while home, the phone rang six times before Joan's voice mail directed Rose to leave a message and make it short, damn it. Rose slotted the phone onto her backpack.

She tapped a pencil on Joan's database, her mind blank. What else could she do? The longer she thought about it, the less she wanted to talk to Vic's cop friend.

Maybe she should just go home.

But her instincts told her Joan was not at the shore sitting in the sun as Vic had suggested or photographing gargoyles at some church not named on the list.

Rose wandered around the small cottage, looking for signs of its previous occupant. The economical use of space with its built-in armoire, its no-nonsense kitchen, yielded no evidence Joan had ever inhabited the space. Not even an errant blonde hair remained on the moss-green carpeting or the beige vinyl bathroom floor.

Rose stretched out on top of the white duvet and looked across at the other twin bed. Joan and she had shared a room until college had parted them. The carton of Joan's belongings sat where Rose had left it on the bed.

Vic's book drew her. She opened the carton and pulled out the book.

Do You Believe in Evil? was just as captivating the third time around. Joan never re-read books. What was the point if you knew the ending, she'd say?

But as Rose read Vic's book, she felt sure Joan *had* read *Do You Believe in Evil?* several times. Marginal notes were written in different colored ink on the same page, many pages were dog-eared at the top and bottom.

Rose's PDA chimed gently on the bedside table. It was three o'clock. She marked her place with a note Harry Watkins had taped to her door earlier. His bold, block letters shouted his disapproval of the invitation.

It came from Mary Garner who wanted to meet at four o'-clock at the library. This time, Rose intended to make full use of the computers.

After a shower, Rose put on the only dress she'd thought to·stuff into her suitcase. It was a long, swishy, yellow and she liked it because she could pack it in a ball and it came out looking pretty decent.

Remembering the perfection of Mary Garner's attire, however, sent Rose hunting for an iron.

At four, she presented herself at the library. Mary patted Rose's hand. "I want to apologize for Harry Watkins. He can be quite unreasonable."

"I'm surprised he delivered your note," Rose said with a laugh. "But don't let it trouble you."

"I would not want you to leave Marleton with the wrong impression. And I've been worrying about Joan all day."

The library was a model of efficiency and neatness. As was the librarian. Every hair of Mary Garner's head was perfect. Joan would admire such perfection. It only made Rose feel grubby and wrinkled despite the ironing frenzy.

"It's a week of worry for me," Rose said.

"You said no one has heard from her. Is that unusual?"

"Very. Joan and I have a daily e-mail correspondence. To be truthful, it's about the only way we communicate without arguing."

How to explain her anxiety without sounding nuts?

"Her e-mails got weird—and then they stopped. So, I just hopped a plane. Then when Harry Watkins said she'd gone . . . well, that was really odd since she'd written she meant to spend July on All Saints. So, I was really worried. I made some calls to her close friends, but no luck. They also tried to reach her by e-mail. None of them could get a response, either."

Mary Garner looked genuinely concerned.

"If not for the weird e-mails before they stopped all together I might not have become alarmed, but . . . well, I'm here, anyway."

"What's weird?" Mary asked.

Rose waited to answer as Mary checked out books for several of the villagers. When they were alone again, Rose said, "You'd have to know Joan to appreciate what I mean."

"She appeared to me to be very business-like. Came in every morning, worked on the computers. Research, it appeared to me. She often wanted to print out material, so we'd chat while she waited for her pages. A rather capable young woman in my estimation."

"Exactly. So you can understand my concern when her e-mail messages had become rambling, confused affairs, as if she were drunk while she typed them. She's usually succinct, to the point."

"And she left no word where she went?"

"None. On the side of there being nothing wrong is the fact that she paid for the month before leaving—she must expect to come back. On the side for concern are the e-mails and the fact that she left some important materials behind. Reference work for her book. Stuff she would never leave unprotected in an empty B-and-B for a day, let alone a week."

Rose watched Mary square up a pile of bookmarks. V. F. Drummond bookmarks, Rose saw with wry amusement.

"Did you save any of her messages? Can you give me an example?"

Rose looked Mary Garner in the eye and knew this sensible woman wouldn't laugh.

"Joan wrote that her head was filled with scary thoughts."

"Did she say what those thoughts were?"

"I asked her that exact thing, 'What kind of scary thoughts,' I asked. All I got back were two words . . . *evil thoughts*."

UNABLE TO WRITE, VIC motored over to Stratford. He recognized that work would not go well with his head full of Rose Early.

He admired the motives that brought her to England after her sister, though he thought it likely to end in embarrassment when Joan was found to be shagging some chap in London.

How different Rose was from Joan. He saw similarities

between the two women around the eyes and mouth, but Joan's cool, blonde exterior, her long lacquered fingernails and caustic tongue contrasted sharply with Rose's softness and more rounded figure.

Not that good-looking?

If he compared them to flowers, Rose was like her name, a lush Damask rose, heady with fragrance. With lots of hooked thorns standing at the ready to protect her.

As for Joan, she was more of a vine. One that appeared to be lovely at the outset, but one it was soon realized would take over the flower beds and choke out the competition.

Vic found Trevor in the bar of the Shakespeare Conference Center.

"Trev?" He clapped his friend on the shoulder. "I thought I'd find you idling about."

They traded a few insults then Vic plunged in. "Do you remember the young woman in my garden? Rose Early?"

"Joan's sister? To be truthful, I've done little else but think about her," Trevor said. "There's a bit of Irish in her face that appeals to me. If you give me her card, I could ring her."

Vic hid a sudden flash of annoyance with a shrug. "It seems Joan's gone missing. Probably off on holiday somewhere, but you can't convince Rose of that."

Vic was impressed with how casual his voice sounded while inside, his gut felt bunched and knotty.

Trev grinned. "So you suggested to the fair Rose that she might consult the police?"

Vic nodded. "I thought you'd be a better choice than PC Alden. He'd have to make an official report of it."

"Why don't I take our Rose to the Bell and suss out the situation?" Trev asked.

The Bell was known for its London menu and intimate atmosphere.

"I need a smoke," Vic said. The two men left the hotel. "Look, it's important I join the two of you."

"Don't you have writing to do?"

"Sure, I've writing to do. I always have writing to do, but it's not like thief-catching, I'm not on a rota."

Trevor went into another favorite diatribe about the low pay of public servants versus that of useless entertaining types like authors.

Vic interrupted him. "I'll pay for dinner. We useless, entertaining types can afford a bit of charity. And Rose knows me now. She'll be more comfortable sharing her story with me there."

"Will she?" Trevor lifted an eyebrow.

Vic ignored his friend's sarcastic tone. "She wants some help finding her sister. That's all."

"So you want me to ride up like a knight in shining armor and save the day? Without any official nonsense?"

Vic's annoyance ratcheted up another notch. He sent a smoke ring in Trevor's direction. "Sure. What time will you finish here?" he asked.

"I can leave now. The priests are all in the bar." The two men walked down Chapel Street to Vic's car.

"Have you told Rose you were shagging her sister yet?" Trevor asked.

Vic folded himself into his mini. "What point would that serve?"

"It just might prove a bit sticky for you later if you don't." Trevor leaned his palms on the car roof and frowned.

"No more than if Rose learns you were shagging the fair Joan as well."

9

WHEN THE DOOR TO her shop opened, Mrs. Bennett looked up from hemming Mrs. Edgar's mother-of-the-bride gown. "Ah, Father Nigel. How may I help you?"

"Mary Garner tells me Joan Early's sister is here. She was in the church with Vic Drummond this noon."

"And what do we care about that?" Mrs. Bennett continued the nearly invisible stitches that had earned her the reputation of the finest seamstress in Gloucestershire . . . and before that, in Nottinghamshire. And before that . . . well, who could remember that far back?

Father Nigel paced across the small shop. "This Rose Early was in the church."

"She's just a tourist visiting one of our historical treasures."

"We differ in opinion on this point, Mrs. Bennett."

"As we often do on others." She ignored the vicar's huffing and puffing as he strode back and forth in the shop. His steps were heavy, shaking the little glass shelves that displayed embroidered scarves and handkerchiefs.

"If you are truly alarmed, I suggest you send Donald to speak to her."

"Donald! You must be mad."

Mrs. Bennett's needle fell still. "Is that not his role as curate? And I shall put your outburst down to a touch of indigestion. Take an anti-acid tablet when you get back to the vicarage."

"Forgive me. I think, that is, I didn't mean anything by it, Mrs. Bennett, but surely not Donald. You know how he feels about Drummond. What if Drummond's with her when Donald calls?"

Mrs. Bennett snipped off the tail end of a piece of thread. "Then Donald will have a chance to practice patience. And forbearance."

ROSE HEARD A KNOCK on her cottage door. She stumbled from the bed, still half asleep, and tripped over her sneakers. The clock read seven o'clock. Her stomach growled. Dinner. She'd missed dinner.

When she jerked open the door, she almost mewed her disappointment when instead of the annoying Vic Drummond, she saw a young man in a black cassock.

"Good day, Miss. I'm Donald Lawry, curate of All Saints. I've come about your sister." Or that's what Rose assumed he'd said. His accent was thick, his delivery rapid.

"Mary Garner said you thought she might be missing and I've come to offer my help, if I may," the curate finished.

Rose led him to a patio table she shared with the next cottage down. She shook the priest's hand. "Thank you for coming."

The young man, as tall as Vic Drummond, had a handsome, patrician face. For a moment, Rose rued the misfortune of all the young ladies of the village who might sigh over this blond, blue-eyed man, then remembered that Anglican priests could marry. She almost smiled thinking this young man blew V. F. Drummond right off the map in the "good-looking" department.

"Oomaelpyou?" Donald asked.

"I beg your pardon?" She realized she'd been studying his sculpted lips rather than concentrating on his words.

The spoke more slowly. "How may I help you?"

This time, Rose understood. "I really don't think you can. I'm not even sure what I need."

"Why don't we start with what brought you here?"

Rose found herself staring at his mouth again, straining to interpret his words. She wished for subtitles.

"My sister came here to work on a book on church art, which I'm sure you know." Rose gave Father Donald the same summary of her reasons for her dash to England that she'd given to Vic and Mary Garner, although with the priest, she put more emphasis on her guilty feelings. "Joan asked me to come over about ten days ago. I'm ashamed that I just shot back a snappy answer that some of us had *real* work to do. I'm ashamed of that answer now."

Father Donald placed his hand over hers. "We all have sins of omission as well as sins of commission."

Rose nodded, but felt no better for his words. "I should have come right away." The curate pressed her hand. "I think something happened to her."

Father Donald frowned and said something that sounded like, "Such as?"

Before she could answer, she saw a tiny lime-green car turn in the Rose and Thistle's driveway. She thought of clown cars from the circus. How many would emerge she wondered as the car headed for her cottage. Just two, she saw as it drew to a halt.

Rose and her guest got to their feet.

"Donald," Vic said, back in his icy gardener mode.

"I'm Detective Inspector Trevor Harrison," said the man Rose was embarrassed to see was the one she'd dubbed Shirt-and-Tie.

Her anxiety kicked up a notch. This time he was not just a stranger in a garden; he represented officialdom and a change in her search for Joan from simple to complicated.

"May I stay?" Donald asked, pulling out a chair beside her. "I might be able to offer—"

"Sit. Sit." Harrison jabbed a finger around the circle at each seat.

"Try not to be so cheerful," Vic said to his friend. He placed a hand over Rose's, squeezing. Somehow it offered more comfort than the curate's had. "I asked Trevor to hop on his white charger and rescue the fair maiden."

Donald bristled. For the first time, he spoke very slowly and very clearly. "I do not think this a time for levity, young man."

Rose wondered at the hostility between the men. And Vic Drummond had to be in his forties to the priest's twenties.

"Let's sheath our swords, shall we? Rose?" Trevor asked.

For the fourth time, Rose detailed her concerns for her sister. "Aren't you going to write any of this down?" she asked the detective.

"Not I. Although Vic didn't want to involve PC Alden, he's the proper person at the moment to start inquires. I'll take you to the station and introduce you. Perhaps we can have dinner at the Bell afterward."

Father Donald jumped to his feet. "There's nothing to bother the police about here, Miss Early. Surely, your sister is—"

"Why don't we let Rose decide if we should bother the coppers?" Vic said, putting his feet on the chair the priest had vacated, making it impossible for the man to retake his seat.

Donald looked from Vic to Trevor. "I think it's a bit premature to call in the police. We don't want to embarrass Rose's sister."

Or so Rose thought he'd said, his last words coming out in an impatient, garbled rush.

"I'm sure Rosie hasn't buckets of cash to stay here indefinitely," Vic said. He yawned and stretched.

"Nevertheless." The curate took a deep breath. "I believe

you're making too much of this. Indeed, I could look for the woman and Rose could go home. We can ring each other daily."

Vic put his hands behind his head and slumped down on his spine, eyes closed.

Rose opened her mouth, but Trevor held up his hand for silence.

"It never hurts to get these things out at the first possible moment," the detective said.

Rose watched the priest's cheeks flush. He leaned toward her. His breath smelled of mint and something else. Gin was the only name she could put to it.

"If money is a concern, you would be better served—"

"Praying for Joan's return?" Vic said.

The curate jerked upright, but he kept his gaze on Rose and directed his words to her. "Belief can accomplish much."

"Stop it, both of you. I can pray *and* talk to the police," Rose said. "Why don't the two of you debate the point while Trevor and I visit PC Alden."

She ran into the cottage to get her keys and bag. When she returned, Vic sat in the backseat of her rented Rover. The priest walked down the stone drive, his cassock swinging about his legs.

"You really should lock your car doors," Trevor said as he settled next to her in the front seat. "You never know when some miscreant will break in."

Vic ignored him with a giant yawn.

"Why were you so crabby to the priest?" Rose asked Vic.

Trevor Harrison answered when Vic just shrugged. "Father Donald was supposed to have paid a call on Vic's Aunt Alice the day she died. He stopped off at the pub instead and when he finally made his visit—"

"Alice was dead," Vic interrupted, leaning forward, his attitude transformed from laid-back to angry in an instant. "If he'd paid his call when he should have, he might have fetched the paramedics."

"Why was Donald seeing your aunt?"

"He wanted her to organize the church fete. She used to do it every year, before she left the church. Maybe he thought it would bring her back into the fold."

Trevor Harrison's cell phone chirped. He swore and plucked it off his belt.

"I'll be leaving you with PC Alden; I've got to get back to Stratford," Trevor said when he finished the call. "A touch of Islamophobia has reared its ugly head, and I've got soothing-over duty. I'm sorry we'll not be having that dinner, though."

Rose ignored Vic Drummond's grin. "Perhaps another time," she said.

THE MARLETON STATION WAS a two-story utilitarian building housing a sergeant and four constables. Vic installed Rose on a wooden bench in the public area until PC Alden called them into his office.

PC Alden, a rangy man with dark eyes and a harassed air, typed Joan's information into his computer with a rapid-fire two-finger typing technique.

Vic thought Rose looked wilted after they were dismissed by the officer. A stolen bicycle now commanded his attention. They returned to the Rose and Thistle.

"Dinner at the Bell?" Vic asked.

"I need a bed, not dinner," Rose said, pinching the bridge of her nose.

"Mine's empty," Vic said before he could stop himself. He felt the heat of his remark. Or it made him feel hot. Rose looked steamed, but the kind that ended in having one's balls kicked.

"Let me rephrase that," he said. "I have an empty bed, and if you'd like to rest, I could look over that research muck your sister left while you do."

Her look of aggression tempered to amusement. "Maybe a fresh eye would help. But we'll do it at my kitchen table."

The kitchen table will suit me fine. Then we can try the carpeting, if the old man is up to it.

He'd never been in Joan's cottage and its stark modern interior was cold and cheerless, devoid of personal items or comfort. He frowned. "Did you cross the pond with only that rucksack?"

She smiled as she dropped the pack dangerously close to his toes. "No. I have a suitcase."

She left him in the tiny kitchen, closing a door behind her. He busied himself by plugging in the kettle. She returned with a cardboard carton.

She plunked it on the table and drew out the contents: the camera lens she'd shown him in the pub, folders, pamphlets, and his book.

"That's it."

"You're shaking," he said as he took *Do You Believe in Evil?* from her hand.

"I guess I need that nap."

"What you *need* is a fry-up."

"What I'm *having* is a nap." She headed for the bedroom.

He riffled the pages of his book as he watched her go. When the bedroom door closed, he leaned on the breakfast bar and read.

He paused now and then to think about Joan Early's margin notes. He began to sweat. He remembered discussing these notes with Joan. In bed. Why hadn't he told Rose how well he'd known Joan? "Because you're a shit, Drummond," he answered himself.

And maybe a coward.

He lost himself in the book.

The shrill scream of the kettle brought him back to reality. He hadn't filled the kettle and he found he'd taken a seat in Rose's sitting room, in an armchair covered in an uncomfortable tweedy fabric. How long had he been reading?

Rose looked rested as she poured the boiling water over a tea bag. She brought him the mug and sat on a footstool by his knee.

"Did you find anything interesting?" she asked.

He read the anxiety in her eyes. He wondered if he'd spoken any of his thoughts aloud. "Not really, I suppose I'm just guilty of self-absorption." He carefully closed the book. "Might I borrow this?"

"Help yourself. I read it through last night, including the notes. Maybe you'll be able to find something I missed, some clue that will tell me where Joan went."

"Damn it. Do you know how long it took me to write this book? And you read it in one night?"

"I'm a fast reader and I'd read it before."

"You're to savor the words, notice the turn of phrase."

"Notice the priest's eyes change from blue to brown on page seventy-three?"

He took a large gulp of tea to tame his tongue, burned his mouth, and swore.

"Don't like your tea?"

"It's so weak an octogenarian nun would scorn it."

She leaned forward and took the mug. Her fingers skimmed along his. "Sorry. I should have realized you were preoccupied and warned you it was hot."

"It's my own fault, mate." He liked the feel of her fingers on his. "Did you enjoy the story, at least?"

A few butterflies burst into flight in his gut. What did he care if she liked the book? It led best-seller lists for weeks.

"I'd have edited out half the profanity."

His butterflies relaxed.

"And the far-fetched stuff."

The butterflies became wasps. He snatched the mug from her hand and pretended nonchalance. "If you took out the far-fetched bits, you wouldn't have any scary bits. And that's what they pay me for."

"I wasn't talking about the scary stuff. I meant the love-at-first-sight stuff."

His wasps morphed back to butterflies. "Don't you believe in love at first sight?"

"Nope. Sorry." She stared down into her mug of instant coffee.

"Been stung?"

Her fingers caressed the mug and he had a thought that he was sure originated in his lap not his brain.

"I've had a few ups and downs."

"Tell me."

"Not a chance."

"Then tell me about Joan. Did she believe in love-at-first-sight?"

10

ROSE EXAMINED VIC DRUMMOND. He looked at home, book in his lap. A thoroughly English gentleman in a thoroughly English parlor, if one ignored his rumpled wrappings.

She felt a bit giddy in the stomach thinking about what was under those wrappings. Or maybe she was just hungry—needed a fry-up, as Vic said. Extra crispy fried chicken. Or chicken wings, hot as Hades.

No. What she needed, she admitted, wasn't food. Watching the changing expressions on Vic's face as he had read, his concentration total, had convinced her of that.

Rose sighed. "Joan was a hedonist. She believed in lust at first sight, second, third sight. She swore she'd never been in love. You're her type. I can't believe she didn't make a play for you while you were signing her book."

She watched color fill his cheeks. It was charming and gave him the appearance of a boy caught in a misdeed by his third grade teacher.

"Joan did not try it when I signed her book. How about another cuppa?"

"Sure."

He followed her around the counter to stand far too close behind her as she filled the kettle. She gave him a sharp elbow to force him back a few paces. It only earned her a mischievous grin. He knew he was having an effect on her, and she decided he needed to be knocked down a peg, before she did something completely stupid and humiliating.

She put the kettle on and turned around. He was inches away. His height intimidated.

"Back to your book. I'd have cut the profanity, lost the love stuff, and also made the ending more definite."

"How?"

"Well, you left the reader wondering if the world was safe from evil."

"That was the point." He reached across the narrow kitchen and grasped a piece of her hair.

She jerked it out of his hand. "I like my stories with happy endings. I don't want to turn off the light and find I can't sleep because some evil killer is lurking outside. Or might be."

He caged her at the counter. His lips were an inch from hers. "If you couldn't sleep, I accomplished my purpose."

He kissed her.

It was a quick, impersonal peck on the lips. Then he was hunting through the cabinets, muttering that he needed a proper tea pot. She tried to suck some air back into her lungs and almost coughed with the effort. How could a nothing kiss deplete all the oxygen in a room?

"Take a lesson," he said, lifting the whistling kettle. "Warm the pot." He swirled some water around in the bottom of a chubby brown teapot he'd plucked from the cupboard. "Empty, then measure your tea. I like two of English Breakfast and . . . two more of English Breakfast."

She watched him put four scoops of loose tea into the pot. "Where'd you find that stuff?"

He tapped a canister she thought held sugar.

"Pour in the water. And make sure it has come to a good boil." He clapped the lid on the pot. "Now let it steep."

"Until it's mud."

"Near enough."

"I'll stick to coffee."

He took the one step separating them and although she leaned away, he managed to skim his lips across hers. "I like the taste of coffee, too."

The air swirled out of the room again. "I can't breathe."

"Good." He slid his arms around her waist and settled his lips on hers.

This time the kiss lacked the speed of the first or the temptation of the second. She flattened her hands on his chest. "You're playing a role. Continental playboy, maybe?"

"Continental playboy?"

He backed off and she sucked some air back into her lungs.

"I've never been called Continental. Thick, thieving, lazy, but never Continental. Sounds like something my grandmother called my granddad."

He poured the ink-black tea into his mug. "Will you spend the evening with me, Rose Early?" he asked.

"Doing what?" she asked suspiciously.

"Acting Continental." He wagged his eyebrows.

She thought of an evening with him. Sparring with words. Kissing. Bouncing ideas about Joan past him.

Joan. "I can't go anywhere with Joan missing out there somewhere."

"Don't wring your hands." He captured hers between his palms. "We'll eat, then really search this place. Maybe she left something you and old Harry missed."

"Okay. But—"

"But what?"

"You have to promise you won't kiss me again."

He feigned a loud groan. "I promise."

"Okay. Dinner and searching."

"I'll fetch a few supplies."

He paused in the doorway. The setting sun framed his long, lean body.

"Oh. One thing, Rose."

"Yes?"

"A famous author once said, 'I write fiction. I lie for a living.' Keep that in mind."

11

NIGEL LOOKED UP FROM his papers. "I really don't have time for this now, Donald. I have my sermon to polish."

Donald smacked a fist on the desk, making the pens and pencils jump. "She's gone to the police."

"Alden's a simpleton."

"*Detective Inspector* Harrison is not."

"Harrison will not look into the matter. Now pull yourself together."

"Pull myself together?" The curate shot to his feet and began to pace. "How can you just sit there? Aren't you concerned even the least by this woman's presence?"

"You cannot allow your emotions to run away with you."

"I feel ill."

Nigel sighed. "Spent too much time in the King's Head?"

"I am not drunk, damn it."

"Lower your voice," Father Nigel ordered. "And control yourself. If you can't, take yourself off."

"All right. That's just what I'll do."

Donald flung out of the office, slamming the heavy oak door behind him.

Nigel almost went after him, but thought better of it. Instead, he went to the phone and punched in a number.

"We've a spot of bother. I think your confidence in our young friend was misplaced. He's feeling rather panicky. Definitely been sucking down the gin. What do you suggest?"

He listened for a moment. "London? Of course. I should have thought of it myself. As ever, your advice is invaluable. Really much ado about nothing. And this sister, the one at the Rose and Thistle?"

He ran a line through several words in his sermon as he listened.

"Let the matter rest? That's what I thought, too, now Donald's spoken to her. Great minds, and all that."

"I'M BEST AT BREAKFAST," Vic said.

A fry-up, Rose discovered, was not the desired burger. It was pretty much a full English breakfast served up at home. She watched as Vic fried eggs, bacon and sausages, tomatoes, mushrooms, and to her horror, bread which he browned in the bacon and sausage grease.

It was, however, delicious. And sitting across from Vic Drummond added greatly to the pleasure. He didn't just cook, he told stories.

"I was a bit of a tearaway. Stole anything not nailed down, broke windows, drove Aunt Alice mad. But she set me straight and it's due to her I'm where I am today."

"Sit still," she said when Vic tried to wash the dishes.

Instead, he took up a cloth and helped her dry.

"She really took care of herself, old Alice did. Walked everywhere. Wouldn't have a car though I tried to give her one."

"Not that clown car of yours? No wonder she refused."

"Clown car?" He looked puzzled.

"Never mind. I'm sorry I interrupted you. Your aunt?"

"Alice." He rubbed at an imaginary spot on a plate. "She ate well, did Alice. Didn't smoke or drink except the odd glass of wine now and then. I have to say I was in shock when they called and said she was dead. The autopsy showed no sign of heart disease, either."

"Sixty-one is far too young to die."

"And last night—"

"Last night?" Rose prompted.

He hesitated. "Never mind." He puffed on and then polished the plate. "Why don't I start searching for clues? I'm feeling rather Inspector Morse right now."

He tucked the dish towel into her back pocket, deliberately copping a feel, Rose thought, but before she could chastise him, he had bounded up the stairs to the second floor.

VIC LOOKED UNDER THE spare bed and pulled out every dresser drawer and checked their backs and sides. He had no idea what he was looking for.

A clever cupboard had been fitted into the space over the stairwell. It held spare linens. He tugged them out and tossed them on the floor. Doing so revealed the cabinet to be deeper than he'd expected. It extended to the cottage's outer wall, filling the dead space that formed the ceiling over the stairwell.

He climbed into the cabinet and contemplated the space that disappeared into gloom. As his eyes adjusted, he saw something between the rafters. Far back. Out of reach.

"Very tempting," Rose said by his feet.

"I think I've found something," Vic said. He'd written enough horrific ends to characters who injudiciously probed dark spaces to feel a bit hesitant to go any farther.

But with Rose watching, he had no choice. He forced himself to crawl forward, to put his hand into the dark recess between the rafters. *Paper*. Probably shelf liner, but he pulled it out anyway. It was a red folder.

"What are you doing?" Rose asked, tugging on the leg of his trousers as he backed up.

"I'm scaring the shit from myself." He felt more than a tinge of pleasure when Rose's face lit up as he dropped the folder at her feet. He jumped down and dusted off his knees and hands.

"Why scared?" she asked, plucking the folder from the rug.

"You've read my book."

"Ah, yes. Didn't rats devour Tony's fingers when he—"

"I don't need to relive that, thank you."

Rose perched on the top step and shuffled the folder's contents. A deep swell of disappointment took the place of her anticipation.

"I don't get it," she said. "It's just more of the same, photos and so on." She thrust the folder into Vic's arms and flopped on the bed.

He sat next to her and examined the folder. "If she separated these from the others and hid them, they must have some significance."

She covered her face with a pillow. She couldn't bear to have him see her cry.

"No wallowing," he said and drew the pillow away.

He stretched at her side. She wanted his comfort. And feared anything else he might offer.

She propped her palms against his chest when he leaned over her. "No kissing," she whispered. "You promised."

But her hands didn't cooperate with the holding-him-off idea. Instead, she pulled on his sweater.

He licked her throat.

She shivered. He licked her again. Slowly. She moaned aloud. He ran his tongue down her throat to the V of her shirt.

She slid her hands into his hair and closed her eyes while long-forgotten sensations surged through her body.

He nuzzled the skin on the rise of her breast. In moments, her nipple was between his teeth. The sensation was exquisite.

"Lie with me." His breath was warm against her breast.

"Oh, Lord. What am I doing?" Rose shoved Vic aside and pulled her shirt and bra back into place.

"You were making us both happy," he said, combing her hair aside.

"Maybe for a few minutes. But tomorrow—"

"Let tomorrow take care of itself."

She shook her head and slid from his embrace. She picked up the folder and headed down the stairs to the kitchen.

He joined her. "Are you one of those repressed Americans?"

"Repressed!" She slapped his chest with the folder, then saw his grin. "Oh, shut up. Let's sort whatever's in here with the other junk. Maybe we can figure out what Joan was up to before she left town."

Her hands, usually surgeon steady when holding a camera, shook a little as she scooped up crumpled sheets of paper and shoved them in his direction.

"Only if you agree to one more kiss," he said.

Her temperature roared into fever range. "One."

He put his hand behind her head and leaned down. She kissed him. She touched her mouth to his, then slid her tongue across his lips, savored the taste of his mouth. Her pulse throbbed against her throat. She could not breathe. Or think.

She broke it off.

"Brilliant," he whispered.

12

"LOOK." VIC HANDED HER a set of official looking documents. "Joan must have borrowed these from the diocese. They have Archdeacon Keeling's stamp on them. Maybe we should nip round to Stratford tomorrow and offer to return them. The man must be at this useless bugger of a convention Trevor's policing."

"What good will that do?"

"We don't actually have to take the documents or return them, just pump the chap for information. It's worth a try."

"You just don't want to sort papers. Did Joan eat anything other than cream teas?" Rose tossed a receipt aside.

"I don't want to sort paper. I want to make love to you."

"Don't go there again, please," she said. Whatever was simmering between them threatened to boil over. She knew it from the exaggerated way they avoided touching hands as they passed photographs back and forth.

And how they touched when it was completely unnecessary. Toes. A knee.

She'd need to change her underwear if things didn't cool down soon. "I can't concentrate when you look at me like that, either. Don't you have a wife or girlfriend you could call?"

"My wife is at my villa in Spain, spending my royalties as fast as I earn them and my girlfriends are . . . well, I don't have one at this moment."

Rose needed an antacid. Her stomach felt as if she'd swallowed a hot charcoal briquette. "So, you have a wife?"

"Had. We're divorced. I also have two sons. Ian is twelve and Phillip is fifteen. They're with their mum for the summer hols."

Cancel the antacid order. "How do your sons feel about having such a famous dad?"

"Ambivalent. They're spoiled rotten. Spend most of their time with their hands out, whining for something. I'm a lousy dad. I was a lousy husband. So when I propose, think twice."

She laughed.

"What a nice sound." He drew her into his arms, across the scattered photos and papers, across his lap. "My invitation to share a bed still stands. Preferably yours, if the sheets are clean. Mine probably aren't."

His words were light, but his chest rose and fell against her breast too quickly for casual intent.

She lay in silence, listening to the sound of his breathing, her body stiff with indecision.

He ran his hand down her arm and linked his fingers with hers. And drew them to his erection. A jolt ran from her belly to her groin. Neither of them drew a breath as he shifted her fingers in a slow caress of his penis.

Rose slipped her hand away, slid from his grip, and headed straight for the cottage door. It took all of her self-control to throw it open and stand aside.

"You have to go, Vic," she called. "I can't do this. Not now."
Or not yet.

Vic looked disappointed though he said nothing, just gave

a shrug. She didn't need an Oxford scholar to point out that he wanted her. And if he pushed—even an inch—she'd be stripping him out of his jeans, discovering the answer to boxers or briefs.

He came close and skimmed his fingertips across her cheek to her lips. "Tomorrow, Rose," he said softly. "The archdeacon. Don't forget." He didn't look back as he climbed into his car.

She headed to the bedroom and threw open the windows to watch him go. The darkness swallowed him but she could hear the crunch of his tires on the stones. Then that sound, too, disappeared.

A face, like a disembodied Cheshire Cat's, appeared before her. She swallowed a shriek.

"You're as immoral as your sister," Harry Watkins said.

"I beg your pardon?" Rose drew back from the window sill.

"You heard me. I'll have no lewd behavior in my place. This is a family place. I told your sister the same. Have another man in, I said, and you're out. Moaning and groaning. It isn't decent and I won't have it."

Watkins faded into the shadows as the Cheshire Cat had, and Rose was left wondering how the man, whose cottage was on the opposite end of the complex, knew what went on in Joan's bedroom.

No ORGAN MUSIC FILLED the church for the midnight service. No doors stood open to welcome casual attendees. The worshipers moved silently down the aisle and took their seats. They filled only one pew. A row of monks filed down the side aisles as well, but the worshipers were oblivious to their presence. Their ghostly garb was felted wool, leather sandals, and rope belts. They gathered in the choir stalls where centuries before they'd worshipped at regular intervals around the clock. Now, they came only in protest of the living who sat in the front pew, who listened to the living in mockery of all the monks believed.

* * *

VIC TOSSED AND TURNED, unable to sleep. He gave it up, pulled on the clothes he'd dropped in a heap on the floor, and headed for his laptop. Before he opened it, he lit a cigarette. He sat in the dark and smoked.

He could still feel Rose's fingers on him. When he'd first come home, he'd thought of masturbating, but changed his mind. There was something in his state of arousal that couldn't, or wouldn't, be satisfied with such a sterile completion.

He wanted to fuck Rose Early until she screamed.

No. That was wrong . . . make love to her until she cried. Or fainted. He drummed his fingertips on the closed laptop.

Make love was too tame for what he wanted. Fuck too coarse.

He was a wordsmith without a word.

When he'd drawn her hand to his lap, he'd done it to break the incredible tension that stood between them, perhaps even get the slap he deserved. Instead, she'd obliged him.

"Shit that's cold. Obliged," he said to the silent parlor. "She fucking obliged me."

He ground out the cigarette and opened his laptop. "Get to work," he told himself.

A ball of food, the sum total of the fried meat and bread he'd eaten, clogged his throat. His fingers clenched into fists.

There, with the teasing, blinking cursor, were the words he'd deleted the night before. Every fucking word.

THERE WERE NO LIGHTS in Rose Early's cottage. Her windows were closed. Vic ran his fingers along the panes, pushing gently. Latched.

He stood back and counted to ten. If the windows had been open as they'd been when he'd left, he'd have climbed over the sill and into her bed.

Silently, he stepped close to the blank windows and peered in. Rose lay curled on her side, one hand beneath her cheek. She'd removed only her jeans.

He rapped his knuckles on the glass.

She started awake and screamed.

He watched recognition cross her face. She grabbed her jeans and pulled them on.

"Are you crazy?" she asked when she opened the window.

He climbed over the sill. "Barking mad."

They stared at each other. The room was filled with her scent. Something clean and innocent like early violets.

"Things are a bit dicey back at Alice's. Thought I'd spend the night here."

She shook her head, but before she could put her refusal into words, he caught her in his arms and pulled her close. She was warm and soft from sleep.

"No sex, Rosie. Just a bed. That's all I need."

But not what I want.

She drew to arm's length and tugged on his hand. He followed her through the cottage to the stairs and up.

The duvets and pillows were still scattered across the floor. Holding his hand, she pitched the bedding onto the mattress and then let him go.

"Rosie—"

She silenced him with a finger to her lips. "Harry said he'll kick me out if there's any lewd behavior going on here."

"Lewd? That's quaint."

"I can't get tossed, not yet."

"Right. No lewd behavior."

Then she was gone. Her bare feet made no sound on the thin carpeting. He stretched out on the bed, fully clothed, and pulled the duvet up.

But it was not lewd behavior that tormented him as he stared up at the ceiling, unable to sleep. And it wasn't thoughts of Rose alone downstairs, her white knickers gleaming in the moonlight against her long, tanned legs.

No, a blinking cursor tormented him.

Words he couldn't delete.

And an itch down the center of his chest. A thin red scratch. A mark that hadn't been there when he'd gone to bed.

13

ROSE HAD DIFFICULTY SWALLOWING her disappointment when instead of a warm, tempting Vic in the upstairs bed, she found only a neatly folded duvet. But as she packed her camera into her backpack, she heard his car rattle into the stone drive, on time for their visit to the archdeacon.

Ten minutes into the journey, at the first rotary, she was no longer smiling. She gritted her teeth and said a rapid string of prayers. He whizzed along the tiny country lanes, narrowly missing other cars, skimmed hedgerows. Every turn felt backwards. From her position on the left side of the car, she gripped an imaginary steering wheel and jammed her foot repeatedly on a non-existent brake.

"Who taught you to drive, the Marquis de Sade?" she asked.

"Taught myself."

"Great." Her stomach slid back and forth as her bottom did likewise on the seat. "Is Harry Watkins the stalker type?" she asked to distract herself from imminent death.

Marleton Village had nothing on Stratford-Upon-Avon for tourists and she hoped they all lived through Vic's visit.

"Wouldn't think so. Just overly concerned with everyone's morals."

"Do you think he was . . . well . . . watching me through the window?"

Vic took his eyes off the road. "I would."

Rose gripped the door handle when the car jerked to a stop in front of a statue of a jester, the perfect parking place for a clown car. He turned off the engine and draped an arm across her shoulders.

"I'm serious. Is Harry dangerous?" she asked.

"For my money, he's harmless."

"He implied that Joan had more than one man overnight. Moaning and groaning, he said."

Vic stared at her a moment, then looked away, tapping his keys on the steering wheel, lost in thought. "Keep your doors locked, just in case," he finally said.

"He came to my window."

"Keep them locked as well, then."

"Yeah," she said, unable to prevent a smile. "You never know who might come in."

ARCHDEACON KEELING, ALONG WITH many of the other church dignitaries at the symposium, was registered at the Shakespeare Conference Center. He came immediately to the page Vic sent through the desk.

Rose found Vic had a charming side. And he used it on the archdeacon when they'd claimed a table in the bar. The man was a fit seventy or so, with fluffy white hair and ruddy cheeks.

"We apologize for interrupting your busy schedule," Vic said.

"I am busy, but your message piqued my interest. You said this was about our book?"

"Yes. May I introduce Joan Early's sister, Rose? She flew over from the States because Joan has not answered her e-mail messages or phone calls in a number of days. Rose is concerned something might have happened to her."

"Hmmm." The archdeacon steepled his fingertips and propped his chin on them. "I'm rather disturbed to hear this. She has a rather significant sum of diocesan money. Her advance was rather handsome."

Rose's stomach did a nose-dive.

"Have you heard from her?" Vic asked.

A waiter came to take their order. Rose opted for a ginger ale in hopes it would settle her stomach.

"I had an e-mail from Joan on the twentieth. I remember because it was my birthday. She asked me if there were more pictures of All Saints Church in our archives. I wrote her back that I'm sure she had them all."

"Did she say why she wanted the photos? We have an assortment of rather important looking documents and photos she left at her bed-and-breakfast," Vic asked.

"No, I just had the one message from her. In truth, I was worried about the older photographs as they're irreplaceable. I chastised my secretary quite strongly for not making copies. Perhaps you could return them?"

"Of course. So you haven't heard from Joan since the twentieth?"

"That's correct. I asked her numerous times in several follow-up e-mails when we might have a return of the materials. At the same time I informed her our publisher is rather anxious that the book is overdue. She never responded."

"Overdue?" Rose asked.

"By more than a month," the archdeacon said.

An acid bubble shot straight up into her throat.

Vic covered her hand. "Rose thinks something has happened to her sister. It's very distressing not to know where she is."

The archdeacon turned a kind gaze on Rose. "Surely she'll turn up. I shall pray you were precipitous in coming so far from home. Perhaps she has found a church not on your list?" he asked with a skeptical note one heard from teachers when they suggested your missing homework might be in your locker, but when they really believed you'd not done it in the first place.

What was it the archdeacon did not believe? That Joan would turn up or that Joan was photographing churches?

"Thank you," was all Rose could manage. The ginger ale had done nothing for her insides. "How much did you give Joan as an advance?"

"Oh, dear. I'm not sure I should divulge that information. Let us just say it was a sizeable amount. Quite adequate she said for her expenses while she did her research. For her car, her plane fare, lodging, and so forth."

Rose knew the cost of the Rose and Thistle. And of rental cars. Plane tickets. She had written the checks for the plane tickets, herself, from the Early Studio accounts.

"The book is terribly important to the diocese. If it's as lovely as her other work, we just know it will be a best-seller."

"Oh?" Vic said.

"Yes, all profits from your sister's book will go directly to church restoration efforts in the diocese."

When the archdeacon returned to his symposium, she gave Vic a wan smile.

"Good Lord, I hope Joan isn't on a cruise with a pocket full of church cash. It might be a bit tough repaying that advance if she doesn't show up. Can I get something stronger?"

"Whiskey?"

"Anything."

Had the "handsome" advance something to do with Joan's disappearance? Had Joan spent the money and run away from the consequences?

When Vic placed a thick tumbler of whiskey into Rose's hand, she couldn't remember asking for it.

"Wakey, wakey, Rosie. And don't worry about the advance. I'm sure it's a pittance."

A pittance. Rose gulped the whiskey. It burned down her throat.

"Maybe compared to your advances. You don't understand. Joan's advances are never enough. She owns half my studio and draws half the profits. What there are of them. Mostly she charges her expenses, swearing her next advance will cover them. If she's done something . . . never mind. I'm being a bitch."

He took her empty glass. "I think we should visit every church on her list. Talk to every priest or their secretary."

"No." Rose stood up. The room tilted. The whiskey had gone straight to her head. "I'm going home. I'm sure you were right the first time. She's probably on the coast somewhere sitting in the sun." She turned away and bumped her hip on a chair. "I'm such a fool."

Vic helped her into the car and had the good sense to keep his lip zipped on the ride back to Marleton.

He drew the car up in front of her cottage.

"Thank you for your help. I'm going to work on changing my plane ticket. With my luck, the penalty will wipe out the rest of my checking account."

Her insides were knotted with a confused sense of sorrow and loss.

When she tried to climb out, he stopped her with a hand on her thigh. "Don't go," he said.

14

VIC'S HAND WAS VERY warm. Too warm. Too tempting. And so was he in an irritating, British lout kind of way.

"Why shouldn't I go?" Rose asked.

He did not respond, just drummed his fingertips on the steering wheel.

She denied the flush of pleasure under the whiskey haze that he wanted her to stay. Her brain fumbled through responses to sexual invitations.

Acceptances. Refusals. Acceptances.

"Look, Rose, someone has to finish that book," he said.

His words wiped out her budding lust.

He came around to her side and took her arm.

Did he think her unable to walk straight? Or get out of a car that could double as a lima bean can?

She felt confused, shaky. Disappointed.

She wrenched from his grip. "Finish her book? You're drunk."

"I'm not and why not? You're a photographer, aren't you?" His expectant, happy look morphed to a worried frown. "One picture's the same as another, isn't it?"

"Is one horror novel the same as another?"

"Ouch."

She plopped into the garden chair and propped her elbows on the glass table top. "And even if I could take the photographs needed—"

"She took dozens, surely there are only a few more necessary. Perhaps she was finished."

She quelled his enthusiasm with a glare. "As I was saying, even if I took the photographs needed, there's the text to go along with them."

"I could do that for you."

Rose shook her head. "You are drunk. Or maybe I am."

Vic pulled his chair close. Their knees bumped beneath the tiny table. "I'm a writer, Rosie. The deadline is sacrosanct to me . . . or getting close to the deadline is sacrosanct."

Rose could not help smiling. "But Joan has already missed her deadline."

"As far as I can see, you have two choices. One, go home and possibly repay that advance. Two, finish the book. The first is costly, the second free. If Joan pops up and objects to what you've done with the bloody book, she can make changes. Later, if an editor wants them."

"Changes?"

"Sure. Replace this photo with that. Strike the odd word here and there. That kind of change."

Rose evaded Vic's intent gaze. She even drew her knees away so she had no contact with him. There was something about him, especially when they touched, that disconnected her brain from her mouth.

"I've never been involved in one of her projects. I'd have no idea where to begin."

"That's easy, mate. We examine her other books."

"I suppose."

"And I know the book business head to toe. I'll call

Joan's editor, have a chat, and you can take it from there. Just think of all the church treasures you'll be saving. You'll be brilliant."

ROSE SAT CROSS-LEGGED ON the cool white duvet in the center of a pool of Joan's contact sheets. Even without notes, there was an undeniable order to the work. The moods of Joan's photographs might be different, but the theme, the celebration of sacred art, remained the same.

"What's the verdict?" Vic asked, stretching out on the opposite bed and lighting a cigarette.

"Smoking is bad for your health. And mine." Rose plucked the cigarette from his mouth and took it to the bathroom where she dropped it into the toilet.

"Not that verdict," he said when she returned.

Rose sighed. He'd lit another cigarette while she'd been flushing the other. "You are a pain in the ass. Smoke outside, would you?"

He propped his head on one hand and squinted through the smoke wafting off the cigarette clamped in the corner of his mouth.

She turned her back, feigning interest in the All Saints altar screen.

He put out his cigarette by flicking it through her open bedroom window, then returned to his lazy posture. "The verdict?"

"I don't know." She slued around and straightened some of the photos. "I'm so surprised by the spirituality of her work."

"Not much on religion, was she?"

"No. My mother drove my father insane with her flits from belief to belief. I remember one month when my mother decided we should be Quakers. That was the proverbial straw to dad. He'd been a photojournalist in Vietnam and was far from pacifist. The phase didn't last long, but that's when my parents separated. Joan and I were Lutheran,

Buddhist, Quaker and Baptist before we were eighteen. I ended up spiritual without being of any particular faith, and Joan ended up like my father . . . without God."

"I understand. My father worshipped at his betting shop and my mum was very High Church. Never the twain shall meet. I learned to nick a few quid to cover my father's losses and to pray for the opportunity with my mum."

Rose laughed.

"I like that sound."

Rose swallowed the laughter. There was a look in his eyes that said he was going to cross the narrow distance between the beds and kiss her. She grabbed several contact sheets and clutched them to her chest.

Of course she had also thought he wanted her to stay in Marleton because . . . he wanted her.

She bit her lip. "I shouldn't be laughing with Joan missing. That is. If something is wrong—"

"If something was wrong she wouldn't be charging her mobile."

Rose frowned. "You're right. She's charging her phone. If she wasn't, I'd get that annoying message, 'Customer Unavailable.' "

"See. Nothing wrong."

"I'll kill her. She deliberately fostered anxiety. I came three thousand miles because of that anxiety."

"There's still the book to be done."

"Yes. The book."

"I'll write the text for you." He changed the subject and the atmosphere with a few words. He took up a sheet of photographs, matched it to the neat database Joan kept for her work. "The majesty of St. Stephen's," he said, "is found in its glorious rib vaulting that reaches like arms toward heaven." He flipped the photograph to Rose.

He had captured the exact nature of Joan's photograph.

"You pick the photos and I'll supply the captions. The larger text can come after we see what's what here." He reached across the separation between the beds and plucked a photo, one yellow with age, from the pile. A receipt fluttered to the floor.

"What's this? More cream teas?" Rose asked, picking up the small, blue paper. "This looks like a receipt for a costume. Now why would Joan need a costume?"

"Fancy dress ball?"

"She didn't mention one." Rose unfolded the receipt. "There's something on the back."

Vic took the receipt and turned it over. "Club 7734. Never heard of it."

"We're letting our attention wander." Rose tucked the scrap of paper into the receipt folder.

Vic leered. "My attention never wanders. It's firmly on your—"

Rose clapped a hand over his mouth. At the same time, he encircled her waist and pulled her down onto his bed. Joan's database crackled beneath them.

His mouth was warm. Hungry. She, too, was starved. The kiss became a feast of tongues. And tastes. The taste of the skin of his throat, then his chest, beneath his soft sweater.

"What happened here?" she whispered. She drew her fingertip parallel to an angry red scratch. It pointed straight to a narrow line of hair that disappeared into the waistband of his khakis.

He covered her hand, but did not slide it over his groin as he had the last time they'd kissed. Instead, he moved her hand to the duvet, rolled off the bed, and away.

"Just a scratch. Have to stop sleeping in the flower beds. And I'd better get back to the roses. Getting leggy, you know."

The image conjured in Rose's mind, of Vic naked, lying among the lush foliage of the gardens, made her insides quiver.

Then he was gone. Not just from her bedroom, but from the cottage. And not through the door, over the sill.

His car coughed once before spitting stones from its rear tires and heading down the drive.

She spent the next hour pretending to sort Joan's photographs. In reality, her mind was firmly on Vic and why a simple question about a scratch had sent him away so precipitously.

She packed Joan's materials into the cardboard carton and restored it behind the buckets and brooms. Some instinct compelled her to secrete the red folder between the rafters over the stairwell.

The costume receipt she tucked into her purse, unable to remember where she'd found it. Without the scattered photos and papers, the cottage seemed barren of human habitation.

Forlorn.

She pulled out her cell phone and touched a key to light the screen. Joan's phone number still remained in the window. Impulsively, Rose hit the call button. Even held in her lap, Rose could hear the repeated rings, the voice mail message.

She called Joan three more times, less because she expected an answer, but to hear her sister's voice. As long as she heard that voice, there was nothing wrong.

Rose put the phone to her ear. "You better get your ass back to Marleton, Joan. I'm going to finish your book. And we both know your opinion of my work. So if you care . . . call . . . come back." Her throat tightened. "I'm keeping the royalties, too."

VIC USED AN INTERNET search engine to find Club 7734. It was a private club in a posh part of London. Not far from his own flat in Caldor Mews. Members only.

"Shit," he muttered and rang a friend who had influence and power. "Oliver? Vic here. No, I am not going to fill in on your cricket team next month." He fumbled for an excuse to avoid the hapless team Oliver captained each summer in a charity event that attracted wealthy, but octogenarian patrons. "I broke my wrist. Oh, I have a secretary to put down the words. She's brilliant. Lovely girl. No, I won't introduce you."

He had a brainstorm. It was almost as lovely as the secretary he'd conjured in his mind. She typed in nothing but lace knickers . . . rather like Rose's.

"Ah. Perhaps I could persuade her to have supper with you, if you can do me a favor." He listened to Oliver go on about cricket for a few minutes before interrupting him. "Listen, Oliver, there's a club I'd like to visit. Club 7734."

Vic held the telephone away from his ear as his friend shouted something about bloody morons who expected the moon.

"That's why I called you. I know you can get in anywhere, anytime . . . What's the secretary look like?" Vic grinned. "An Irish colleen with a dreadful American accent. Now can you get me in the club? The website says no entry without a card."

Oliver promised to hunt up a membership card in exchange for supper with Vic's secretary. Vic felt only a slight twinge of guilt. What woman wouldn't enjoy dinner with one of Britain's most popular and eligible MPs?

Would Rose lie for him?

He rubbed his perfectly functioning wrist. The dinner was a non-starter. Then he brightened. He'd make it up to Oliver by doubling his donation to the charity cricket match.

Next, Vic researched Joan's costume shop. It, too, was in London. Its website was not unlike the one for Stitches here in Marleton, and Stitches was known to produce a costume or two for church pageants. Now why had Joan gone to London, rather than patronize the local seamstress?

He leaned back in his chair and pondered the kind of fancy dress Joan might order. Leather corset and a whip, he imagined. Not the sort of thing the very proper Mrs. Bennett might stitch up.

MRS. BENNETT LICKED THE end of the thread and drew it through her fingertips. The muted shades of blue and red were difficult to match, so were the lovely beiges and tans needed for the crusaders' faces. Shadows were important. It was the shadows that brought the characters to life in a tapestry.

Several tourists, here for the morning service, asked questions about her work. She dutifully answered them and suggested they purchase the textile book in the gift shop. But they were not very interested and wandered on to look at the twisted, tortured faces of the martyrs on the altar screen.

Mrs. Bennett hummed and stitched until Father Nigel appeared, then she discretely packed up her little sewing basket, folded her stool, and took a seat near the rear of the participants. Few attended on a daily basis anymore.

Harry Watkins and his mother who played the organ did, of course. Jack Carey, their venerable tour guide. Three tourists. The obligatory servers and of course, lovely Father Donald.

Nigel conducted a pathetic service, stumbling through the liturgy like a student who has not quite done his lessons and must recite before the class. She let her attention wander. The church was lovely. It held all the vestiges of medieval times. She could almost smell the unwashed at worship.

Mrs. Bennett remained in place when the service ended. She caught Father Donald's gaze. She smiled and beckoned him near. He came down the aisle with long, agitated strides, his color high.

"Mrs. Bennett." He shook her hand as the first wave of tourists surged past them on the way to the gift shop and the first tour.

"Father. Have you been to London?"

His already flushed skin colored as bright at the scarlet thread on one of the tapestry lilies.

"Please. Not here."

"Why not here, luv? You've nothing to be ashamed of. A little recreation is good for the soul, is it not?"

"Nigel says so."

"And Nigel knows best."

VIC WROTE UNTIL NOONwhen Oliver's call interrupted him. The pass to the club would arrive by private messenger at

Vic's London flat after five that evening. He was entitled to invite one guest.

Although Vic's mind was on an evening wining and dining Rose at Club 7734, he wrote for another hour.

His fingers ached when he finally called a halt. "Wish I had broken my bloody wrist," he muttered. He rubbed his chest. The scratch that had embarrassed him and sent him from Rose's comfy bedroom looked infected. He dabbed it with antiseptic before heading back to the Rose and Thistle.

Rose's bedroom window was latched, so he circled around to the front door and eased it open. She sat perched on a stool at the breakfast bar. She held a lens like a jeweler's loupe and moved it from picture to picture on the contact sheets, writing in a small notebook he'd noticed when she'd been calling her American partner, Max. Her pink shirt did not reach her low-slung jeans. The bumps of her spine might be nice to count. His fingers itched.

"In or out," she said, but did not look up.

He stood behind her and stroked the bare skin between her shirt and jeans. He felt her muscles tense, but she didn't seem to mind until he slid his hands around to her stomach. She clamped her hands over his.

"Whoa, buddy." She shoved his hands away and indicated the loupe. "I picked this up in the village. You've a really nice photo shop here, by the way."

"Thank the tourists. We also have good wine, cheese, a library. We're rather civilized. We're going to Club 7734 tonight if you're game."

"No kidding! You are a marvel."

"My friend Oliver is. He's filthy rich, like me, and my MP. We often scratch each other's backs." He tried to scratch Rose's but she swiveled out of his reach. "I'd like to look over this club before we waste our money on costumes, though, so let's go."

* * *

ROSE INSISTED ON DRIVING them to London. Vic complained she drove like a snail. She silently chanted her driving mantra. *Keep left.*

She stopped twice to take photographs. Not of churches, but of cottages, fields, and stone walls. Vic waited patiently while she indulged herself.

"Come here," she called at one point "Stand by this stile. No," she tugged on his arm. "Lean. Think about your book. Worry about your deadline." He frowned and she took the shot. "Thanks, that was perfect."

She looked in the viewfinder again, not to take his picture, but just to indulge an inner need.

I'll title this English Wastrel on a Stile.

His baggy sweater, sleeves pushed up to his elbows, his wrinkled khakis, could not be improved upon. He turned his head. The sun lay across his cheekbones, rendering him timeless. Her finger and instincts reacted.

Back home in her studio, she would play with the color values, turn him into a nineteenth-century rake.

"Vic! I have the most incredible brainstorm for Joan's book. What if we took the old photos—Joan has releases for all of them—did a blending, make it appear as if the scene was aging on the page. I mean, isn't that what makes it all so beautiful? The patina of age? The muted colors of the tapestries, the fading of the banners, the martyrs?"

He smiled. "Brilliant."

But as they climbed into the car, her enthusiasm cooled. The idea was too radically different from Joan's plans, plans that had become more clear as Rose examined the work with closer attention.

"What's wrong?" Vic asked, taking the driver's seat.

"Oh, nothing."

"Qualms?"

"Are you a mind reader?" She returned his smile.

Of course he scorned his seatbelt, but she gripped hers as the road narrowed into a one lane path. The hedgerows threatened to scrape the car doors.

They stopped for a dozen sheep who were being led across the lane by a man who might have stepped from the nineteenth century, himself. She begged Vic's patience to photograph the scene.

"You're divorced," Vic said when the sheep had made it safely crossed the lane.

"Oh, yes. Doug was great. We just married too young—right out of college—and woke up one morning to find we had nothing in common except my friend Sarah." She gave him a wry grin.

"I also married young. Before fame and fortune. She developed a taste for the money and a distaste for the solitary chap who provided it."

THEY ADMIRED THE MAGNIFICENTGeorgian building that housed Club 7734.

"Are you sure this is it?" she asked.

He pointed to the discreet brass sign over a bell push with nothing more than the numbers 7734 to indicate they were in the correct place.

"But these look like houses, not clubs."

"Not anymore. No one can afford the upkeep and taxes on these places, today. Most likely these are offices for solicitors, physicians, and so forth."

No one answered their ring.

Vic poked the bell a few more times. "I'm sorry no one is about. I thought we might learn something about Joan without—"

"Putting on costumes? Making fools of ourselves?"

Vic nodded and headed for the corner pub. "I was having second thoughts about this adventure. Let's ask the barman at that pub when the club opens."

The barman at the St. George Arms smirked at Vic when he asked about the club.

"Don't open ever for the likes of you and me," the man said.

"Private is it?" Vic asked, as if he knew nothing of the club.

The man nodded. "Strange things go on there, we hear. Under investigation, or so rumors say. Wouldn't take the likes of her in there." The man indicated Rose with a blunt-tipped finger.

Rose sat at an outside table. The sun shone across her face, burnished her hair, shadowed her eyes.

"I was just asking for myself." Vic ordered a pint of beer and a lemonade for Rose.

The man leered and handed off the drinks.

"What did the bartender say?" she asked when he settled across from her.

Vic took a long drink from his glass. "He said the club's not for the likes of you and me, so maybe you should stay at my place instead."

"And that won't corrupt me?" Rose said.

Vic decided not to respond and start an argument. He hadn't meant anything nefarious. To the contrary, he was having second thoughts about taking Rose to a place dubbed strange by a man who was local and should know.

He sensed a stubbornness in his colleen that did not bode well for keeping her home by the hearth. "According to Oliver, most people go to Club 7734 in fancy dress as they don't want it getting about they frequent the place. If Joan wanted to be incognito, we might not have much luck tracking her down."

"No, it also means she probably went there. Why else would she buy a costume? And a pricey one at that?"

"Still, if the place is under investigation—"

"I think we should have theme costumes."

He frowned. "Theme?"

"Yes. You could be the Wizard of Oz, I could be Dorothy."

"I think you should wait at my flat—"

"Or maybe you could be the backend of a horse and I could be the front."

"Are you saying I'm an ass?" Then he grinned. "On second thought, imagine where my face would be in that costume."

Her cheeks flushed. Every freckle gleamed like cinnamon sprinkled on cream.

He finished his beer. "If you won't listen to reason, next stop, SewFun."

VIC PARKED IN FRONT of a Tudor building undergoing restoration. SewFun's windows displayed French maid costumes, whips, and scanty lingerie.

"This should be so fun."

"For whom?"

"Well . . . me. You will model a few costumes for me, won't you? After all, I've seen you in your knickers, so why be shy?"

"When? Where?" She remained on the curb, eyes wide.

"The other night. You shouldn't sleep in your clothes, damned uncomfortable."

She shrugged but tugged her pink T-shirt down to meet her jeans.

God Bless women's fashions. Lacy thongs and bare midriffs.

Inside, Rose wandered past the leather corsets and whips he'd imagined for Joan. He also saw racks of items that brought a blush even to his cheeks. He hustled over to Rose who was frowning over a tray of manacles.

"I doubt I'll find a costume in here. And I can't imagine this being to Joan's taste either," she said.

Vic blocked her view of clips and harnesses. "Yet, she did purchase a costume here."

Rose sighed and pulled the small, blue receipt from her back pocket. "Maybe we won't need to buy anything or go anywhere."

As if on cue, the shop girl dropped her tabloid and approached.

"We need some fancy dress," he said.

"We need to ask a few questions first," Rose said and poked an elbow in his ribs. "My sister bought a costume here. Can you tell what she bought from this?"

The girl, who was rather drably dressed in a loose sundress and cardigan sweater to match, scratched some of the pimples on her chin. "I sold this. A dominatrix set."

Bingo, Vic thought.

"Can you remember who bought it?" Rose asked. "It's really important."

"Yeah, I remember her. We don't sell too much custom stuff, except near Halloween. American, really crackin'. Said she was going to some posh club."

"Can you remember anything else?" Rose looked at him.

"Yeah, we like to match our costumes."

"Like Dorothy and the Wizard of Oz," Rose said.

The girl smirked. "More like Domination Dora and Passive Peter."

Vic watched a blush bloom on Rose's cheeks.

"Her companion was a fallen angel, which doesn't go with her, see?"

They dutifully nodded.

"I think she liked the props." The girl stroked a hand along a rack of domination accessories. "She said she intended to whip some answers out of him."

15

Vic sat in a low armchair covered in faded chintz in the back room of SewFun. The place smelled of dusty fabrics and old furniture. Although the front of the shop held eye-popping costumes for every taste—if one liked one's breasts, arse, and cheeks on display. Here, in the dressing area, he couldn't imagine buying a tea cozy from whomever had run up the rather grimy lace curtains.

He wondered who Joan's fallen angel was. Not himself and not Trevor. Or maybe Trevor. Vic wasn't sure if Trevor would opt for a night of debauchery with the fair Joan.

For the tenth time Vic glanced at his watch. If the shop couldn't come up with something pretty posh in the next few minutes, they'd need to search elsewhere. Time was flying.

"Vic?"

He looked up and gave a low whistle. "Search no more."

Rose remained half-hidden by the dressing room curtain, biting her lip. He lifted a hand and silently beckoned her near.

He didn't trust his voice. She floated within reach of his hand that lay on the armrest.

An ice princess, he thought. *And I'm going into meltdown.*

"Too . . . weird?" she asked.

There was nothing in the front of the shop to compare to this gown. Custom, the shop girl had promised.

We suit the man or woman.

He fluttered his fingers through the ribbony silver fabric that draped Rose from breast to mid-calf. She looked ravaged by wind and storm. His heart beat too quickly.

In a minute he'd be committing a crime.

There seemed to be nothing beneath the wispy shreds of cloth. He felt well suited, so well suited he might have a coronary.

He slid his fingertips between the slivers of icy silk and stroked the back of her knee. She made a sound in her throat. He urged her close with a small pressure. She nestled her other knee between his thighs for balance.

The warm pressure on his testicles spiraled arousal through his body. Was it deliberate? Or accidental?

"Do you like it?" she asked, her voice not much above a whisper. "I told her I didn't want anything too risqué." Her cheeks went pink.

Accidental.

He swallowed hard. "If the arctic had a king, you would be his queen."

"That doesn't sound so hot."

"On the contrary—it's very hot." He placed his palms on the back of her thighs and stroked his fingers up to her bum. A tidal wave of lust crashed into disappointment when he discovered her warm skin demurely covered with something that felt like a rather ordinary undergarment.

"A body suit," she said. "Flesh-colored."

"Damn." He cupped her buttocks and pulled her close, pressing his mouth to the sheer fabric on her stomach.

She threaded her fingers in his hair. "I'm not sure this is a good idea."

"If you can come up with a better one, I'm all ears. Until then . . ." He nuzzled her middle, separating the gauzy strips, finding the sleek undergarment. Her navel was a silky indentation. The undergarment suggested every luscious inch of her. He licked from her navel to the hand she slapped on her midriff to stop him.

"I don't own this costume."

With a groan, he set her aside. "Where's the shop girl?" he asked.

VIC TOOK ROSE TO his flat at Caldor Mews to wait for the club pass. Rose imagined everyone who lived in the elegant houses that lined the oasis of quiet made more than a pittance at whatever they did.

She felt self-conscious of her knock-off jeans and shirt as he pulled a key from under a pot of red geraniums and opened his front door.

Rose looked around. The entry was a schizophrenic mix of kids sports equipment and polished antiques.

As she dropped her backpack, a phone rang. She stepped into a high-ceilinged living room to give Vic privacy to speak with someone he called Ian. His younger son, she remembered.

Vic's living room revealed an expected addiction to books. She wandered about, read titles, was happy to see he was eclectic in his tastes. Tattered history books leaned against classics that rubbed shoulders with the latest in popular fiction.

She stood before his fireplace and tried to reconcile Vic's slapdash appearance with the man who'd furnished and decorated the room with such simple taste.

The walls were a dove gray, with glossy white paint on the mantle, bookshelves, and molding. The furniture, deep, comfortable sofas and chairs, was upholstered in a darker gray.

She skimmed her fingers on the only splotch of color in the room, yellow roses, and realized that Vic was like this living room, all shades of gray.

He was possibly immoral, possibly devious, and equally probably an honorable man. He had certainly been devoted to his aunt and sounded as if he cared greatly for his sons, she thought, as she eavesdropped on his side of the phone conversation.

Vic was being very parental, refusing to allow the boy an advance on his allowance for something Vic referred to as video rubbish. He sounded as authoritative as any other father might when dealing with a boy of twelve or so.

"Sorry," Vic said after he'd won the argument. "Ian tries it on every now and then. His mother always tells him to ring me as I'm the pot at the end of the rainbow. Ring the pot, she says."

Rose smiled and perched on the edge of the sofa.

"Do you see your children often?"

"They live with me during the school term and their mother on holidays."

"I suppose they go to some ritzy boarding school?"

"No, the humble one two streets over. I make up for my misspent youth by watching them like a hawk—something they take in stride." He grinned. "But we all enjoy a bit of time apart. Make yourself comfortable. I think I'd like a glass of wine."

Rose felt anything but comfortable. At his aunt's, Rose found the atmosphere cozy, homey. Here, she felt like an American tourist in a rich writer's apartment.

Vic returned with a black lacquered tray with a bottle of wine and two crystal glasses.

"Who did the flowers?" she asked.

"My man."

"Your man?" Rose took the proffered wine glass.

"Yes. I've slaves aplenty. Jasper is just one of them. Keep him in the dungeon when I'm not about."

Rose laughed.

"Actually, Jasper is a rather pretty young man who is madly in love with one of the footmen at Buckingham Palace."

"I'm impressed."

He laid his arm across the back of the sofa. "My only connection to royalty is through my butler."

"At least you have a butler."

"He butles very well, I've heard. I only know my clothes are clean when I open the drawers and there's always a fine wine about. Although it might be for the seduction of footmen not pretty ladies from King of Prussia." Vic leaned over and kissed her throat.

Rose stood up and went to one of the side chairs. "If you do that—"

"You'll end up seeing the cracks in my bedroom ceiling."

Rose now knew what was meant by a hot flash. Her entire body flushed to a boiling temperature. Perspiration broke on her skin.

The doorbell chimed.

"Our club pass, I presume. As you Americans say, 'It's party time.'" He raised his glass to her.

16

ROSE FELT NAKED IN the dress. It made her feel insubstantial and incredibly vulnerable. And hot. And breathless.

And each time she met Vic's eyes, she saw her arousal mirrored in his gaze.

Vic put a floor-length velvet cape over her shoulders. "This was my aunt's. For the symphony."

It was not the clown car waiting outside Vic's door, but a large, silver car with a roomy, leather-scented interior.

Her heart beat in time to the music Vic put in the stereo. His driving still terrified, but at least she was not two inches from the road.

Club 7734 still looked closed, although there were now real gas-fed flames in the brass lamps that flanked its walkway.

Vic wore black from head to toe. He had disdained all efforts by the shop clerk to put him in something "matching" her icy concoction. Instead, he'd insisted on contrast.

Although club guests must wear a special mask to designate them as such, members wore what suited them—mask, face paint, nothing.

As far as Rose was concerned, Vic was more masked tonight than if he'd donned one that covered him head to throat. His face was deathly white, his eyes lost in deep shadow and radiating streaks of black. In the gaslight, she saw blue throughout his spiked hair. The spikes went well with the ones on the heavy leather collar he wore about his neck.

The door clicked open. They entered a lofty entry, the floor checked with marble tiles of black and white. A massive flower arrangement sat on a mahogany table in the center of the lobby. The floral scent filled the space with a cloying, funereal atmosphere.

A man dressed in a pinstriped suit approached them.

"The undertaker," she whispered to Vic. "And we're the dead folks."

"Welcome." The man held out his hand, palm up. Vic placed the card that he'd gotten from his friend, Oliver, on the man's palm.

"The lady will need a mask." The gentleman opened a door concealed in the wood paneling and ushered them into a cloakroom.

Vic placed her cape on a hanger while their host handed her a mask from a rainbow assortment in a deep bowl. Hers was silver and covered only her eyes and nose while tying at the back of her head.

The host directed them to another door hidden in the wallpaper that opened to reveal a tiny elevator. As they descended in the lift, she wondered if she was dropping into hell.

Vic held her hand and took the lead when the elevator came to a halt. Flashing lights and pounding music assaulted them when the doors slid open. The silence and elegance of the entry above and in the elevator, made the club, itself, both a physical shock and a disappointment.

"Not much different from a New York City dance club," she shouted near Vic's ear as if she clubbed in the Big Apple every week.

"Or London, for that matter," he said. "Let's see if one of the barmen remembers Joan."

"If she wore this mask, we haven't a prayer," she returned. That thought led her to another. Who was Joan's fallen angel?"

They maneuvered, hand-in-hand, through the crush of dancers. As her senses adjusted to the club, she realized there were very few guest masks visible.

The three men and one woman who tended the bar in the huge chamber wore crisp white shirts and black trousers. They shook their heads as Vic questioned them. Rose could not hear what they or Vic said. She felt as if she had fallen into a television show in which only the actors were muted. She watched the dancers, instead.

The variety of clothing confused her. Some patrons wore business suits, and except for the macabre assortment of masks they wore to hide their identities, looked as if they'd stepped from the office. But they were in the minority. Most of the guests wore costumes Rose could only say belonged in the windows of SewFun. Or they wore not much at all.

She saw glimpses of breasts, paunches, bottoms in the strobing, pulsing lights. And lots of leather. It almost felt as if she were viewing the scene through her camera lens as her mask narrowed her vision and blocked the peripheral world.

"They have a privacy policy," Vic said in a brief lull in the thundering music, his lips near hers, his breath warm on her skin. "No questions. No answers."

"Shit," she muttered.

"Let's look around." With some effort, they negotiated their way from the dancing hall and into what looked like hell's waiting room.

This room was as black and dark as the first had been brilliant and pulsing. The music deafened although it was completely different in nature—slower, sultrier, almost hypnotic.

"I could have saved a ton of money," she shouted at Vic, "and just worn my underwear."

He leered and nodded as two women in just that waltzed by arm in arm.

Smoky candles on spikes gave barely enough illumination to navigate to the bar. As her eyes adjusted to the gloom, Rose realized this room's dance floor was ringed by large oval tables over which were red spotlights. From the center of each table sprouted a brass pole and a glittering naked woman to slither up and down it.

Yikes, pole dancers, she thought as Vic left the bar.

"Same answers, mate. Privacy policy and all that."

"I don't think this is my kind of place."

"Spoil sport," he quipped, but steered her along to yet a third room.

At the entrance, they passed two men wearing nothing but tiny leather briefs and equally tiny leather masks. Their skin was as white as Vic's, though their pallor looked natural. They wore fine silver chains connecting their pierced nipples to somewhere or something in their little pants. She giggled.

The men held hands and circled Vic, gesturing for him to follow, but he just grinned and pushed Rose along.

"This isn't very productive is it?" Rose asked as they moved from room to room, sometimes taking a flight of stairs down and sometimes up. She felt disoriented, lost in the maze of rooms. Every room battered the senses through sight and sound. Although she never finished any one drink, the combined sips made her lightheaded.

Their inquiries yielded nothing. Rose realized Vic was folding money into the palms of the bartenders as he asked his questions, but to no avail. Either the policy of privacy was not subject to bribery, or so many beautiful women dressed as a dominatrix that Joan hadn't made any impression. Nor had her fallen angel.

Vic hustled her down a hallway, past alcoves draped with curtains whose spangles gleamed in the strange lighting. She caught a glimpse of a cot-sized bed within one.

"No place for good girls," he said. "Come on."

She held on tight as he negotiated crowds, dancers, and groping hands to reach another bar. She wasn't sure if they'd been in the room before. They were blending together. Or was it the heavy layer of pot she realized hung in the air along with the incense?

VIC STOOD BEHIND ROSE at the bar in one of the endless rooms. They'd been here before. This was the room with the snake charmer theme.

An incipient headache hovered behind his eyes. He fought a war with himself. Half of him wanted to grab Rose and take her home. The other half of him wanted to come back another time—alone.

"Let's dance," she said.

"I don't dance."

"I'll teach you."

She put her hands on his hips. He felt the heat of her as he quested through the silvery ribbons for the woman beneath.

He found the nearly imperceptible edge of the undergarment that arched over her hip. She shivered when he slipped his fingers beneath the hem of the undergarment, stroked the silky skin where her hip and thigh met.

She enflamed him with every slow, rhythmic shift of her body on his. The music might be frenetic, but she danced, eyes closed, to her own rhythm, an old familiar one.

He wanted to feel that rhythm in bed, feel the slip and slide of her supple body on his bare skin.

She guided his caress much as he had done the day before with her. Her body was warm, furnace warm. He nipped her shoulder and suckled in imitation of what he wanted to do where his fingers stroked.

A man jostled him, swept Rose into a tight embrace, and danced away with her.

Vic felt the ebb and flow of dizziness as he watched her. Each undulation of her body shifted the ribbons across her breasts, her hips, buttocks, her thighs. He stared at the shadows of her body, the contours emphasized by the fabric that fell away over her breasts. Her nipples stood out taut against the sheer undergarment.

She belonged in another venue, not here. He wanted her on the lawn. In her tulip-yellow dress. He could pluck a daisy, put one in her navel, use one to stroke—"

"I'm stiff as a fucking pole," he said to one of the leather clad chaps who couldn't hear him over the pounding music.

The room tilted. Where was he? Why wasn't Rose helping him with his pole problem? He took a deep breath, but coughed from the thick smoke that swirled through the room. Smoke laced with the smell of incense, pot, and cigarettes.

In a moment of clarity, Vic realized the problem wasn't with his cock. In a chamber of thundering music, his silence about Joan resounded so loudly he felt it like a blow.

"Sorry, chaps, I have a confession to make." He ducked the leather clad twins.

No sylph in icicles swirled on the dance floor.

Rose was gone.

Frantically, he searched the crowd. He stumbled into the next room.

Rose stood in front of the bar. Alone. The flickering candles on nearby tables rendered her gown as transparent as the thinnest of ice. But in his mind's eye, she was standing in the garden, in a yellow dress, gathering daisies.

ROSE FOUND THE MURAL behind the bar like a mirror—hard to look away from. The figure painted there was not a man, though he had a man's muscular body. The thing's skin was burnished bronze with shadowy sinew, black and ropy on his thighs and arms. But it was the long, thick phallus between his thighs that drew the eyes. It ended in a glowing barb as if tipped with cinders from hell's flames.

The creature had the thick ears of a pig, a face twisted with evil intent. It was the perfect face for an All Saints gargoyle though the rest of it might offend the parishioners. Rose could almost smell the brimstone beneath the gargoyle's feet.

Vic dropped a hand on her shoulder.

"That will be hard to measure up to," she said.

"Sheath the claws."

"I think I'm drunk." *Or intoxicated by the forbidden nature of the place.* Her head ached as if she'd downed at least four glasses of wine. Had she? She could no longer remember.

"Let's go home," he said by her ear. He led her through a casino room. Lights at the tables spotlighted hands on black tablecloths, but kept the faces of players in shadow. Rose wished for her camera, to capture the hands in their disembodied play.

"We should have brought a picture of Joan." She wasn't sure if he heard her. Vic's eyes looked like black holes in his white face. For a moment, the room stretched away behind him, a kaleidoscope formed only of black and white.

Her head cleared when they left the casino room, pushing open a door with a light above it that said "Exit" in a variety of languages. Rose recognized the first room of the club with the elevator doors to the street level. The sudden contrast of bright lights to the secretive atmosphere of the gaming room made her stumble against Vic. She caught hold of his shirt.

The music changed to an eerie, sensual sound, something that made her think of pipes blown by Native Americans in the desert.

Or was it just in her head?

Thick smoke filled the air. One deep breath and her head spun. People no longer danced to the music here. They milled around, turning in the swirling lights, laughing. Ceiling spots revolved, throwing wreaths of light across the dancers, then swathing them in gloom.

The music pounded like an animal's heartbeat. The throb reached into her head and deep into her groin.

She leaned her head and hands on the wall and took deep breaths. Vic stood so close, she could feel his body heat. Even in this chamber of mingled perfumes, pot, and incense, she could smell him.

An undefined and undeniable Vic kind of scent.

She felt cocooned by the anonymity of her mask and his large form behind her. He cupped her breasts, pressed his hips to her buttocks. She shifted against him unable to ask for what she wanted. His response was immediate, cool air sweeping down her back in the wake of her zipper.

He tugged her zipper down past her buttocks, put his hands between her thighs, and opened her body suit.

She savored the heat of his fingertips, slipping and sliding along her most intimate places.

The music beat in her blood.

He withdrew his hands and she almost screamed in frustration. Then he planted his hands next to hers on the wall. Something probed between her thighs. A jolt of pleasure spun out from the heat of it.

The room shifted, throbbed. Something acrid filled her nostrils.

Vic's hands looked dark. Leathery. His fingers stretched, looked strong enough to crush her.

She tried to break away, but her body felt paralyzed. The blood pounded in her veins and rushed to the flesh rocking between her thighs.

Acid rose in Rose's throat as Vic's arms continued to transform. They desiccated down to the muscle fibers.

In her mind's eye she saw the figure in the bar mural and the barbed phallus now shifting and probing to enter her. She called out for him to stop, but only a croak came from her throat.

The room spun, the lights flashing more quickly, the bass throbbing more deeply, the pipes shrill. Vic's breath seared her skin as he dragged his tongue down her back.

"Stop," she managed again, louder this time, though scarcely above a hoarse whisper.

The metal-hot shaft whipped from between her thighs, like a snake darting away.

VIC TRIED TO ZIP Rose's costume while supporting her boneless body.

He shouted her name two more times and felt a tremor of

response. She shoved his hands. He released her, but remained ready to catch her if she fell.

She groped at her mask, tugging, gasping.

Damn the rules. He yanked her mask away. She stared past him. Sweat plastered her hair on her cheeks.

"Let me fasten you," he said. Rose ignored him. Or didn't hear. She stared past him, at the dancers who were in their own worlds, spinning, laughing, groping each other.

"Rose? Rose." He shook her. Hard. Her head flopped back and forth like a rag doll's.

Her eyes snapped to his face, mouth open in a small O.

"Turn around," he ordered her.

She obeyed.

He tugged her costume together and then paused. An inflamed, raw looking line ran from her nape to her buttocks.

Her thighs were a furnace hot when he drew the bodysuit together and pressed the edges of the clever fabric fastener together. Touching her only enflamed him further, but he ignored his baser urges and finished zipping her dress.

He clasped her shoulders and drew her back against him. "Sorry for shaking you, mate, but you scared me. Let's get out of here."

She stumbled along with him, a zombie, not speaking, or reacting as they rode the lift to the cloakroom. He swapped her mask for his aunt's cape.

Outside, in the cool night air, he held her against the car and let the wind blow the cobwebs and intoxication from his head.

There was no thought of going to his London flat. It was Marleton he needed. His aunt's cottage. A great breath of her flowers and the clean country air.

They stopped only once, at a level crossing. Nothing stirred in the surrounding countryside. It must be after three o'clock in the morning.

"Did you . . . did you?" Her voice was a breathy whisper nearly lost in the push of air from the passing train.

He tipped up her chin and examined her face. Her lips looked dry, her expression flat. "Did I what, mate?"

"Mate." She licked her lips and her tongue looked dry too.

"Mate? I think I might have been a touch forward of things, but no, we didn't mate, mate." What did she think had happened? "I may have put my hands where I shouldn't, but I can't be faulted for more."

She shivered and ducked her head. He lifted her chin again and touched her lips with his. No response.

"What's wrong, Rose?"

Her breath had a sulfurous quality to it. "You changed."

A horn blew. He drew back with reluctance and put the car in gear.

Marleton rushed toward them. Instead of heading for the Rose and Thistle, he turned into his lane and parked at a neighbor's garage where he kept his car.

Rose followed him up the lane, and across the plank bridge to Alice's cottage without demur. Inside, on an impulse, he asked her to turn around.

"I love this new cooperative you," he quipped, but she showed no sign she heard him. He tugged the zip down a few inches and saw the red line. "Sorry, it looks like this zip really irritated your skin."

She shrugged.

The cottage sitting room lay bathed in moonlight. He struck a match and lit a cigarette. At the sound, she whipped around and for the first time, he saw animation in her face.

"Vic?"

"Who else?"

"Maybe a gargoyle?"

"I guess that's my clue to wash off this paint."

He went into the cottage's miniature downstairs loo and dropped his shirt and collar on the floor. He scrubbed his face free of the itchy makeup, dunked his head under the faucet. When he looked at his face in the mirror, he tried to see what Rose had. All he saw was a rather ordinary man.

* * *

Rose shivered. The cottage didn't seem cold though. The chill felt inside her, deep inside, yet the flesh between her thighs throbbed with a sharply contrasting heat.

Her back itched.

Vic came to the doorway, rubbing his neck with a towel. "There's something I want to tell you."

He'd discarded his black shirt. Water ran down his chest. He looked intimidating in the moonlight, but driven by some impulse that felt centered in the throb between her thighs, she approached him and licked a drop from his chest.

He discarded his towel and thrust his hands into her hair. Another drop beckoned. She followed it to his nipple, sucked it to a hard point, then chased another drip down the center of his chest, across his belly, to where it disappeared into the waistband of his black trousers.

Vic's penis was a hard ridge against her palm. He wore no underwear.

His belly moved quickly in and out with the escalation of his breathing. The tiny cottage overflowed with the sound. It joined the rush of the wind outside, filled her ears, her head.

He groaned when she put her mouth on him. A vision floated into her mind, the mural in the bar, the barbed, swollen phallus of the gargoyle.

She opened her eyes. But it was just Vic. With a sigh, she stroked him, tasted the essence of him that beaded on the tip of his penis.

"Rose. Stop." He tugged her from her knees.

They stood there a moment, two feet apart. The moonlight washed the room to blacks and white, him to his shades of gray. Shadows hollowed his cheeks. "I'll call this one, Demon in a Country Cottage."

He tipped his head. "What are you talking about?"

She touched his lips with her fingertips. "I want to take your picture. While you're like this. Ready—"

He grabbed her, embraced her, lips hard against hers.

Then she was naked, her gown on the floor with his clothing furnishing a pillow for him. She climbed astride his hips and bent her head to his.

"I'll focus on this . . . and this," she said licking across his shoulder, up his throat. "And here." She touched her lips to his eyelids.

He murmured unintelligible words against her breast, stroking all the hot, slick surfaces of her. His tongue traced circles on her skin, teased her nipples to painful points.

She wanted something, but couldn't name it. He scrabbled in the mess of their clothes, drew out a condom and tore at the packet with his teeth.

"I'll do it," she said.

He growled like a feral beast and arched under her as she caressed the thin latex over him. "I need you inside me, Vic. Now. Right now."

He cupped her buttocks, rolled her over, and plunged into her.

He rocked her, pounded into her in a frantic wild rhythm, thrusting her along the floor, sliding on the polished wood and the sled of their clothing.

He drew back, lifted her hips, pushed into her and held still.

She watched him, suddenly outside herself, afraid he might metamorphose into the gargoyle of the club. The scratch on his chest pulled her eyes down—to where they joined.

But he was Vic. Just a man. His body went taut. He closed his eyes and groaned.

A clock nearby chimed four delicate notes.

Every nerve in her body screamed for completion. But whatever spell had come over her, that had made her lick his chest and tear his trousers open like a wild thing, was gone.

She could no more ask him to touch her, banish the frantic sensations between her thighs, than she could tell him of the hallucination she'd experienced in the club.

"Hey, mate," he said. "Not much in that for you, was there?" He kissed her and ran a hand from her breast to her knee.

She held her breath as his fingertips explored the contours of her stomach, breasts, and finally between her thighs.

His tongue jousted hers, stabbing into the heat of her mouth.

Her world narrowed as it did when she put her eye to the viewfinder of a camera. She could only focus on two places—those he laved with his tongue and those aroused by the slip and slide of his clever fingers.

Then it was done. A wrenching, almost painful explosion of sensation radiated from his hand to her chest in waves so tangible she thought she saw them ripple over her skin.

He looked down at her, shadows concealing his expression. "What the hell happened in the club?"

She shifted from his hold and dug in the pile of clothing for her costume. "I think I was a little stoned. Let's leave it at that."

"No." He jerked the dress from her hand and stood up. "Stop fucking with me and give me a straight answer. Whether you were stoned or not, you zombied out on me in a way that was almost . . . what happened? And you don't get this back until you give me an answer." He shook the costume at her.

"You changed."

"How?"

"The mural."

"I turned into a bloody gargoyle?" He threw back his head and laughed.

"Isn't this just dandy." She had no trouble snatching the costume from his fingers.

If she thought he looked intimidating naked and bathed in moonlight, he looked maniacal laughing and naked in the moonlight.

"What am I doing here?" She felt heat rise on her face and chest as she tried to regain some dignity in the ridiculous costume that would only fasten as far as her waist in the back. The discarded condom, the man standing naked with his hands on his hips must be some nightmare.

She threw open the door and ran down Vic's garden path

to the gate. She fumbled the latch open. The air was cold on her bare skin, heightening her awareness she must make a bizarre picture. The path was black with shadow, but the moon dusted the far fields with enough light to guide her.

Vic did not come after her and she imagined she could hear his laughter following her up to the village and past it to the Rose and Thistle.

"I am insane," she said aloud. "I've been rolling on the floor with a guy who thinks I'm a riot." Her body felt swollen, still half-aroused. The chilly air did nothing for the heat of her embarrassment.

Harry Watkins sat before his cottage, at his table, a mug in his hand.

Did the man ever sleep?

With as confident a stride as she could manage, she crossed the lawn to her door. She felt Harry's gaze on her with every step. Surely, he could see that the back of her dress was unzipped?

In the safety of her bedroom, she pulled the curtains closed on the locked windows and discarded her costume in the bottom of the closet. Out of sight. Out of mind.

After a long shower she toweled off and caught a glimpse of herself in the mirror. She rubbed away the steam.

Same old boring Rose. No sign of her confusion was painted on her face.

She drew the towel in a sawing motion across her rear, then up her back and cried out with pain. Looking over her shoulder, she saw the enflamed line.

She began to shake. The room darkened, the scent of sulfur filled her nostrils. She gripped the sink and took deep breaths.

Her cell phone vibrated in the kitchen.

"Hello," she said.

"I'm an ass—" Vic started.

"Can you come over here?"

"You read my mind."

"Harry Watkins is sitting outside."

"Open your window and turn off your bedroom light." The phone clicked.

Vic came in the window, just one shadow emerging from another.

"What is it?"

He was still dressed in all black. He looked so good, her teeth ached.

"Rose?"

"Will you laugh?"

In answer, he drew her carefully into his arms. She poured out what she had seen in the club chamber, how he'd changed, how she'd imagined his tongue, the barbed phallus.

This time he didn't laugh. "Let's have a look."

She turned around for him and he drew the towel down to her buttocks.

"This wasn't caused by that little zip."

He put his hands on her waist. "This is all I did."

He kissed her nape, licked down the column of her spine. She stood so still, she could hear water drip in the shower, hear her heart beat. She dropped the towel. He caressed her lightly between her thighs and said softly, "That's all, mate. Just my hand."

She turned around and took a deep breath. This time, it was Vic on his knees before her. His hands were warm as he rubbed them up and down her hips, his lips warmer, pressed to her stomach.

"It's just me," he whispered. He stood up and took her hand, led her to the bed. They stretched out on their sides, nose to nose. "Whatever you thought, it was the wine, the atmosphere, not me. I can't explain your scratch, I've my own that doesn't make sense, so let's just put it down to drunkenness."

She could only nod. His lips were warm on hers, a whisper of sensation. Why am I no longer cold, she wondered, lying on this bed, him clothed, while I'm not? He pulled her against him, opened his thighs so she could nestle hers between them and she *was* warm.

They lay that way until the room grew gray with dawn light. He rose and pulled the curtains open. Color bled back into the room. He lifted a brow in question.

In answer, she undressed him.

This time, when he fitted himself to her, he rocked slowly in and out in a languid rhythm. Time stretched. She closed her eyes and learned every inch of his back, buttocks, and thighs with her fingers while her mouth learned the taste of his throat, mouth, the palms of his hands.

A knot of need centered where they touched in such an intimate joining. "Now, Vic. Now would be nice," she whispered against his lips.

Every vestige of gentleness disappeared as he granted her wish. She dug her fingers into his shoulders and hung on. Each hard push of his hips, each withdrawal, sent her to the edge of pleasure and set her there to beg for the fall over.

When he came, he cried her name, and drove into her so hard she gasped. Her own climax followed his, a sweeping shiver of sensation that rocketed along every fiber of her body. And every nerve.

They collapsed in a sweaty tangle of limbs. He fell into a deep sleep. This time, contentment settled on her along with the weight of his body. She dozed.

A rustle of ivy startled her awake.

With a sudden wash of fear, she turned her head.

No Cheshire cat face hung in the window. Only a small bird, a wren, she thought, perched on a slender leaf to twist its head and question what the hell she was doing.

VIC BEHAVED LIKE A nervous cat when he emerged from the bedroom. She looked up from her black coffee and toast. "I made you some tea." She hefted the squat brown pot.

When he settled on one of the counter stools, she sighed. He wore only his black trousers. Nothing under them, she now knew. Gotta touch him again, she thought. Soon.

And she did, under the guise of examining the scratch on his chest. "How did we get these?"

"Now there's a question I don't want to explore."

"Oh, I love exploring." She ran her hands up his chest to encircle his neck.

Every muscle she caressed was taut. "Relax," she said.

He pulled her arms away. "We need to talk. But later. I have some business to take care of." He fetched his shirt and grass-stained sneakers from the bedroom floor and in a moment was gone, her mug in his hand.

Rose felt a familiar chill, a little twist in her stomach.

We need to talk.

"Great. I'm history already."

DONALD WATCHED HARRY WATKINS water the tubs of flowers that flanked each cottage. "Do you think it wise, letting this Rose Early stay in Joan's cottage? We don't know what their relationship was. They might be dire enemies. The woman might be stalking Joan. That might be why Joan left, she heard Rose was coming and ran away."

"I'm seeing your point. Hadn't thought of it that way." Watkins shaded his eyes and frowned.

"We think you should ask her to leave."

"We?"

"We."

"I'll do it now," Watkins said.

"Don't tell Ms. Early we suggested she leave, will you?"

"That I won't, Father, you can depend on me."

ROSE RUBBED HER NOSE and sighed over the contact sheets she'd fanned out on the kitchen counter. A thump on the door broke her concentration. She squared the contact sheets, glanced at her reflection in the microwave door, and fluffed her hair.

Instead of the expected Vic, she found Harry on her doorstep, a hose dribbling water near his shoes.

"You're to go. Today," he said.

"What?"

"I've been thinking that maybe your sister won't be best pleased if she comes back and finds you here. I mean, she didn't leave me word you were coming."

"But I'm her sister—"

"Don't care about that. She didn't leave any word you were coming, so I'm asking you to go. And don't be taking her things when you do. Leave her box where you found it."

Rose felt rudderless. Speechless.

"By four, miss," Harry said and stalked away.

"Well, if I needed a sign, that's it," she said and closed the door. She wandered around the barren cottage, gathering her few personal items.

As she set the carton on the counter, she paused. How did Harry know about the box? Her skin crawled. Had he been in here? Snooping?

Wobbly with indecision, a raging hang-over definitely on the horizon, she finally packed some cleaning supplies in the box in defiance of Harry's dictum.

She tucked the research materials, the red folder, and all of Joan's photographs into her suitcase. The costume she left in the closet. Let Harry get his jollies with that.

Where could she go? Her thoughts went immediately to Vic. She rejected the thought as quickly as it formed. Despite their new physical intimacy, Rose sensed Vic would throw up a drawbridge at any sign she was taking advantage of it.

No, she needed a nice, neutral place to bunk. She straightened the bed, eradicating all evidence of lovemaking.

As she slung her bags into her car, precisely at four, she still had nowhere to go. "Screw you," she said under her breath and waved at Harry Watkins who sat in front of his cottage with his mother.

Her first destination was the camera shop. With a little cajoling, the shopkeeper allowed her to play with some of Joan's images on his computer. When the shop closed, she headed across the street to the library.

Mary Garner smiled with a look of real pleasure when Rose propped her elbows on the circulation desk.

"Can you recommend an inexpensive place to stay?" Rose asked. "Harry Watkins decided I shouldn't stay in my sister's cottage."

"Shall I have a word with him?" Mary asked. She patted Rose's hand. "He's a right bastard when he wants to be."

Rose shook her head. "No, don't say anything. But I need a place to stay."

"Here." Mary placed a brochure on the attractions of Marleton on the counter. "You can use my phone."

Rose settled at Mary's desk. She had no luck. It was the height of the tourist season. With reluctance, she called Vic.

"Hi," she said.

"Hi, mate." He sounded normal. Or normal for Vic. She could hear him sucking the smoke into his lungs.

"You know, smoking will kill you."

"What made you say that?" he asked, a touch of chill entering his voice.

"Forget it. Listen, Harry tossed me."

Vic was silent for a moment. "For lewd behavior?"

"No, he developed a conscience and decided Joan and I might be at odds, and if she returned, she'd be upset that he let me camp there."

"Come here."

It was what she'd **wanted, hoped for**, but now he'd made the offer, she felt as secure as a hedgehog on a lane when he was driving.

"Look, I'm checking my e-mail at the library. Why don't you think about it? I won't be offended if you change your mind. If you still feel the same in an hour, call me here."

She cradled the phone and sat at one of the computers. She checked her e-mail. Still nothing from Joan. Just spam and Max with his tasteless jokes. With forty-five minutes to spare before she expected to hear from Vic, she did a search of the area surrounding Marleton, but found nothing available that was not twice what she could afford.

Mary trundled a cart of books over to where she sat. "Did you have any luck?" she asked.

"No, but Vic Drummond offered to let me stay at his aunt's."

"Joan can find you there when she comes back."

Rose pulled out her phone. "I should leave another message on her voice mail—tell her how to get to his house."

"She knows." Mary smiled. "She ate dinner with him often enough *not* to know where he lived."

"At the pub?" It was all Rose could manage.

Mary swung her cart around and headed back toward the stacks. "Oh, no. The Bell. Our little dining treasure. I always eat there with my Jack. Vic and Joan were very set on the salmon mousse, though I'm more partial to the fillet steak."

ROSE SAT IN HER car for an hour. Her chest felt as if someone had reached in and knotted all the arteries, twisted the veins. Her head throbbed with a pain she knew would not be cured by aspirin.

We need to talk.

"Of course we do, Vic. We need to talk about your lies."

He had warned her.

"I am the biggest, stupidest—"

Her cell phone rang.

"Where are you?" Vic asked. "Mary said you'd done a bunk."

"I'm in my car."

"On your way here, I hope," he said.

"Actually, I'm thinking of going to the Bell for an early dinner. Mary Garner highly recommends it. Says you and Joan really enjoyed their salmon mousse."

17

VIC TAPPED THE HOOD of Rose's car with his knuckles and looked around. Where was she? He scanned the street, busy with tourists, despite the imminent danger of rain. She stood on the bridge, camera pointed at the water. He loped over to where she leaned, bracing her camera.

"I wanted to tell you about Joan," he said without preamble.

"Why did you lie?" Rose moved her camera a fraction of an inch and fired off a half-dozen shots. The hood of her windcheater hid her face.

He hated being in the wrong. Especially when he probably was. It brewed an acid burn in his gut.

"I didn't lie. I just left it too late," he said.

She rounded on him and thrust the camera forward like a weapon, nearly smacking him in the chest. "Just? You lied, Vic. I asked if Joan had made a play for you—"

"She didn't when I autographed her book."

She blinked; her camera lifted. If it had been a spear, he'd be gored.

"Ah, semantics. How could I have forgotten that you play with words? So, she didn't make a play for you then. Must have been *later*. How much later, Vic? A day? An hour? Ten minutes?"

"This isn't helpful—"

"It is for me. I need to know who you really are. What was the nature of your relationship with Joan?"

"It wasn't a relationship. If she were here, she'd tell you we were bloody bored with one another after the first time."

She turned away and put her eye to her camera, but not before she'd drawn her hood closer about her face. It was protective and dismissive.

The lowering sky mirrored his mood. It layered mist across the fields as he had layered excuses between himself and Rose. "I wish I had a bright, shiny explanation to give you, Rosie, but I don't. I met you and thought that despite your differences, you and Joan were probably much the same inside. So, I didn't explain myself; I just wanted you."

"Fine." She dodged through traffic to the other side of the bridge and resumed her photo-taking.

He was stuck on his side until a gap in the traffic appeared. She edged away when he joined her.

"Here's the difference between you and Joan. I asked her to tell me about herself, and I learned she was a photojournalist, what books she'd done, why she was in Marleton, her grievances with her agent, but I never learned she had a lovely and charming sister, or had been taught by a father who'd worked in Vietnam. I thought she lived in New York City. Alone!"

The rain began in a light patter of drops on his shoulders and hair. Rose quickly put the camera in her bag. When she looked up at him, her eyes were as green as Ireland's grass.

He grabbed her bag to prevent her from leaving. "I just scratched an itch with Joan. I made love to Rose."

Rose jerked the bag from his hands and slung it onto her back. "Well, I'm sorry to say that I was just scratching an itch with you." She walked past him. Away.

"I deserved that," he called, but she kept on walking.

"Scratch be damned." He jogged after her. He knew he needed to choose his next words more carefully than he'd ever done when writing.

His mind went blank.

He was out of breath when he reached her car. He clapped a hand on the door to prevent her opening it and driving out of his life. His mind was still a blank. "I'll quit smoking if you stay."

She stared at him. "You're the biggest asshole I've ever met. As if you'd quit smoking."

"I was trying to think of something to say that would keep you here."

"That's not it."

"I know. Give me a minute. I'm thinking as fast as I can."

He saw a ghost of a smile hover on her lips, but it vaporized as quickly as a spirit faced with exorcism.

"We have stigmata, Rose."

"Stigmata? We have *scratches*." She shook her head and tried again to get her car door open.

"I'm filthy rich."

She dropped a fist on the car roof, dangerously near his hand. "That's something that would appeal to Joan, not me." Her anger radiated at him like a hand slap.

"No, I don't mean it that way. I meant, I'm filthyrich@dybie.com. Remember that first day? I said I'd e-mailed my answer to your question. 'Do you believe in evil?' you asked. I answered."

ROSE LEANED ON HER car and puffed out an exasperated sigh. Mist cobwebbed his dark, disheveled hair and moth-eaten sweater.

"I'm going to have a beer at the Pig and Pie." She headed toward the pub. "Then I'm going to twist your ears off."

When they were settled at a window table, she tried to reconcile her anger, frustration, and envy. She figured Vic was something akin to the steak and kidney pie being served to a nearby table. She had the crust figured out. It was the insides that remained a mystery. She liked the steak, but wasn't sure about the kidneys. And the kidneys were ruining the whole meal.

Vic set two dark beers on stained mats.

"So, we've come full circle," she said. "Do you believe in evil?"

"Maybe." He took out his cigarettes.

She lifted one eyebrow. He sighed, crumpled the pack, and tossed it onto the dusty window sill by his elbow.

"Look, Rose, I'm not sure *I* believe in evil, but I do believe Alice thought it alive and well in Marleton." He rubbed the center of his chest with his palm. "You can't deny our stigmata."

"What we have is not stigmata. We have scratches. I don't know how you got your—probably screwing some village wench. But I'm sure I got mine from a zipper. It's just a scratch." She rubbed a thumb down the beer glass in illustration. "You're just avoiding the real issue here. You had so many opportunities to tell me you knew Joan but you didn't."

He took her hand.

"When I first met you, it wasn't important. You were simply . . . a challenge, of sorts." He tightened his fingers.

She'd need to make a scene to retrieve her hand.

"Then you became too important."

Her heart did a little dance. *Caution, Rose, he's a master at playing with words.* Her heart settled into a lump of gristle, maybe something she'd find—and reject—in her steak and kidney pie. "It's never a good idea to toy with the truth."

"I've done it so long, I can't stop. Auntie Alice always called me on it. I loved her for it." He looked toward the rain-streaked window.

The tears that crowded Rose's eyes embarrassed her, and she looked there, too, pretended to examine the picturesque street with tourists dashing for shelter in the tiny shops.

"Are you wanting something to eat?" Nell, the barmaid asked.

Rose took the opportunity to pull her hand from Vic's and mask her confusion with a perusal of the blackboard menu.

"Sure, Nell, the fish and chips will do for me. Rose?"

"The same," she said to Nell, and to Vic, "maybe you'll choke on a bone."

She sipped the foam from her beer, then licked her lips, and felt a touch of satisfaction when the action drew his eyes.

Vic leaned close. "I expected Joan to appear on your doorstep. She'll tell you, I thought. But before I knew it, I was in deep, and it was too late. If we'd not gotten drunk at the club, I would have come clean."

There was an invisible perimeter of danger about him. Touching wasn't necessary for her to fall under his spell, just proximity. She tucked her hands under the table.

"Maybe we should make this conversation about Joan, and what's happened to her."

"This conversation *is* about Joan. I shagged her. You know now, and I want it behind us."

"That's such a guy statement. I don't think there's much more to say, Vic."

"Have you never done something you regret?"

"I think I made that pretty clear."

"I don't mean us. I mean, isn't there something you intended to do, but before you knew it, time had passed and it was too late?"

Yes, I didn't come when Joan asked me.

But Rose no longer felt she could share with this man, so she didn't. "Sure. Once I broke a window playing softball and never owned up. What's your point?"

He slid his chair closer, put an arm around the back of hers. He tucked her hair behind her ear. The tender gesture set her nerves on fire.

"I've broken a bloody window, Rose. I need forgiveness."

She drank off the last of the beer. "I forgive you, and when I've had the fish and chips, I'm heading home."

"What about the book? No matter what's between us, you need to finish it."

"I won't be finishing the book."

"I'm disappointed you'd let your anger with me change your mind about Joan's book."

"Don't flatter yourself. I can't finish the book because I don't have the right cameras. They're at home."

"Buy some."

She shook her head. "You can't just pick up a camera and expect to do your best work. Would you be comfortable with someone else's computer? I don't have the time and quite frankly, I don't have the money."

Vic picked up her backpack.

"What are you doing?"

He pulled out her cell phone. She yelped and made a grab for it, but he threw up an arm and blocked her.

"Max? Sorry for the late call. I'm one of Rose Early's new mates."

Rose felt her face go hot with indignation as he and Max bonded across the miles.

"Can you do Rose a favor? She needs to take pictures of tapestries and altar screens. Pack up whatever she might need to take pictures inside churches. Outside, too."

She made another attempt for the phone and met his forearm in another block.

"Ship them off overnight express, that's a good chap."

She listened as Vic reeled off his aunt's address.

"Half a mo," he said, scrabbled through a set of tattered papers in his wallet and read off some numbers. "That's my FedEx account. Pack her babies with care," he finished. He tossed her the phone. "You call your cameras 'babies?'"

"What's wrong with you? You're crazy."

"Crazy, am I?" He grinned. "I'm as sane as the next man. I'm just eliminating excuses."

The anger was like snakes seething in her stomach. "Fine. So my stuff's coming tomorrow. It doesn't matter. I don't have the software I need. I'm short of cash. I have no place to stay—"

"Software's easy. Computers abound. And although I'm in the shit, my offer still stands—stay at my place."

Nell separated them with plates of fish and chips. She put a bottle of malt vinegar in front of Vic and a bottle of catsup in front of Rose.

With a smile, Nell poured more beer into their glasses. "The rain's worsening. All the tourists will go home and leave us in peace." She put a hand on Rose's shoulder. "Not meaning any offense to you, miss."

They ate in silence. The supper gave Rose time to gather her thoughts. She felt defeated and exhausted. What was she going to do? Where was she going to stay? What about Joan's book? "You'll just have to ship my stuff back. I won't be here to get them."

Vic shoved his empty plate aside. "What's your next excuse? Maybe you're not as good as our Joan?"

"Not as good? I'm every bit as—" She snapped her lips on the rest of it. He was goading her. "Maybe I'm not."

"Then the book will be a disappointment." He stood up and stretched. It lifted his misshapen sweater, revealed his flat stomach and the tantalizing swathe of dark hair on his belly. "Come along, mate. Let's get you settled. And you can tell me what's so fascinating about my bridge."

"Trolls, Vic. I assumed you knew them intimately since you're one yourself."

18

Rose lay curled on Vic's sofa, fully dressed, under a soft blanket, listening to the china mantle clock chime midnight, then one. At two, she conceded defeat and admitted she was not really angry with Mr. V. F. Drummond. Her churning emotions were just a relapse into old familiar territory. It was a land where Joan's ability to claim someone's attention rubbed Rose's emotions raw.

Vic just represented a bigger than usual abrasion on feelings thought long reconciled. At the same time, Rose admitted Vic didn't owe her hindsight loyalty. She wasn't sure if that was how a therapist would tell her to look at it, but Rose knew that if the woman had been anyone but Joan, she would have defended Vic's right to keep his personal life personal.

An hour later, Vic came down the stairs. She heard the whisper of his feet on the polished wooden floor.

He's just looking for his smokes, she thought. They lay next to his laptop. But he didn't reach for the cigarettes; he lifted the blanket and slid next to her, using his hip to shove her over.

"This is highly uncomfortable," she said.

"I can't sleep, knowing you're angry." He kissed her eyebrows.

Heat trailed in the wake of his mouth. He unbuttoned her blouse, shifted it open, eased her bra strap off her shoulder.

"I was jealous that you'd done this with her," she whispered.

"I never did." He skimmed his thumb over the rise of her breast. "I never sought her out because I couldn't sleep worrying about her. I never thought of her after. You're like words I can't delete. Make love with me, Rose."

"Okay." She tried to sound as casual as she could, when inside she was as taut with need as he was.

She drew down the zipper of his jeans.

When they were naked, he linked his fingers with hers and made a cradle of their arms about her head. She embraced his hips with her thighs, took him in. As he penetrated her body, he also pushed her into a realization—she could hide a truth from him, but not from herself.

19

VIC PULLED A SINGLE item from the packing material. "This is it? A tripod? No cameras?"

"I lied. It must be your bad influence." Rose felt the heat on her cheeks. "The camera I have is fine. Actually, it's the best."

He brandished the lightweight, travel tripod at her like a sword. "I was right, you were making excuses."

She scooped up some of the packing material, unable to think of something clever to say. She had made excuses that avoided the real issue. Was she good enough to work on Joan's book? Would the work she did be appreciated by Joan or scorned by her?

"What's this?" Vic asked, holding up the red folder with a penciled list on the front.

"At first," she explained to Vic, "I didn't think I'd need to take more photographs, but there are two series that need redoing. I really can't believe Joan did such a poor job on Marleton's altar screen and tapestry. Without the loupe you'd never notice it, but they're just enough out of focus to be useless. I played with them over at the camera shop, on their computer, but I wasn't able to fix them."

"Did Joan have a laptop with her?"

Rose shook her head. "Liked computers about as little as she did digital photography. She still uses the darkroom at our studio, whereas I'm a computer junkie."

"Let me see." Vic took the contact sheet Rose held and sat down at his aunt's kitchen table. "I know how she took these. On her back." He wagged his eyebrows.

Rose found the innuendo didn't hurt. They'd crossed more than one proverbial bridge between their first lovemaking of the night and before their last, interrupted by the express mail.

"I'm not joking. I think she was lying on the floor."

Rose considered the picture. "The lighting's what matters. I guess I'll have to ask one of the ministers if I can get in at night."

Vic surged from his chair. "Why ask? If Father Nigel says no, you're stuck."

He left her in the kitchen. She heard him rummaging in the desk in the sitting room. A few moments later, he returned with a piece of braided leather. At the end of it was a large brass key.

"Alice's key to the church. We can get in anytime."

"No way, Vic. That's breaking and entering."

"My specialty . . . well, pinching donations isn't a break."

"Any other crimes I should know about?"

"I stole a car once."

"Am I supposed to be at ease with that idea?"

"I was nine. I drove rather well, I thought, at the time." He went to his computer for the third time that morning, opened a file, and skimmed it.

And your driving hasn't improved much since.

"If you'd prefer to write, I could—"

"No. No. The last thing I want to do is write."

"Why not?"

"I meant what I said last night, you're like words I can't delete. I have more of those than I can handle."

"What are you getting at?"

"It's like our scratches. Unexplainable."

He ran his fingers through his hair, making it stand up on end. She resisted the urge to do something about it, sure she'd end up on her back if she got that close—or he'd end up on his.

"What's the smile for? You think I'm full of shit, don't you?"

She put her camera down. This was the serious Vic she'd not seen often. "I'm sorry. Why don't you explain this unexplainable thing."

He did more damage to his hair. "I've written something I don't remember writing and then, when I delete it, it's back the next day."

A shiver raised the hair on her neck. She knew immediately he was sharing something that he had not disclosed to anyone else, was giving something of himself he didn't often give. Trust.

"You're giving me the willies," she said.

"I'm given myself more than that," he said. "The bit's about Alice. She's telling me not to smoke, telling me the smokes will kill me."

"And?"

"And I get scratched." He rubbed his chest. "When I delete the words, they pop up the next time I open that file."

"Maybe you're writing them without being aware you're doing it."

He shrugged. "If I believed that, I'd believe my own books."

"What are you working on now?"

"A new book. I've created a new file, but if I go back to the old one, the words are there."

"I'm the first person to tell you I don't believe in therapy, but maybe it has something to do with your anger about your Aunt Alice's death."

He plucked one of his books from a shelf. He opened the front cover and pulled out a letter tucked into the front flap of the dust jacket.

"She wrote to me a number of times, asked me to come for a visit. I kept putting her off. Deadline, you know. Then she died." He put the letter back where he'd found it, and replaced the book. "I regret not being here."

"Kind of like Father Donald must . . . knowing he stopped off for a drink and might have saved your aunt if he hadn't."

Vic rounded on her and stabbed his finger at her. "It's not the same. I was in London, he was down the lane. She changed plans to meet him. If she'd been with Mary—"

He dropped his hand. "Sorry, I guess I'm a bit tense without the cigarettes.

"You're right. It isn't the same." It was and it wasn't, but if Vic was feeling even one tenth as bad as she felt for ignoring Joan's entreaty to come to England, his guilt must be appalling. Vic owed his aunt for years of care. She only had competition for their father's attention between her and Joan.

20

Rose frowned. "I'm not sure I understand, sir. You're saying I can't take photographs in the church?"

Father Nigel folded his smooth, plump hands across his ample stomach. "I feel it would be contrary to our policy of sanctity to allow you to take photographs after hours."

"But my sister did. She took dozens of pictures, most of them can't be during daylight." She set a contact sheet on the desk.

Nigel studied it, then handed it back. "I'm afraid you're mistaken. Your sister only took photographs during tourist hours as per our agreement. She, along with any member of the public, is welcome to photograph the church at those times. Beyond that, the church maintains a strict policy of no photography."

"Since this is the brainchild of Archdeacon Keeling, would you mind calling him for his permission? I believe you'll find him at the Shakespeare Conference Center in Stratford." Vic asked.

He extended a business card, one of Trevor's Rose saw.

Father Nigel turned his gaze on Vic for a long moment before he read the hand-written number on the reverse of the card. "If you wish." He picked up the phone. After a few minutes conversation, he hung up. "The archdeacon is sympathetic, but agrees it is my place to make such a decision."

"Don't you want All Saints Church represented?" Rose asked.

Father Nigel stood up and dropped Trevor Harrison's card on his leather blotter. "It is immaterial to me if All Saints is in the book. If you will excuse me, I have another appointment."

Rose followed Vic. "I don't understand him."

Vic shrugged. "There've had a few burglaries recently. Maybe he's just overly concerned about security."

"If he knows your reputation, he probably thinks you're behind them."

"Before his time." Vic hooked his arm through hers and led her toward the public footpath.

"Let's just cut across the field," she said.

"Can't. That would be trespassing."

"You're concerned about trespassing when you suggested a bit of B and E this morning?"

He grinned and wagged his eyebrows. "I have standards." They followed the path between two meadows. The sky opened and they finished the distance to his cottage at a mad run.

"I feel utterly frustrated," she called from the kitchen as she rubbed her hair with a towel.

Vic scattered papers on the desk, swearing something beneath his breath about matches.

"I could eliminate All Saints Church completely, but it's a gem. The tapestry alone should have a double-page spread. And the altar screen is spectacular. Imagine what it must have looked like when it was first unveiled. The gilding must have been magnificent." She sighed, rearranging the contact sheets on the table. "These are just . . . poorly done."

Vic shook his aunt's key in her face.

"No. Now knock it off." She ducked under his arm and took the contact sheets to the sitting room. A fire burned in the grate. Rain drummed on the windows. The scent of flowers filled the room. "Without All Saints, the book will have a big, fat gap in it."

She knelt on the rug and used the pattern of vines around the center rose medallion to lay out the contact sheets.

Vic knelt behind her. Desire ignited as he stroked his hands up under her T-shirt and cupped her breasts.

His hands sent tiny shocks along her nerves. His breath bathed her neck and shoulder in heat. She pretended it was just another afternoon, just a casual lover stroking her nipples so tight they might burst.

She'd never had a casual lover.

Vic pulled her T-shirt off and tossed it among the photographs. He stroked his hands over her in a long slow passage to her waist. He slid his fingers inside her waistband then deep between her thighs.

"Sweet Rose," he said against her ear.

There was nothing sweet about her thoughts. And nothing casual.

21

SENSATIONS LIKE THE FLAMES in the hearth licked through Vic's body. Rose's hips were warm beneath his hands. Red glinted in the glossy hair that swung from her shoulders in rhythm to his stroke.

She looked over her shoulder at him, lips parted.

From the moment he'd pulled off her shirt, he'd wanted to watch the flex of her back muscles, see the shadows along her spine, touch that valley, damp with sweat. He wanted to feel again the powerful surges of sensation that had gripped him in the club.

Tremors ran through her body as he licked his fingers and drew them from her nape to the cleft of her buttocks, tracing the ugly scratch. What caused the mark? The zip? Or his tongue?

She met each thrust of his hips with her own ferocity.

He wrapped his arms around her waist and buried his face in her hair as he came. The waves of pleasure surged up from deep in his body. The eruption knocked them over.

Rose rocked against him, making breathy sounds, her nails digging into his forearms.

"Come for me," he demanded. He played on her until her thighs tightened on his hand and her hips churned.

Words rushed into his mouth, but he held them back. They were like lines he couldn't quite get right, that needed rewriting before being fit for an editor's eyes.

They lay spent in each other's arms, their legs tangled in clothing, contact sheets crumpled and scattered. A log shifted and a spark landed on the rug. He groaned and flailed out of his jeans, then put out the ember with a slap of a discarded shoe.

"Vic?"

He cupped her face. "You're brilliant."

She lowered her gaze, shook her head. "I can't be that smart. Every time I tell myself I'm going to keep my pants on, I find them around my ankles."

"And lovely the sight is," he said, lifting her face and smoothing back the wild mane of her hair. "Lovely."

A knot in his throat threatened to unravel into words he might regret. He set them aside for another time. *Or never.*

And wasn't it procrastination that had torpedoed his ship with her the night before? "I don't think I've ever wanted a woman during writing hours before."

She burst into laughter. "How unromantic. I'm interrupting the writing. I guess the public should be glad you don't write romance." She broke from his embrace.

He prevented her pulling on her underwear and jeans by cupping her buttocks and licking her navel. "You smell like roses."

"No, I smell like lavender and patchouli, or so my shower gel says. How can you live here and not know what roses smell like?"

He let her hop away, enjoying the vision of her dressing almost as much as he'd enjoyed the disrobing. She contorted to clasp her bra and one breast spilled from the cup.

"Let me get that for you," he said, caressing the mound

back within its lacy confines. "I can't smell a damned thing because I smoke. I guessed about the roses."

Her breast was heavy and warm in his hand. Her belly was warm as well when he drew her jeans back down.

VIC WORKED AT HIS computer, and Rose wrote a tentative order for the chapters of Joan's book. As the afternoon waned, she found herself filled with indecision about the progression of certain elements of the work.

Her gaze drifted to the rose medallion rug. Had Vic made love to Joan on this rug? Had he run out of condoms with Joan and settled for mutual oral pleasure as they had?

Settled? No, she was lying if she thought there'd been anything settling about it. Just the opposite. Instead, she'd been so unnerved by the joy of tasting every inch of Vic's body while he pleasured her with his rough-gentle mouth, she'd wept.

How embarrassing.

"No, I didn't." Vic no longer sat facing his computer. He had turned and propped his feet on the seat of a nearby armchair.

She felt the flush of heat on her cheeks. "Didn't what?"

"Shag Joan here."

"Did I ask you?"

"I read it on your face."

The flush extended down her body. "I was thinking of how embarrassed I'll be if the book sucks."

He smiled. "Liar. You were embarrassed that you'd been making love on the same rug as your sister. So, don't be. Joan never came here. There are women you take home, and women you don't."

His words were double-barbed. They gave her flush the edge of pleasure, and they reminded her he'd been Joan's lover.

"I'm feeling restless. I'm going to take my camera up to the church. Maybe I can simply get someone to turn the spotlights off. It might be dark enough on a day like this to work."

"I'll come along."

"No. Stay here and write."

He hooked her waist and drew her near. His kiss landed on her midriff, the action almost overturning his chair. It was endearing and rather Vic-like in its comic outcome. It was also tempting to remain in the circle of his arms, maybe climb astride his lap. She had to force herself to disentangle from his embrace and pick up her jacket.

The rain pelted her shoulders as she walked up the lane to the looming church. It filled the landscape, its stone facade looking black and slick in the storm.

She edged past a couple admiring the baptismal font and entered the gift shop. It smelled strongly of wet wool.

The sour Fiona Sayer still manned the counter.

"Excuse me," Rose said. "Is there a maintenance man around?"

"Why?" The woman had large, thick glasses that magnified her eyes, dark as tarnished pennies.

"Father Nigel gave me permission to take photographs of the altar screen and tapestry. I'd like to know if I can have the lights off for a moment or two."

It wasn't technically a lie. Father Nigel had not objected to her photography during regular hours. The vicar's name caused a change in the woman's demeanor. Some of her hostility abated.

"Cleaners only come in on alternate Saturdays, but Father Donald is hanging about. Ask him."

"Thank you." Rose walked slowly down the nave. She lifted her camera and took some shots of banners hanging overhead. Some were as gauzy as cobwebs, giving new meaning to the word "threadbare."

Vertigo clutched at her and she shook it off by concentrating on the narrow world of her viewfinder.

She also took a shot of the man coming toward her down the nave. He wore a black suit that flowed with his body and made Vic's sweaters and khakis look even more rummage sale than usual. Several teenage girls reading the flagstone grave markers in the north aisle stopped and stared at him with appreciation.

Father Donald might have been walking a runway, modeling clothing except for his clerical collar. His hair gleamed gold as he came closer, stepping from pools of light into pools of shadow. She took another shot of him.

"Ms. Early?" Donald shook her hand. "I didn't know you were still in Marleton."

"Rose, please. And yes, I'm still here. I'm working on my sister's book."

"Her book?" He looked puzzled.

Hadn't they talked about the book the other day? "Archdeacon Keeling hired my sister to do a book on the more famous pieces in the diocese. I'm finishing it for her."

"Ah. Now I remember."

"You could help me," she said, skirting around him and heading for the chancel.

"How?" He paced her and she smiled as the teenagers did the same, gaze fixed on her fashion-model handsome escort.

"I'd like to take some photographs of the tapestry and altar screen." As she said the words, a wave of putrid air surrounded them. She coughed and glanced around for a grate of some kind that might lead to a sewer somewhere. She saw nothing but worn stone.

"How may I help you?" With his words the sensation passed.

"Could you turn the spotlights off for me after I get set-up here."

"Turn out the lights?" Father Donald frowned. It marred the perfection of his tawny brows.

Rose indicated the tall, thick candles on spikes. "If I could light these and have the spots off, I think I might get the image I'm looking for."

"I, that is, I'm not sure." He ran a hand over his hair. The gesture reminded her of Vic, though the curate smoothed where Vic rumpled.

"I promise to work quickly."

"Well, I suppose . . . that is. . . ."

A feeling of lethargy came over her as Donald stammered through his excuses. She thought he did not really have a reason at hand, but just an instinct that he should refuse.

He ground to a halt, rubbed his hands together. "I'll just see to those lights," he finally said and headed back toward the bays of the north aisle.

Rose struck a match from a pack she'd purloined from Vic. The sulfurous scent lingered as she touched each huge candle's pristine wick.

The giggling teenagers watched her. Their chatter sounded far away, as distant as those of the tour guide, leading a group of a dozen or more tourists to the bell tower stairs.

What was it about the church that made her sick? She wanted to question the girls who lingered for another glimpse of Archangel Donald.

To distract herself from the miasma of lethargy and nausea that wrapped chilly arms around her, she set up her tripod and camera, checked her settings.

Suddenly, the eastern end of the church went dark.

The teenagers ooohhhed and Rose looked up at the altar screen to allow her eyes to adjust to the limited light.

She could barely manage a smile. It was not the sudden shift from spotlight to candlelight that had dazzled the girls, but the curate who was even more alluring by the light of flickering flames.

The girls intercepted him, drawing him into a discussion of the choir stalls, or so Rose assumed although she could not really hear their conversation.

In fact, a buzz filled her ears. She shook her head and felt dizzy again.

She ignored her discomfort, but could not hurry the work. She used time exposure with the candlelight and hoped for Donald's continued distraction with his giggling entourage.

A little halo appeared around each flame. The floor felt as insecure as the attic gangway. She more fell than sat on the floor beside the small tripod, the flagstones cold and hard even through her jeans. She adjusted the tripod so the camera captured the tapestry soldiers as they galloped uphill in their ferocious progress over peasants, other crusaders, and priests.

The images filled her viewfinder. She took several pictures, cross-legged by the tripod, uncomfortable as she never was when crawling around on the floor to capture the attention of a child or beloved pet.

She centered her attention on a crusader's courser that reared his hooves over a ragged, cowering man. The warrior's lance dripped blood on the peasant's smock. Tendrils of smoke rose from every spot.

"Ms. Early. What are you doing?" Black filled her viewfinder. She looked up to find the curate blocking her view of the tapestry.

"Taking photographs," she said and thought she needed a picture of the border with its lurid lilies. The candlelight reflected on the gold thread turning the veins on leaves and petals molten.

"This is most inappropriate. You must get up. Please, miss. Now. I insist." He fluttered about her like a young crow.

Translating his rushed speech with a buzz in her head made her weary.

"I'm almost finished."

"Get up." He spoke slowly and distinctly. "You tourists have no respect."

He grabbed her arm and hauled her to her feet. His fan club hid their grins behind their pamphlets.

"I'm not a tourist, Father, I'm working."

"I can't allow it."

"Donald." A little woman, in a matching gray skirt and blouse appeared from the chancel. She touched the young man's arm. "I don't think she meant any harm."

Donald's mouth worked. Myriad expressions crossed his face.

Sweat dampened her underarms. Bubbles of indigestion

broke in her throat. More moldy drafts entwined her body. She imagined centuries of spores incubating in the tapestry. Her head pounded.

"Never mind," she managed. "I'm finished for now. Thank you for turning off the lights."

She grabbed her equipment, turned, and walked unsteadily along the nave. The huge open space smelled cleaner, the air cooler than in the stagnant area of the damaged north transept.

Once outside, she crouched on the church porch and took a few deep breaths to clear her head before collapsing the tripod and shoving it into her backpack. The village lay before her, washed in spangles of light. The rain had stopped, the sun rising over the hedgerows. Her hands shook as she tried to capture the stripes of color weaving through the fog over the meadow. What was wrong with her?

She headed for Vic's cottage, watching the swollen creek that fronted the cottages as it ran over mossy rocks toward the troll bridge. She remembered her trepidation about crossing the plank bridge walkway to his cottage just a few days before.

This time, before she knocked, she took out her digital camera. Her hands were steadier now, her stomach settling down. She captured the bright blue door and lush roses that wreathed it. She would enlarge this and hang it beside the one of Vic leaning on the stile. She shifted her settings to frame the entire cottage frontage and fired off a series of shots. Something moved.

She lowered the camera, examined the window without the restriction of her lens. There was nothing but glass and cloud patterns reflected there. What had she seen? Or imagined?

Some trick of light had created the features of a face.

She raised the camera again and centered it on the gargoyle door knocker, then shifted quickly to the window panes. Twice more, she played with the camera, but no matter how she attempted to recreate the moment, she could not capture the elusive shadows that had momentarily coalesced into a face.

As she reviewed the last few pictures on the camera screen, she was grateful she had put the camera into automatic mode. On the first image she'd captured the face. Or maybe she had. The screen was too small, the sun behind her too bright to really tell. She needed a computer. And software.

VIC WAS STRETCHED OUT on the rug, on his back, examining Joan's contact sheets. "How'd it go?" he asked.

"I've changed my mind about the B and E."

"Bondage and Ecstasy?"

She grinned and kicked the unopened cigarette pack away from his side. "Maybe after."

"Come help me," he said, patting the rug.

"I have some photos to upload."

As she worked, Vic continued to look through Joan's work.

"Hey, Vic," she said as she loaded the digital pictures into the computer, "Were you looking out of the window just now?"

"Not me," he said, getting to his feet.

He propped one hand on the desktop and the other on the back of her chair. He sniffed her hair. "You smell musty."

"I was sitting on the church floor. Check this out."

She pointed to a picture that now filled her computer screen.

"And?" He yawned and scratched his chin, now covered with two day's stubble.

"Can't you just feel this man's terror?" She indicated the cringing peasant.

"What's the smoke?"

"Not cigarettes." She expanded the view to include the charging horse and dripping lance.

"Bugger," Vic said.

"Looks like the blood is rather acidic—"

"Sulfuric."

"Strange touch."

Vic nuzzled her neck. "We need to nip upstairs and give you a bath."

"How about after we do our B and E tonight? I'll just stink of mold again."

"Unlimited water in the pipes, mate." He plucked her digital camera from the desk. "I'd like to take a few pictures of you in bubbles."

Rose reached for the camera, but he backed away. She feigned unconcern, though her heart kicked up a few revs. The last thing she wanted to do was be part of a nude photo op. "Only if I can take a few pictures of you."

His expression changed from bright to shadowed. He dropped the camera into her hands. "Not on. I can't afford them appearing on the web somewhere, maybe with a gargoyle head on the end of my penis."

She took the camera from him. "Is that why your picture isn't on your books?"

"Exactly. You have to build a few walls to keep the stalkers out."

"Anyone ever scale your walls?" she asked, putting her camera back in her bag.

"No more than a toe." He hacked the air. "Loped it off, I did."

THEY ENTERED THE CHURCH from the north porch, using Vic's key. Nausea crept up on her with each footstep closer to the altar screen.

"If this is what morning sickness feels like," she said when Vic put his arm around her waist, "I'm never getting pregnant."

"I've never done that bit, but the little nippers are worth it, most of the time."

She tried to smile, but had to swallow down an urge to vomit. "They have a serious mold problem here."

"I'm not feeling so hot myself." He urged her toward a seat in the choir loft, but she pulled away.

"No dawdling. If we're caught here, you won't have to worry about stalkers scaling walls, you'll be front page news."

"Never caught yet."

She went to the altar screen but swayed as nausea overwhelmed her. Vic tugged her to a small stool before the tapestry. He shoved her head between her knees. Rose took two deep shuddering breaths.

"Maybe there's some swamp beneath this ruin," she said.

Something scurried along the wall.

"Shit," Vic whispered and directed his torch beam toward the wall. "A rat."

"Mouse," she said.

The tiny rodent stood poised, head turned to them, as it paused in its progress along the wall, then it continued on, disappearing behind the choir stalls.

"It was a rat."

"Mouse," she muttered.

"Lighting, Vic?"

He ignored her climbing the pulpit steps. Wax lay in thick streamers down the sides of the candles around the nave altar. She pushed her fingernail into the soft wax. "Are there any afternoon or evening services here?"

Vic pantomimed a sermon from the pulpit, his flashlight beneath his chin.

"Nothing past evensong."

Rose set up her tripod and camera in time to catch the fluid expressions that crossed Vic's face. "But this candle wax is soft. Doesn't that mean they were burning recently?"

"Probably a coven sacrificing virgins on the altar."

"Is there such a thing?"

"As a coven?"

"As a virgin." The shadows flickered behind him. She lifted her head. It was still there—a glimmer. A giant bird swooping skyward. "Vic. Behind you," she cried.

"Shhh. You'll wake the dead."

"Behind you."

He spun around and swept the pillars with his flashlight. Nothing moved. The swinging beam sketched only the carved saint who adorned the column.

"Settle down," Vic said, coming down from the pulpit.

"You're letting this place get to you." He combed the hair from her forehead. "You feel cold."

"Maybe." She took a deep breath. "Or I'm getting a disease from this stinky place." She swept the beam of her flashlight back and forth. "What's there?"

His torch beam settled on a small arched doorway in the south aisle. It looked ancient, weathered, its iron studs rusty with age.

"A crypt."

"Can we get in there?"

"Why? Just old bones."

Rose went to the door. "Joan has notes on a crypt. She had it slotted in between the tapestry and the altar screen. But why would she be taking pictures down there?"

"Ghoulish of her, but let's give it a look."

A cool draft swirled around her ankles.

Vic's key turned smoothly in the lock and when he drew open the door, a black maul yawned before them.

The odor of decay swirled up the steps. Vic coughed. "Christ, when did they last clean this place?"

Rose shined her flashlight down the steep stone steps worn concave in the center. Poised at the foot of the steps was another mouse.

"More rats." Vic swore.

The creature's tiny red eyes gleamed up at her. "Think of him as Stuart Little and you'll be fine."

He brushed by her and charged the hapless rodent, sending it scuttling off into the darkness.

When she put her foot on the first step, the vertigo returned with a vengeance. Her shoulder skidded along the wall as she descended the steps.

The power of their combined flashlights revealed a small vaulted chamber.

"What a bloody mess," Vic said. "I'll get some bloody candles to chase the rats away."

"Mice."

Rose imagined the circular crypt as it might have been

when the blue and gold paint were fresh. Now dampness had blackened the gilding and stained the delicate arches with long swathes of mold.

But what drew the eye, and the hand, was the medieval lady who lay at rest in the forgotten space, her marble robes draping a small sarcophagus.

Vic came down the steps with the huge candelabras from the bay honoring the British war dead.

"I see what drew Joan. The artist who carved this is a master." She stumbled against the cold stone.

"Steady on," Vic said, grabbing her arm.

Rose ran her hand over the marble figure that lay so silently in the dank tomb. "It will take more talent than I have to do this lady justice." She licked her dry lips and leaned on the wall. "Who is she?"

"Lady Agnes," Vic said. "Lively little tart . . . or so history says. How's the lighting?" He set a candelabra at the head and foot of the coffin. He struck a match.

His voice drifted away. He *was* far away and growing more distant.

Rose eased herself to her knees, not to pray, but to press her head to the cold stone.

A moldy miasma filled Rose's nostrils along with something beneath it. Rodents. Dead rodents.

"Let's get out of here," Vic said and pulled her up.

"No, we need to get the job done." She tried to drum up spit, but failed. "I can't come back."

She wondered if she had the strength to attach the camera to the tripod. It was hard to breathe, harder to concentrate as knots tightened in her stomach and chest.

"I'm feeling dizzy, myself," Vic said, propping his hand on her shoulder.

"Don't faint," Rose said through her clenched teeth, but wasn't sure if she was speaking to him or to herself.

"Men don't faint."

"Can you . . . move the candles a foot . . . closer . . . to Agnes? I need more light . . . on her . . . skirt."

As Vic adjusted the light, Rose peered through her viewfinder on the medieval tart, but could not keep her centered.

She pressed the back of her hand to her mouth and moaned. Vic grabbed her, and half carried, half dragged her up the narrow stone steps.

He tossed her on the church lawn. She stretched out her arms and legs and stared up at the spinning night sky while he returned the candles and found her backpack.

The earth slowly stopped rotating. The stars sharpened into individual points of light.

"Did you lock all the doors?" she asked the gigantic shadow looming over her, but not really caring if he had.

"Right and tight. Camera and legs are inside." He set her bag next to her on the grass. "Fetching as you are there, I think we'd better go." He snapped his fingers.

Suddenly aware of the picture she painted on the church lawn, Rose rolled to her feet and followed him down the road.

VIC BREWED EARL GREY tea back at the cottage and was pleased to see the color return to Rose's cheeks.

"I'm already feeling much better, so I don't need this stuff." She looked into the mug. "Did you put something in this? It tastes . . . weird. Do you have any wine?"

"Try the biscuits." He plunked two boxes on the table.

"Gingerbread Gentlemen?" Rose read the label on a small blue box.

Vic opened another carton. "Personally, I like the Little Lemon Ladies." He gave her a smile and was pleased to see her effort to return it. Thoughts of Lemon Ladies reminded him of her buttery dress. He fought an overwhelming urge to lick her lips and anywhere else he could reach.

Instead, he placed the biscuits on one of Alice's treasured china plates.

Rose crumbled two biscuits for each one she ate.

"I want that key," she said. "I want to go back and finish

the damn job. I can't let this mold allergy, or whatever it is, defeat me."

He poured himself more tea.

"Hand the key over, Vic." She put out her hand and snapped her fingers at him as he had at her in the church yard.

He closed his fist around her hand and jerked her forward. Her mouth was sweet with gingerbread, warm and moist. "One thing I've learned is never break into the same place twice in one night. We'll try again tomorrow."

He pulled her up and lifted her into his arms, carried her up the narrow stairs. He chose his childhood bedroom over Alice's for its narrow bed. Rose couldn't avoid him there.

She looked far from tired as she undressed, shucking clothes as fast as a fishmonger shucked cockles, then diving under the duvet. He tugged the chain on the light in the loo next door and extinguished the one in the bedroom. He wanted to see her, but not put her in the spotlight.

"You're warm," he said, smoothing his hand over her forehead. Her skin was fever-hot compared to the crisp, cool linens he'd had the foresight to put on the bed that morning.

He tossed the duvet back. It slithered onto the rug. She sat up and drew her legs in toward her body, folding her arms around her knees while he undressed. When he settled on the bed next to her, she remained contained, protective.

"I love your downy skin," he murmured, stroking her arm. "You have freckles everywhere. I think they each have their own little hair."

She extended her legs a touch, her arms loosening. He kissed her thigh, nuzzled the crook of her elbow. An inch of space appeared between her legs and arms.

He gathered her bunched, taut body into his embrace and kissed her mouth. He savored the softness of her lips, was heartened that it took only a moment for her to put an arm around his neck and kiss him back.

She bloomed against his body like one of Alice's flowers, softening, stretching out her legs, relaxing her arms as he ran his lips over her chin, cheeks, brows.

He pulled open the drawer in the bedside chest and dumped a handful of condoms on the mattress. "I've been shopping."

"You'll kill me," she whispered.

"You'll die happy."

She wriggled her moist center against him. Every nerve in his body went on alert.

Her hair floated across his shoulder. The sensation was more powerful than any drug. The light silhouetted her in a nimbus of gold and copper as she moved her lips in a slow journey down his center.

A shudder ran through his body. This image of her would return, again and again, he knew, when she was gone. A pang of regret filled him that she would leave. "I hope the book takes weeks. No, months," he said.

"Why?"

"I need time."

"For what?" She rubbed her nose on his belly. He felt it behind his testicles.

"For you to believe my apology."

She licked around his navel. "Honesty is the best policy."

"I've always had a bloody time with honesty. It doesn't mean—"

"Shhh." She eased down onto his cock. "Explain later. Put it in an e-mail."

"I've not wanted to be honest with someone before . . . or after."

He drew her forward to bury his face between her breasts, kiss her hard nipples. He scraped his cheek, his lips, back and forth across them.

As warm as he had thought her lips, her insides as she sheathed him were a furnace. The condom did nothing to quell the sensation that he might be incinerated if he remained within her.

"Brilliant," he said as she slid slowly up and down on him, shifting, teasing. He had a momentary vision of himself stretched on the green grass, her riding him like this, but in her buttercup yellow dress. And he would fill her with cum, without condoms, and when she stood, holding her skirt high at her waist, he would see the slick wet on her inner thighs. He arched beneath her and cried out as the fantasy overwhelmed him.

She slipped off his hips and curled at his side, one hand on his stomach.

He touched her breast, her navel, between her thighs. It was not fantasy, her heat, nor the pebble-hard flesh he caressed, as taut as her nipples.

"You've a fever, mate," he said. "Something in the church has made you sick."

"Kiss me."

He knew she did not intend mouth to mouth. He forgot what he wanted to say. Forgot his name.

"Grant my wish, Vic."

ROSE WOKE WHEN MORNING sun filtered through the window ivy. She spent a few moments looking around at a room that must have once been decorated for a young boy, but now felt like a neutral guest room, despite the family photos on the dresser. She examined the faces, recognized Vic in the immature faces of his sons, and in one of two women who stood arm-in-arm at a sea resort.

Alice Drummond and Vic's mother, she presumed.

She found Vic in the garden, snipping the topiaries. "I'm impressed that you're so dedicated to the garden," she said.

"One of Alice's hobbies. I wish the customers would come for the buggers."

"The topiaries?" She saw they were in individual pots sunk among the poppies and foxglove.

"She sold them, mostly to posh restaurants. Unfortunately, she didn't keep records so I don't know if I'm trimming them for a customer or for no purpose."

"Shame about that one's nose." Rose pointed to the rabbit he'd been snipping when she'd first met him.

"I'll wire a raspberry on."

The word came out razbree. "Father Donald's rather hard to understand, where's he from?"

"Cornwall. Been transferred a few times, I imagine." He mimed drinking. "The rest of us are starting to sound like the idiots on American telly."

Rose carried a chair into the grassy center of the lawn to enjoy the warm morning sun—and admire Vic's ass as he bent over to pluck errant weeds from the beds. "What does the F in V. F. Drummond stand for?"

"Fitzwilliam. My mum wanted to name me after Mr. Darcy. A Jane Austen fan she was. But my father won on my first name."

"Victor?"

"Vickers."

"Vickers? Poor boy."

He grinned. "I was born on a day my father was rather lucky at the racecourse. I'm named for his favorite bookie, Lester Vickers. I suppose your mother loved flowers."

"Joan and I are named for our grandmothers. My maternal grandmother's name was Rosamond. Unfortunately, her middle name was Daisy." She kicked off her sandals and rubbed her toes on the cool grass. "How's that for pitiable? Rose and Daisy?"

He stopped weeding. His eyes were wide as if he'd been given the key to the smoke shop. "You're my soul mate," he said.

"Why on earth?"

"I have this fantasy about you." He dumped the shears on the table. "You're lying here naked, with a daisy in your navel."

Rose began to laugh. "Where did that come from?"

"Inside my head. It's what I kept thinking in Club 7734." He gave her a sheepish grin.

"And here, I thought you were thinking about glittery pole dancers."

He shook his head.

"I don't see any daisies here," she said softly, sweeping her hand out to the emerald carpet.

He strode to the end of the garden, opened the gate, and disappeared for a few minutes. Her heart began to beat. It stuttered when he returned and dropped dozens of tiny daisies in her lap. Each white flower gleamed with drops of dew.

She held her skirt like a basket and left her chair to kneel by his feet. He settled next to her. One by one, she plucked the tiny petals from a daisy. Each petal floated to rest between them.

Vic put his hand behind her head, drew her close and touched her mouth with his. "I was more aroused by thoughts of you here, in my garden, than I was by any scenario at the club."

"I've never been anyone's fantasy before."

They dueled tongues for a few minutes.

"Grant an old man his fantasy?" He used one of the flowers to tuck her hair behind her ear.

"Only if you're not too old to act on it." She scattered the daisies on the grass, stood up and slipped out of her underwear, though she kept the dress on. The high stone wall, the trees, gave her a sense of security, but not enough. Someone might do as she had, come around the side of the cottage unannounced. She didn't want to be completely naked.

Vic, however, had no such qualms. He blithely stripped out of his clothes. She decided to torture him a bit by folding his jeans and T-shirt in neat squares.

Finally, she stretched out beside him, on her back, her head on one arm. His hand shook a bit as he drew her hem to her waist and placed a flower in her navel. She gripped his wrist and pulled him close. "Where else did you see daisies in this fantasy?"

He tucked a daisy in her pubic hair. "You're brilliant, Rosie. I'll remember this day forever. If I don't die of a coronary."

22

MRS. BENNETT SNIPPED A thread and sighed. Her work was exceptional.

"Have you read this?" Father Nigel held out a copy of *The Times*.

The headline said, "Religious Leaders Agree on Youth."

"Much ado about nothing," she said and stood up, rubbing her back. "The weather will change again. I feel it in my bones."

"I feel this in my bones." He shook the paper. "It says we'll all be answering to this—this committee. It will be nothing but forms and—"

"Stop it, Nigel. You know as well as I that the truly important ones here will not be influenced by such nonsense. Simply bring them in as servers, as we always have, teach them well, and they're ours forever."

"I wish I had your confidence."

"I know committees; they come and go. We need only

wait a bit and this one, too, will go." She sorted through her silks for her beloved ebony thread.

"We've another matter to discuss. I saw photos yesterday that were taken here, at night. In the dark."

Mrs. Bennett looked up, ebony thread forgotten. "At night?"

"I only saw a glimpse of the pictures, but there's no doubt someone let that woman in here."

Mrs. Bennett felt a surge of anger. "Who has the pictures?"

"Her sister, Rose Early. She wanted to retake them, they weren't satisfactory in some way. I said no."

Mrs. Bennett nodded. "She was here yesterday, asked Donald to turn out the spots. Perhaps she'll be content with what she got." She made a decision and shut her sewing kit. "But as to Joan Early getting in here at night. That matter needs more attention."

"How did she do it?"

"Do what?" Mrs. Bennett asked, folding her stool.

"Get in?"

"Don't be thick. Who do you *think* let her in? Who has a key? And we'll need to see he's punished for that little disobedience."

ROSE WAITED UNTIL VIC fell asleep. He was restless, rolling his head on the pillow. When he finally settled, she slipped from under his hand. The church key was in the back pocket of his jeans. With her business card.

"I'll have to send for Jasper." She grabbed some clothes and tiptoed from the room. She dressed in the kitchen, eased the door open, and stepped back into the night.

Despite the village lights, the path to the church was dark.

"Shit, you scared me," she said when Vic came up behind her.

"Where the hell are you going?"

"Look, I can't stay here indefinitely."

"What's that got to do with going into a church at night, *alone*?"

"Probably nothing."

"I always think women who go where they shouldn't deserve what they get."

"You are the man who said 'tomorrow,' aren't you? It's tomorrow."

"You must be thick if you think I'd let you go in there alone."

"Come on, then, don't dawdle." She tossed him the key.

The ancient door creaked as Vic unlocked it. As she walked along the silent nave, no longer dark, filled with ambient light from the narrow stained-glass windows, she thought she heard the whisper of sandals, the murmur of prayers.

"They're not there," she said softly to herself.

"Who's not here?"

"The monks. They whisper."

"This place is making you bonkers."

She shot a series of photos of the tapestry and altar screen while Vic raised and lowered candles to her demands. She stopped now and then to put her head between her knees.

It was only through concentrating on the small area visible through the lens that she could stem the sickness and remain upright.

She grabbed her tripod and headed for the crypt. "Will you be my rat chaser?" she whispered.

Vic gave her a wide-eyed look. "You'll owe me."

They unlocked the crypt door and let some of the miasma of fetid air mingle with the fresher air of the sanctuary before descending.

Vic sat on the crypt steps and she took a shot of him, head down, flashlight dangling from his fingertips. She adjusted the candles he'd lit for her and captured some of the crypt's former beauty, the murky atmosphere creating the illusion the gilding remained intact.

"Are you almost done?" he asked. "I feel like shit."

"Not yet. They're all time-exposures. I have to get them right the first time. I don't want to come back."

He headed back up the steps.

Rose allowed the camera to work its magic. Now that she no longer had the viewfinder to her eye, illness returned with a vengeance. The flames danced, giving the illusion Lady Agnes's skirt had moved.

Finally, Rose was satisfied. She took the camera off the tripod and set it aside, then snuffed the candles. Her flashlight illuminated only a tiny circle of space and she wished Vic had waited.

Her hands betrayed her again when she tried to put away the tripod. She knocked over her backpack. The contents scattered across the smooth stone floor. Her phone disappeared.

"Shit." Rose went down on her knees and flicked the flashlight beam around in case Stuart Little decided to come out to play.

Her head pounded. A bead of sweat ran down her temple.

Rose found her agenda book and phone against the marble base of the sarcophagus. Her thumb touched the phone's keypad as she scooped it up, lighting the screen and the small crypt in a blue gleam.

Joan's number was there as it always was.

Rose sat on the bottom step of Lady Agnes's crypt. She put her head on her knees and swallowed down bubbles of acid. She had no energy to gather her other belongings.

A whisper of sound came from above. Not the sandals of ghostly monks. Probably Vic nicking the candlesticks, she thought with a wan smile.

She rubbed her fingertips over the screen that still glowed with Joan's number. She hit the call button.

Deep inside the crypt, a phone rang.

23

VIC ACCOMPANIED TREVOR ACROSS the church lawn to the vicarage where Rose was installed with a Family Liaison Officer. Within a few hours, ancient All Saints Church had transformed from a place of worship to a crime scene.

An ambulance drove off. Silently.

Vehicles clogged the street as the press stowed their cameras and pulled away in the ambulance's wake. With Joan's removal from the crypt, there was little left to titillate. Rose could head home without having a microphone or camera thrust into her face.

No, not home. Rose's home was in America. With Joan found there was nothing to keep Rose in Marleton.

"So, if Joan's been dead for over a week . . . how'd her phone ring?" Vic asked.

"Haven't a clue. I agree with you that the battery in Joan's phone has to be dead. Forensic Science Service will examine it and tell us for certain."

"There has to be an explanation."

"You, who dwell in the supernatural, want an explanation?" Trevor shook his head. "A spark maybe? Possibly there was just enough residual power in the battery to get the job done."

Vic thought Trevor was balmy, but didn't say so.

"Or it was Rose's imagination. You heard nothing," Trevor finished.

"I was . . . looking about. And if it was only imagination, why open Lady Agnes's coffin?"

"Because I told the Criminal Investigation Department Rose was to be taken seriously."

"That was enough?"

Trevor was silent for a moment. "I told Munson, who'll be the lead on this, that I'd done some private inquiries on Joan's car. It hasn't turned up."

They reached the vicarage.

"I'll be honest, it was more that I like Rose. I shagged her sister without caring what became of her. I owed it to Rose," Trevor admitted.

That Vic understood.

Trevor knocked on the vicarage door. Donald frowned when he saw who stood on the porch. "Rose has had quite enough upset for one day."

"I want to offer Rose my condolences," Trevor said. Without asking permission he shouldered past the priest. Vic drifted in on Trevor's tail.

Rose sat in the vicarage office, an untouched cup of coffee on the desk by her elbow. The local constabulary in the person of PC Alden stood with a protective attitude by Rose's side. He'd been brought from bed, Vic assumed as he wore his civvies. A woman in a smart black suit wrote in a notebook. Her attitude stiffened when Trevor squatted by Rose's knee.

Trevor took her hand. "Your sister's been taken away, now."

Rose's face crumpled. Tears ran down her cheeks, dripped unheeded on her chest. Donald handed her a handkerchief. She buried her face in the clean cotton.

They waited in uncomfortable silence as Rose wept. Vic felt as if someone had jerked his tie too tight. He rubbed his throat where his sweater gaped, but it did nothing to relieve the sensation.

Finally, Rose wiped her face and reached out. For Trevor.

"Joan's phone?" she asked.

"In her handbag," Trevor said.

"I was right then. It *did* ring."

"We haven't examined the phone, miss. You'll be going now, Harrison?" the woman asked.

"Yes. I just wanted to offer my condolences. They've taken your statement?" Trevor asked Rose.

She nodded. Her eyes gleamed again. "Don't go."

Why the hell should Rose want Trevor? Irritation hatched a desire to put a fist in his friend's face. Vic balled his fingers into fists.

Trevor shook his head. "I'm so very sorry, but this isn't my patch. You've PC Alden as your Family Liaison Officer and you know him already. He'll look after you, answer all your questions."

"And you are?" Vic asked the small woman who Vic suspected appreciated Trevor's presence as little as he.

The woman thrust her hand out. "I'm Detective Sergeant Molly Munson. I'll be heading the inquiry. You can go, Harrison."

"Don't, please. I need to know what happened to my sister."

Anger surged through Vic like electricity through wire when Rose clung to Trevor's hand.

"I don't believe she suffered." Trevor ignored the sniff of disapproval from Munson.

"A blow to the head, wasn't it?" Donald said. They all turned to look at him. "I . . . that is . . . I asked when I took coffee to the men," the curate stammered.

Trevor gave him a cold look-over, but spoke only to Rose. "These last few hours must have been grueling for you. Try to get some sleep. You might be more comfortable back at the Rose and Thistle. I'll speak to Watkins about allowing you Joan's space."

How dare Trevor try to separate Rose from him? The electrical charge spiraled like lightning through Vic's veins.

Rose touched Vic's arm. One fleeting touch. A moth wing brush of her fingertips. With the contact, the need to strike died. It zinged away as if she'd grounded him somehow.

"Munson and Alden will answer your questions," Trevor said.

"What's next?" Rose asked.

"We'll make our inquiries," Munson said before Trevor could speak. "There will be an inquest. Please remember that PC Alden is at your disposal twenty-four hours a day. Any concerns you have, any questions, he's your man."

Vic looked Alden over. No competition there. A cozy family man who'd be holding nothing more than the metaphoric hand.

"Thank you. Everyone." Fresh tears ran down Rose's cheeks.

Despite the grateful nature of the hug Rose gave Trevor, Vic disliked the length of time Trevor held her, how he ran his hand up and down her back, whispered words of encouragement.

Vic imagined how a lance from the church tapestry, a good sharp one, might look protruding from between Trevor's shoulder blades.

Trevor set Rose away with a kiss to her forehead.

Donald took Trevor's place. His embrace was shorter, but no less aggravating. Vic mentally hefted a lance for the curate as well.

"I'm ready to go," Rose said, softly.

"I'll take you to the Rose and Thistle if you like." PC Alden spoke for the first time.

Rose tucked her arm in Vic's. "That's very kind of you," she said. "But I can find my way."

Outside, a mizzling rain fell, fogging the headlights of Trevor's car as he pulled away.

Lances in coppers and curates seemed ludicrous in the sharp, wet air.

"Vic?"

"Rose?"

"The phone rang."

24

THE DAWN FILLED THE sitting room with a wan gray light. Rain ran down the windows, pattered on the creeper that wreathed them.

Vic stretched. His back ached from a night in an armchair. His head ached from wrestling demons in his imagination. He knelt beside Rose and drew the rug from her shoulders. He kissed the warm skin of her throat. His feelings of unreasonable possessiveness felt bizarre here in Alice's cottage.

Rose opened her eyes and he realized she'd not been asleep.

"I dreamt about the crypt, Vic. I felt like I was there, inside that dark space."

He kissed her lips, her red swollen eyes, her forehead. "You're not. You're here."

"Convince me," she whispered and drew him down.

Her skin was soft as swan's down when he undressed her.

He stroked her from shoulder to knee, smoothed his hand over her as if he were pressing wrinkles from silk. When she shivered, he pulled her against his body, and pulled a knitted blanket over them.

Her breasts were criss-crossed with lines from sleeping in her clothes. He traced each one with his tongue. He nuzzled her stomach, laved her navel, and when she lifted her hips, opened her thighs, he caressed her until she wept and shuddered. This time he thought the tears cleansing.

She drifted to sleep, but not a restful one. She whimpered, murmured unintelligible words, twisted and turned, finally waking and staring at him.

He lifted her into his arms.

The warmth of the tiny bathroom cocooned them as he settled with her in Alice's old tub. Sweat dripped from her face, trickled between her breasts from water he'd run too hot.

He lapped the salty drops from her nipples.

She soaped her hands and caressed his testicles until he begged her to stop.

"Shut up. Sit back." She shoved his shoulders, forcing him against the tub back, and crouched astride him.

When he opened his mouth to explain that he was on the edge, would erupt like Mount-Bloody-Vesuvius, he realized she wasn't listening, her gaze fixed on a point over his shoulder.

He said her name twice, but she didn't respond.

He cupped her face for a kiss. Her lips barely moved, though her hands were busy on him. She soaped and stroked him until he was mad with it, sliding toward oblivion in her hands.

She was deep inside her head somewhere, staring again at the wall, lost in her passions when she took him in.

She rode him hard.

Was she aware of the way she looked, water beaded on her skin, her hair? Did she feel the molten heat between them that had nothing to do with the steaming water?

And her scent. Even as dull as that sense was for him, he could smell her. It intoxicated him.

He cupped his hands behind her head and drew her mouth

to his. He tried to spar her tongue, but she was quiescent, not returning his caress.

His heart beat so loudly it sounded like drumming.

Pounding.

Not his heart. Not rain.

Someone hammered on the door, slamming the knocker against the wood as wildly as his heart beat in his chest. "Shit," he muttered.

Rose squeezed some internal muscles that took him over the edge.

An orgasm ripped through his body. He groaned as the throbbing sensations subsided.

The hammering continued on in a familiar cadence. "It's bloody Trevor."

Rose's gaze went to Vic's face. Her eyes widened. She jerked away, sloshing water over the rim of the tub.

Without a word, she snatched up a towel and threw one at him.

"What's wrong with me?" she asked, but he knew it wasn't a question he should answer.

ROSE SAT ON VIC'S bed and cringed. Although she couldn't distinguish individual words, it was Trevor's voice below. She closed her eyes on the image of the two men in the front room, chatting, her clothing in a heap near their feet.

What had come over her? One minute she remembered waking on the couch, the next waking again in Vic's tub.

And between? What had come between?

A quiver went through her. She clutched the towel tighter to her breasts and snapped on the bedside lamp. As light washed over the room, she remembered the dream she'd had before waking.

She'd been in the crypt. She remembered the smells. A being crouched over her. The mural from Club 7734 swept the crypt vision aside and her insides ached as if the crea-ture's huge phallus had impaled her, not Vic's.

With a cry of anguish, she covered her mouth.

Vic came up the stairs, her clothing in his hand. "That was Trev and Alden—" He dropped her clothes and set his hands on her shoulders. "What's wrong?"

"Nothing. Nothing's wrong."

Vic smoothed her hair away from her face. "Alden went to the Rose and Thistle and found out you'd not been back. He rang Trevor who offered to hunt you down. He's a touch out of sorts over it."

Color stained his cheeks. He wore only his jeans. The scratch stood out in a livid line down his chest.

"Oh, shit," she said and took her clothes. "I suppose they think we were rolling around on the floor. And Joan's not even been—"

"They don't think anything of the sort. I put your clothes in the kitchen and told them you were sleeping."

"I'm sorry. I shouldn't have snapped at you."

"You'll have to dress. I sent Alden off with a promise I'd take you to the station."

Her stomach tightened. "Why? What's left to say?"

"Don't fret, mate."

Rose watched Vic strip. He dressed in front of her with a casual nonchalance she could not match. She wriggled into her underwear with the towel still wrapped around her.

"I'll make us some breakfast shall I?" he said.

"I can't eat anything."

But he didn't hear her. He was gone.

In the tiny bathroom, a pool of water surrounded the bathtub. She mopped it up with her towel and his. She hung them to dry, and did her best to repair the damage to her face by scrubbing off the remnants of makeup and splashing cold water on her swollen eyes.

As she pulled her hair back in a knot, she examined her face in an oval mirror, its frame painted as was the wainscoting with flowers and vines. She looked like an ancient crone.

The face staring at her crumpled. She dropped onto the toilet seat and buried her face in her hands. "Oh, Joan, why didn't I come when you asked me to?"

* * *

VIC FORCED A CUP of coffee and toast with marmalade on Rose. As she ate, he regaled her with gossip he'd heard about the detective sergeant heading the case, and had the good sense to keep silent when Rose left more than half her breakfast on her plate.

At the door, Rose put her hand flat on his chest. "I'd like see Alden by myself. You've been great, but I want to be alone."

He backed off, covered her hand with his and squeezed. "If you're sure? Can you find the station on your own? Left by Edgar's Tea Shop, over the stone bridge?"

She nodded. "I have to do this by myself."

"Give me your mobile, then."

She dug it from her backpack. Her fingers shook as she handed it over.

Was Joan's number still in the window?

Vic punched some keys and handed it back. "I've put my number in. Ring me if you need me. I'm staying right here."

On impulse, she rose on her toes and kissed his mouth. "I won't get lost."

When she passed the church, she saw the police were still very much in attendance. Several officers watched her openly. From their position, she imagined they were stationed to turn aside the tourists. Sensations of guilt, of having failed Joan, made her quicken her pace until she had crossed the troll bridge.

As she passed Edgar's, Rose knew she would never again think of tea without remembering the many times Joan had sat at one of these tables eating scones and clotted cream.

Detective Sergeant Munson had her own office at the station. PC Alden, now in his customary black and white uniform, ushered her in. Rose was grateful for his familiar presence.

The detective wore a dark blue suit with a white, open-collared blouse. Her elfin appearance negated the information Vic had given her that DS Munson excelled at quelling domestic disputes.

"Where's Trevor? I mean DI Harrison?" Rose asked.

"Trevor has returned to Stratford. As he knew your sister, we decided it would not be appropriate for him to involve himself in this matter."

With Trevor gone, the world of officialdom looked bleak. Rose calmed herself.

"We wanted you to know that tests done with a chemical called luminol indicate that your sister fell, or was pushed, down the crypt steps. There are marks on the floor that indicate she was dragged to the coffin and then placed inside. An estimation of time of death would be anywhere from ten days ago to possibly only seven. Establishing time of death might be a bit dicey because of the climate conditions in the crypt. It's damp, but it's also quite cold."

Rose's coffee burned in her throat. Her mind shied from thoughts of Joan lying so close-by each time she'd visited the church.

Munson placed a clear pouch on the desk. It contained a designer leather purse. "This was with your sister. Do you recognize it?"

"No. But Joan had lots of clothes, bags. Shoes."

"Her mobile phone was not operating."

Rose's gaze jerked from the purse to Munson's face.

"I'm not a lunatic, officer."

Alden spoke for the first time. "No one's suggesting such a thing."

"However, I've talked to her phone service, Ms. Early." Munson consulted a sheaf of papers in front of her. "Global International Wireless indicates the phone has been off for ten days. That may help us fix the time of death as well."

"Impossible." Emotions—anger, grief, incredulity—formed a lump in her chest. "I called my sister repeatedly. I called her yesterday. I got her voice mail. The phone was on!" The room tipped. "I left messages," she repeated.

"There were none on her mobile."

Alden offered her his handkerchief.

A buzz filled Rose's ears. "You must think I'm crazy," she said, embarrassed her voice sounded as tremulous as she felt.

"No, you've had a shock, miss. You're confused," Alden said.

"I'm not confused!" She leaped to her feet and paced the tiny office. "I called Joan probably a dozen times this week. I got her voice mail every time."

She stood behind her chair and gripped the back for strength, and wished Vic were there to say something profane for her.

"Why dance around the real point here? You're wondering why I thought Joan was in that coffin. How could I make such an accurate guess? Maybe I knew and covered it up by saying the phone rang. Maybe I'm too stupid to know batteries don't hold their charge for more than a week!"

Munson got to her feet and rubbed a hand wearily over her short, spiky hair. "No, Miss Early, that's not what I'm thinking. You were in America when Joan's phone was turned off. I'm just wondering out loud how a phone could ring when it's supposed to be dead."

They all cringed.

"Sorry," Munson said. "Poor choice of words. The messages can be explained in many ways. You rang a wrong number—"

"No. *No.* I called Joan."

"We can't ignore the fact that GIW says the mobile has been off for ten days. That is, by the way, the same date we have that someone last saw Joan. Mary Garner saw your sister at the Bell that evening."

A heavy silence fell between them.

"And?"

"She was dining with V. F. Drummond."

PC ALDEN ACCOMPANIED HER as far as the bridge. He reminded her he was at her disposal twenty-four hours a day. His cheeks flushed red when he asked if it was best to find her at Drummond's.

Rose leaned on the bridge with no desire to take out a camera. Rain drops dimpled the water's surface. Pale green leaves twirled dizzily along and disappeared beneath the bridge.

She felt like the leaves. She had no direction, no one to talk to, no friends here beyond Vic. That wasn't really true. There was Mary and Trevor.

But unburdening her fears and guilt to either made Rose cringe. Mary might think her crazy, and Trevor represented officialdom even if Joan's death was "not his patch."

Rose thought of the curate, Donald. He, at least, offered conventional comfort. But when Rose walked up to the vicarage, Donald was not there. The police barriers were still up though their presence had decreased to just two officers on guard.

"Needs reconsecration."

"I beg your pardon?" Rose recognized the woman who'd defended her picture-taking to Father Donald.

The woman's shiny red bike contrasted sharply with her skirt and sweater in dull shades of tan. "The church is locked until the crypt can be reconsecrated. The Bishop is expected any time now. They found a body, you know. Murder, it was."

Rose felt the burn of tears again.

"Oh, dear. You look upset. Did you know her, luv? A tourist they said in the village. I'm Mrs. Bennett." The old woman slid her bicycle into a stand by the church gate. "I look after the vestments and tapestry."

"She was my sister," Rose blurted out.

Mrs. Bennett slanted a look at the police, then whispered, "Would you like to come in? You could sit a while. Pray for her."

Rose followed the old woman past the vicarage and then back along the footpath that separated the church grounds from a meadow behind. Mrs. Bennett put a finger to her lips, and smiled. She threw open a small door in the rear of the south transept. A staircase led down to a maintenance area. So much for the police guards.

Mrs. Bennett wove through a maze of folding chairs and

tables, unused candle stands, mops and buckets toward another set of stairs that emerged behind the chancel.

"The Bishop's a nasty man," Mrs. Bennett said. "So I thought I'd get my work out of the way before he arrives. How the man elevated himself to such a position, I don't know. No people skills. Skimpy sermons. And gossip! He'll chatter for hours. *Some* people have real work to do."

Mrs. Bennett set a stool padded with a worn velvet cushion behind the high pulpit. "Sit here. No one will see you there. It's nice and comfy."

Rose felt sick. "I'm not sure this was a good idea."

"Sit. Sit." Mrs. Bennett urged her. "Look at the lovely tapestry. Think about the lovely work."

Her legs rubbery, Rose sank onto the stool. From her place, Rose saw straight into the depths of the choir stalls, saw the grotesque figures carved beneath the fold-up seats. She also saw the stricken faces of the martyrs on the altar screen. It seemed they all wept for Joan.

How many pictures had she and Joan taken of those faces? I'm surrounded by tragedy, she thought, looking at one crusader on the huge wall hanging whose horse's hoofs crushed a hapless farmer.

Everywhere she rested her eyes, the tapestry, altar screen, the pillars behind the pulpit, she saw images of death and destruction.

Bubbles of bile and black coffee burned her throat. How long must she sit here? What polite interval must pass before she could sneak away?

With each touch of the seamstress's hand, the tapestry's surface shimmered in the altar screen floodlight.

"Is that gold thread?" Rose asked. Only conversation kept her mind from thoughts of Joan.

"Whisper, luv. We're being a little naughty here; mustn't get caught."

Rose lowered her voice. "Is the thread gold?"

"Indeed. Silver and gold." Mrs. Bennett stroked the tapestry. "Loomed in the sixteenth century, it was. Flemish. Made of the finest wool, silk, and metal thread. There's not a finer one in all of England."

"I've seen the Unicorn Tapestries in New York."

Mrs. Bennett waved off the Unicorn Tapestries. "Milleflora's not my favorite. I like ones that have stories to tell."

Rose knew the Unicorn Tapestries told a tale, but could muster no strength to argue.

At the sound of a petulant voice at the west end doors, Mrs. Bennett put a finger to her lips. The voice complained about the interruption of a golf game. Other, less distinct voices soothed. Rose peeked round the pulpit and saw Father Nigel and several other men in religious garb disappear down the crypt steps.

"The Bishop. Lives for golf, he does. Once had professional aspirations, but he . . . I believe the word is "choked," Mrs. Bennett whispered.

Rose shrank into the shadows. Mrs. Bennett moved her center of operations to the floral border.

"This tapestry honors our men who fought in the crusades."

And trampled peasants. A wave of nausea swept the uncharitable thought aside.

She could not take her gaze from the spot where the woman had plied her needle until interrupted by the clergymen. The knight whose rearing horse crushed a peasant wielded a long sword with which he skewered a woman in the chest.

Rose blinked. The suggestion of nipples showed at the woman's low neckline. Another woman was bound between two men who dragged her toward a priest.

The images of bondage and religion seemed ill-mixed. Although the tapestry was undoubtedly a work of art, the subject matter revolted her.

Rose shivered and rubbed her arms. Where had her energy gone? It had drained away when she'd found out Joan was dead.

Or had while she was conscious. Unconsciously, she'd exerted great energy screwing Vic. Her sense of propriety prickled at the unchurchlike thought.

"Have you family, luv?" Mrs. Bennett asked.

"Only my mother." The only silver lining to the terrible tragedy of Joan's death was that their mother would never know, nor suffer over the news. Rose and Joan had long ceased to be names their mother knew or faces she recognized.

An errant, ugly thought, swept all peace aside. She closed her eyes. *Had Joan angered Vic so much he'd pushed her down the crypt stairs and hidden her body?*

No. Not Vic.

He hid knowing Joan.

Voluptuous lilies with swollen pistils and dripping stamens bordered the Marleton tapestry. The misericords featured lewd figures with grotesque faces and suggestive postures, so why shouldn't the tapestry have more of the same? The seamstress hummed softly as she worked on veins of a lily. Priestly voices now muted in prayer droned in the background. They morphed into the troublesome whine of a mosquito.

Rose closed her eyes and repeated her own tapestry of prayers learned in various churches and faiths. Her head cleared the longer she meditated. Her strength returned. The nausea subsided. Rose got quietly to her feet and slipped out of the church through the basement maintenance door.

Wind buffeted her as she crossed the back of the vicarage.

Thoughts of Vic and Joan, of pushes, of lies churned in her head.

Movement in the meadow drew her eyes. Father Donald, walked rapidly away from the village. He's trespassing, Rose thought, with a touch of surprise.

And why wasn't he at the reconsecration?

VIC PRINTED A PHOTOGRAPH of Joan off the Internet. Amazing, he thought, how quickly the press worked. The photograph was from Joan's book covers, a typical promotional shot. The news story with Joan's photograph also featured one of All Saints Church, Father Nigel on the steps, Donald by his side. Another file photograph. Vic remembered it as one sent to him by Alice when Donald had been chosen curate more than three years before.

Almost handsome enough to make me want to attend All Saints again, Alice had written.

The man fascinated Vic. When the curate had embraced Rose, Vic had seen the scars of a suicide attempt on the young man's wrist. He'd seen Donald's scars many times before, and every time Vic wondered what had compelled Donald to want to end his life? His writer's soul itched to know. Had the church become Donald's refuge? Or had the suicide attempt come after ordination?

Vic looked up the lane, but didn't see Rose. His thoughts returned to the curate. Vic didn't expect Donald to talk to him about suicide after the scene over Alice's death—ugly words said there.

"Called you a drunken shit, I did," Vic muttered. Anger resurfaced with almost as much force as it had when he'd learned the truth. If Donald hadn't been dawdling down the pub, he might have saved Alice.

And who might have saved Joan? *Him?*

No. Vic had sensed nothing ill in store for Joan on their last dinner together. She talked of nothing but her discontent with her agent. Over the pudding, she had finally admitted why she'd asked him to The Bell. She'd wanted an introduction to his agent. And he'd made some coarse remark about it being the tat for the tits, so to speak. But he'd agreed and been given an impersonal peck on the cheek before Joan had dashed off to her car.

Where had she gone? Whom had she met? What had she done to get herself killed?

Vic placed Joan's photograph on the mantle and wished he'd thought to take one to Club 7734. Despite the masks, someone might have remembered her.

He tucked secateurs into his back pocket and headed to the garden. He paced the flower beds, wanting to make up something for Rose. Something hopeful. He settled on violets.

Rose must have come in the front door while he'd been in

the garden. He picked up the handwritten message lying on his laptop. He read it several times, then crumpled it. When he looked upstairs, her bags were gone.

He almost reached for a cigarette. Instead, he grabbed the phone. "What are you doing?" he asked, impressed by the casual sound of his voice. "You weren't imposing. What do I care what Alden thinks? Who's going to scrub my back?" He listened a moment to Rose's excuses. "Sure. I understand." He cradled the phone, then called her back. "Did Trevor talk you into this?"

She asked him a question.

"Yeah, I can spend one night without you." He slammed the phone down as hard as he could. He looked down at the violets. "You look a bloody fool."

He shoved the flowers into a water glass. He wanted a cigarette. Badly. To avoid temptation, he went to his computer. But when he opened his word processor, the words were there.

The deleted words.

His chest itched.

Ten minutes later, he was on the way to London. On the seat beside him lay an unopened packet of cigarettes, the pass to Club 7734, and Joan's photograph.

25

ON HIS SECOND VISIT, Vic viewed Club 7734 with his vision unclouded by Rosie distractions. He saw beyond the titillation of the customer attractions to the set. Club 7734 was top drawer. No faux marble, even in the loo. No cheap liquor behind the bar.

He wandered from room to room. This time he ignored the eye-popping women who cavorted half-naked in masked anonymity.

Curiosity sent him to the gargoyle barroom. As he ruefully examined the huge phallus that had figured in Rose's hallucination, he caught a whiff of smoke. His heart kicked in his chest. He scanned the room for a carelessly discarded cigarette or candles flaming where they shouldn't, but saw nothing. Luckily, an exit was only a few feet away.

The room pulsed with spinning spotlights set in an ebony ceiling. The smoky smell wafted by again, and he realized it might be part of the room's theme of fire, brimstone and demons. A man and woman, leaning on the bar near him, swallowed each other's tongues.

Vic slid his drink a few feet away from the entwined couple. The man looked like he was wearing nothing but a coating of something brown as Rose's coffee, possibly latex. He was muscular, uninhibitedly aroused, and masked like a demon. His persona fit the chamber, but not the woman who rubbed against him in a gyrating frenzy. She wore Savile Row pinstripes and sensible shoes, a white shirt and waistcoat. Her mask was a Liberty of London tie, with slits for viewing her partner's phallic display.

A sudden influx of demonic patrons filtered into the room. Vic found that the women among them, who also looked dipped in latex, failed to arouse in him the visceral reaction he'd had with Rose in her wispy dress— or Rose in her jeans and T-shirt for that matter.

One woman in particular repulsed him with her thick tail and sharp, curling claws. Each time she sipped from her pink, frothy drink, her small porcine eyes roved the room as if looking for prey.

A veritable demon convention, he thought, making a quick exit. What would Trev think of this symposium of fiends that was in direct opposition to his clerical assignment? Thoughts of Trevor led him back to Joan and Rose. He could not dredge up sorrow for Joan. Nor could he squelch his empathy for Rose.

He roved through several chambers, hunting his own prey, the Fallen Angel, returning to the brimstone chamber without any luck.

The latexed patrons had driven away the more sedate with their braying laughter and aggressive possession of the dance floor.

If asked, Vic would have said he was comfortable in his body, comfortable in most situations, unfazed by the sexual displays of others, but as he made his way along the perimeter of the brimstone room, he found his skin crawling as two "demons" with long, leathery wings folded tightly against their flanks shoved past him. A scent clung to them as if they'd walked through the aftermath of a fire. Nothing of their bodies from nipples to scars to testicles was concealed by their form-fitting costumes.

The room tilted. The floor rocked like the deck of a ship. Vic took a tentative step and bumped into a familiar pair.

Vic's leather-clad friends steadied him with happy hugs. He forced a grin. The two young men had donned high-laced Doc Marten's to compliment their leather briefs. In a harmonious duet, they urged Vic to their table in what he thought of as the performance room.

"What are your names?" he asked.

"I'm Scatty, and he's Skiver," one of them said and Vic knew they might not be wearing masks, but they were hiding behind their slang names.

"I'm assuming you chaps are short of cash."

Skiver opened his eyes wide. "What gives you that impression?"

"You don't seem to have much to wear."

They laughed and relaxed their thin bodies against him. The air was thick with cigarette smoke, though without the underlying hint of brimstone from the previous chamber, and Vic drew it hungrily into his lungs, feeling a touch guilty as he did so.

The stage show tonight was not golden syrup being lapped from naked women. Instead, people took turns hanging from hooks they attached to various body parts. It was macabre and something Vic thought he might be able to use in a book one day.

Unlike the barmen, there seemed to be no brakes on his new friends' tongues. Vic bought them drinks and settled at a small table, one on each side. They draped their arms over his shoulders and admired his fine, strong physique.

"Want to give it a go?" Skiver asked Vic as Scatty left them to join the fun.

"No, I'll like my arms the length they are, sorry." They watched Scatty join the queue of volunteers, behind a female demon who hooked a noose-like device to her ankle.

Moments later, she dangled upside down, her wings folded about her like a bat's in a belfry. "What's with the demons?" Vic asked the young man beside him.

"Wednesday."

"And?"

"Their night. Never see them any other time."

"Must be a bank holiday in hell."

Skiver convulsed with laughter to the point Vic needed to pound him between his narrow shoulders.

He took advantage of the time alone with the boy. "Look, I'm trying to find someone."

Disappointment filled the boy's face and his slight withdraw told Vic he'd blundered. "I don't mean for . . . fun. I mean I have business with him."

"Oh." Skiver shimmied his chains with renewed delight. "Who? We know just everyone."

Vic felt a pang of parental angst that this chap was not much older than his son but had attended this place long enough to be familiar with the regular patrons.

He would send his sons to a boarding school in Antarctica for the next school term.

"I think this man I'm after might be a member. He brought a woman here, a lovely American in dominatrix gear." He showed the young man Joan's photo.

The boy shrugged, jangling his chains. "Lots of *those*, although I wouldn't know American from Chinese if she was a guest."

Stupid. The fucking mask. "She'd have been with this man I'm after. Dressed as a Fallen Angel—"

"Oh, our Fallen Angel. He's a dear, isn't he?" Skiver asked Scatty who'd returned from his dangle.

They chatted across Vic's lap. Scatty sighed. "He always dresses in white robes. Has the most lovely fair hair—everywhere." They giggled. "Generous he is sometimes and others, well, he'll be after you to buy him drinks and not offer *anything* in return. A sponger. Always whining about his pay."

"That's why I need to see him. He owes me money," Vic ad-libbed. "Is he here tonight?"

"You'll get nothing from him." Scatty stroked Vic's thigh. "And you're not his type. He likes women, he does, the older the better." He snickered. "Must enjoy rubbing it in all the wrinkles."

Vic stood up and threw a few tenners on the table. "That's for anything he owes you." He held out fifty quid. "And that's if you see him here tonight and tell me before he leaves . . . or knows I'm after him."

He wandered through the maze of chambers, was groped repeatedly, offered drugs, sex, false credit cards, and worst of all, cigarettes, the last by a demon whose latex enrobed penis drooped to mid-thigh, while his wings loomed menacingly over his shoulders.

Vic refused all offers but showed each propositioner Joan's photo. No one knew her. He'd thought a man in white robes would stand out, but the variety of costuming from bizarre to business suit negated any one man's garb as eye-catching.

Sometimes Vic sweetened the pot with money, others babbled for the price of a free drink. Female members knew the Fallen Angel well, the male less so. Demons of both genders returned his enquiries with blank stares.

But known or unknown, Vic sensed few would point his quarry out. Likely members were reticent as they had their own sins to keep close to their vests. One woman, who promised to tell him everything there was to know about his quarry, would only do so if he joined her ménage a trois.

"Not on," he said. He wanted only one woman—a rather thorny one back in Marleton.

ROSE KNOCKED WITHOUT LUCK on the vicarage door for the second time that day. She gnawed her lip. She'd counted on talking to Father Donald.

She needed to make a confession about failing Joan. And who better to hear it and understand, than a man who had the same sin on his head?

Who else would understand the utter shame she felt for ignoring Joan's requests? Father Donald might not have saved Alice Drummond if he'd kept his appointment, but Rose imagined he would understand her wretched feelings.

Her luck was out at Vic's cottage, too. Both his back gate and front door were latched. Her head throbbed with an ache aspirin could not soothe. So, where was he?

And what right did she have to know his whereabouts anyway? Hadn't she given that up along with her place in his guestroom?

She sat on his front step and leaned against a stone planter stuffed with strawberries. The climbing roses over the door filled the air with a lush scent. She thought about Joan, the book, her sister's relationship with Vic.

Part of Rose wanted to renege on her decision to stay at the bed-and-breakfast. She could break in and be in Vic's bed when he came home. Maybe mindless sex would assuage some of the pain she felt. But Rose knew the sex wouldn't be mindless and when it was done, she'd still have this uneasy, sick feeling about Joan inside.

Should she just climb into her rental car and head to Heathrow? Leave the business of who killed Joan to the police?

Vic's number was in her cell phone directory, so was Alden's, but it was Trevor Harrison's she punched in.

Without hesitation, he agreed to meet her at the Rose and Thistle. After setting a time for late that afternoon, she wondered what she'd do till then. She thumbed through the recent numbers she'd called. Joan's appeared in the window.

Rose hit the call button.

"We're sorry, but that Global International Wireless customer is unavailable," said a mechanical, computer generated voice.

Unavailable.

Rose put her head on her knees and cried.

VIC WAS HALF-DRUNK WHEN his leather chaps danced in front of him.

"He's here," one said by his ear, licking it at the same time. "Come with us."

The young men were in raptures over their success, or so Vic assumed, as their tiny briefs were distended with tiny erections. He followed them through the maze of chambers to a corridor of curtained alcoves similar to the ones he'd seen on his first visit.

This corridor, painted a blood red, had iridescent flames licking up the walls. Spotlights swung like upside-down klieg lights, cutting paths back and forth across the corridor.

A musky-scented smoke, not unlike that in the brimstone chamber, drifted along the floor, swirling about their legs, as the leather-clad chaps led the way.

Just props—dry ice and hidden fans. Vic craved something real. He craved Rose.

The alcoves were mostly empty, their black vinyl curtains held back by hooks if the cubicle was not in use. Vic saw cots in the unoccupied spaces, as well as manacles and tables with bottles of oil and jars of cream.

Scatty put a finger to his lips and pointed at a drawn curtain. The heavy material did not close well. A gap of at least six inches allowed a shaft of light to penetrate the alcove with rhythmic regularity.

Vic took the young man's place. The lads giggled behind their palms.

The man in the alcove was garbed in a white, hooded robe which he'd hiked to his waist. His head was down watching an old woman who knelt in front of him, her back to Vic. She was starkers.

At second glance, Vic wasn't sure the woman was old. Although she had gray hair her body looked youthful, her skin smooth. Vic could not see the man's face because his hood covered him well, was not even sure the man was blond. But instinct told him this was the Fallen Angel.

Vic scattered the fifty quid into the misty vapors by his friends' booted feet, slipped into the next alcove and dropped the curtain.

He passed the time waiting for the happy pair to end their

coupling by reading the labels on the bottles and jars, a touch shocked at some of the detailed applications. He played with the manacles and almost locked himself to the wall, barely managing to unfetter himself, and peek out, when he heard the woman leave the room next door.

She was dressed in a drab gray twin set, pearls at her throat, heavy black brogues on her feet. She wore a narrow mask of black silk that made him think, *Zorro's mother*. He was sure her gray hair was a wig. Her age might be anywhere from thirty to forty, though her "costume" made her look twice that.

The man stepped out before Vic could retreat into the shadows. Blond hair glistened in the quick flash of the strobing lights.

"Trevor?" Vic said.

26

TREVOR WAS MORE THAN an hour late. Just as Rose gave up on him, his non-descript gray Ford turned into the Rose and Thistle's driveway.

He apologized, citing a crisis in Stratford. "For decorum's sake, I think we should remain outside. Whatever we do, it should be public. I don't want to look as if I'm hiding something," Trevor said.

Rose glanced around, but Harry was not in sight. When she locked the door, Trevor put his arm around her waist. She leaned instinctively against his shoulder. They headed to the rows of pear trees bordering the Rose and Thistle's drive. They chatted of the weather, of tourist traffic, of Rose's mother at home in King of Prussia.

"I've spoken to my DCI about knowing you. He may assign me elsewhere."

"Oh, no. You can't leave—I need you." Rose took a deep breath. "Look, I have a list of suspects for you to investigate."

Trevor's arm tightened on her waist. "It's your FLO you should be talking to."

She ignored his caution. "Harry Watkins for one. Then there's some guy called the Fallen Angel. And you should add anyone else Joan slept with . . . or annoyed. Maybe Vic." Her voice cracked on his name.

Although Trevor's body stiffened at Vic's name, she heard what she suspected was amusement in his voice when he said, "Why start with Harry Watkins?"

"Harry implied Joan had a number of men in. Moaning and groaning, he said. How would he know that unless he was *spying*?" She stabbed a finger at first Harry's office and then at her cottage. "He can't possibly know what's going on in my bedroom in back, unless he's right up at the window. Arrest him for peeping, if nothing else."

"Easy," Trevor said and led her deeper into the orchard.

The fragrance of pears, the low hum of bees, filled the space with peace, but Rose would not be soothed.

"If Harry killed Joan, he might kill other women who book this place. He might be a serial killer."

"Then I suppose bringing you here was a mistake. I'll give Harry's name to Munson, but you must understand I can't be a part of this investigation."

"And this guy who calls himself the Fallen Angel, he took Joan to a London sex club—"

"How do you know that?" Trevor's voice went sharp.

"Ah . . . from the woman who sold Joan a costume."

Trevor pulled a small notebook from his shirt pocket. "What costume? Where? When? I could get the sack for this."

Exasperation and anger mingled in his rapid-fire questions. She tried to explain without revealing the depth of her roiling emotions.

"And after SewFun, where did you go?" Trevor asked.

"To the London club."

An expression of mingled sadness and disappointment crossed Trevor's face. "With Vic?"

* * *

"Shit," Vic felt as if he'd walked five miles in his hunt through the club rooms.

The instant Vic had said Trevor's name, a pair of latexed demons had backed out of an alcove, blocking Vic's path. They'd danced together, right and left, Vic swearing, them laughing.

When Vic had extricated himself, Trevor was gone.

Each time Vic glimpsed something white, it was not his friend. He'd accosted a man in a white rabbit suit and a woman whose nearly naked body was so pale, he'd recommended a week in Costa del Sol as a cure before hurrying off.

Swirling masses of dancers frustrated his efforts. Deep inside, Vic was shocked that Trevor would frequent this club. For a moment, he considered chucking the whole effort and leaving his friend in peace.

Another flash of white caught Vic's eye. He came up from behind and jerked the hood off Trevor's head. "Christ, Trev."

It was not Trevor.

"Well, well. Never saw these robes in church, *Father* Donald."

The curate bolted. He pulled open a blood-red door, then slammed it behind him.

"Shit." Vic took only one step after Donald. Three women, garbed in pink satin demi-masks, scanty bustiers, and fishnet tights that concealed nothing, circled him. They linked hands, trapping him.

"Another time." His smile soon turned to a frown.

The women shimmied against his body, thrusting their slippery hips and crotches against him. There was no polite way to free himself from their prison. The effort was futile.

He captured one woman about her narrow waist and pulled her hard against his hips. She kissed him with lipstick-thick lips and a rum-infused tongue. The others dropped their linked hands and stroked his back and balls. He twirled the woman around and released her. She cannoned into her partners and they fell in a heap on the floor.

The red door was nothing more than the way to the loo. It was a long, marble palace with five stalls for privacy. He drew curses and invitations as he peered under closed doors before taking another exit into the casino room.

Frustrated enough to chew through chains, Vic began another circuit of the club.

"Bugger this," Vic thought just as the trio of pink-satin women spotted him and headed his way, vengeance clear in the pout of their lips. He threw open a utilitarian door one might see leading to a maintenance cupboard.

He found a tunnel. The air was cold and damp as he stepped from the heated club room. Vic assumed the passageway might be an exit club members used to avoid possible embarrassing encounters at the front entrance.

The music settled to a faint throb behind him. The stone block walls were stained here and there with mineral scale. Bare bulbs, spaced widely apart, illuminated patches of space along the corridor. A musty scent transported him to his childhood, to dirty alleys outside pubs and betting shops where he waited for his dad.

The tunnel sloped down.

A hundred yards later, Vic saw a glimmer. He heard music. A plaintive violin. At the end of the tunnel, he stood at the top of an iron spiral staircase. He realized he'd stumbled into an abandoned section of the underground, left as it might have been when first constructed in the early 1900s. Remnants of maroon and cream tiles could be seen on the walls of the station far below.

On the decaying platform, men in costumes stood in a queue before a folding table. Two men Vic thought looked like his accountants, from their smart business suits to their somber faces, sat at the table, a book and cash box before them. Four women sat on the floor beside the accountants, hands bound in their laps. A man at the table called out and one of the women was led forward. She wore a dress that reminded him of medieval peasant garb. She struggled and wept, but the club members paid her no attention.

Revulsion washed over him, along with a sense of deja

vu. Where had he seen such a tableau? At the cinema? Read it in a book? Written it himself, sometime?

The sensation of watching something he'd seen before grew more overwhelming as cash exchanged hands. A length of rope was attached to the woman's bindings. Her captor, one of the latexed demons, dragged her to the edge of the platform and tossed her onto the rusting rails.

Bile rose in Vic's throat. Was this yet another scenario to please someone's baser nature, everyone a voluntary player, or was it what it looked like—the sale of an unwilling woman to a man?

And if the latter, what could he do about it?

Before he could stop himself, he was down the stairs and running along the platform. One of the accountant types stepped into his path. Vic shoved the man, spinning him into the table.

Vic leaped to the rails, slipped, and jarred his spine.

The demon faced him, the woman screaming and jerking on her rope behind him. Vic's heart pounded. His mouth went dry. The man was huge, muscular, grinning.

Voices called out, but the woman's screams obscured their words. Vic got to his feet. He fisted his hands. Adrenalin pumped through his veins. "Let her go," he said.

A buffet of air behind him, like a train approaching, made him half-turn. Pain burst in his head.

27

VIC WOKE IN AN alley. He staggered to his feet. His head felt
as if someone had put a hammer through it. He touched the
back of his head and winced. His fingers came away bloody.

When the world stopped spinning, he inspected his surroundings. He was no longer underground. He wasn't even
far from where he'd parked his car. He judged it to be about
six in the evening. He'd been unconscious for only a few
minutes.

A rising wind scoured the alley of debris. The distinctive
two tones of the police floated on the night air. A childhood
instinct made him turn away from the sound. He jogged
down the alley and through a fashionable mews. He found
himself in a garden and jumped a low fence, landing hard on
his hands and knees.

When he reached the street where he'd parked his car, he
slowed to a walk. What the hell was he running for?

He opened his car door, his head throbbing, blood wet on
the back of his neck and shirt.

"I'm too old for this," he said, gratified when he settled into the leather cocoon of his Astin Martin. He plucked the car's mobile phone from the glove box and thumbed in Trevor's number.

"CAN YOU FIND THIS Fallen Angel who took Joan to the club?" Rose said as they left the grounds of the inn for the village.

Trevor's phone chirped.

"Vic?" Trevor said, his gaze sliding from Rose's face. "Yeah. I know the club, thanks to Rose. Why didn't *you* tell me about it? What the devil were you doing playing amateur investigator—" He broke off and listened for a moment. "Yeah, I know someone in London CID who will be interested. Now get the hell out of there."

Trevor snapped his phone shut. "It seems Vic's been clubbing again. Without you."

A pang of uncertainty united with her jealousy. She thought of all the temptations in the club, the half-dressed women, the glittery pole dancers.

"Look, I don't know what Joan was up to at this sex club, but I don't want you or Vic caught up in something you can't handle."

The village shops were closing, the tourists shifting from shopping to sipping beer and wine. Between some of the medieval half-timbered buildings were narrow alleys with low roofs that led to quaint courts.

Trevor paused by one and pulled her into its shadows. "I want you to promise me you'll stay out of that club."

"I promise," she said.

"Good girl." Trevor put his hands on her shoulders.

For a brief instant, Rose thought he might kiss her. His next words were just as unsettling.

"If things were different, I'd put you up at my flat."

28

VIC PARKED ON THE verge beyond the Rose and Thistle's drive. He kept to the grass as he approached Rose's cottage. No light streamed from her windows though Trevor's car sat in front.

Anger built inside him like pus in a boil. He drummed a fist on the hood of Trevor's car. Cold. Been parked a long time. *Long enough for ten fucking sessions of . . . fucking.*

His head throbbed from injury and mental frustration.

He circled around to the side of Rose's cottage, slapped his hands on the window panes of her bedroom and peered in. No bodies rutted on the neatly folded bedding. He hammered on the windowpanes, thumped his foot on the stones till the mortar crumbled over his shoe.

"You'll be paying for that damage," Harry Watkins said.

Vic whirled around. "Where's Miss America?"

Harry shrugged, but his gaze slid to the tower of All Saints Church visible over the treetops.

Without an adieu, Vic jogged up the lane to the church. He

heard the dwindling notes of an organ, the low tones of male voices singing, "Amen." He paused, one foot on the step. It was past evensong, hours past choir practice.

A shaft of ice-like sensation ran through his body, shrinking his testicles, raising the hair on his nape. Despite a desire to head for Alice's cottage and dive under a blanket, he went silently up the steps, under the ancient portico.

Voices raised in song seeped through the narrow gap between the great oak doors. Vic eased one side open and slipped through.

The chilly sensation came with him like a grave-cold embrace.

Ranks of candles threw shadows up the walls and watery patterns across the windows. He dropped into a seat in the back row and stared about him. No congregation sat in rapt attention though Nigel stood upon the pulpit.

He's holding a bloody rehearsal, Vic thought.

Vic knew what his Auntie Alice would say. *Nigel on the pulpit tasted like day old bread put out for company. No one would dispute that food shouldn't be wasted, but no one would much enjoy it, either.*

Vic realized no choir stood in the stalls. No singing filled the cavernous space. Where had the choristers gone? The silence magnified the sermon. The words beat against Vic's eardrums.

Remnants of the club clung to him as smells and tastes. His imagination filled the gaps in Nigel's halting delivery with the strains of a single violin.

He shifted in his seat. Odors floated on the drafts that fluttered the banners overhead—the odors of old underground stations, cigarettes, and a woman's seductive perfume.

Vic tried a trick from childhood. He looked about for something to set his mind and eyes on. The glint of gold in the tapestry to the left of the pulpit caught his attention. The candles picked up the gleaming threads and drew his gaze from knight to knight.

In the lower corner, a bound woman stood between two men. Images from the underground came back to him in sharp, cinematic relief, complete with odors of mold and age. The lump on the back of his head flared with pain.

ROSE SAT WITH TREVOR at the Pig and Pie, feeling on stage, no longer an anonymous tourist. "Everyone's going to be gossiping over their full English breakfasts tomorrow that the sister of the murdered woman was eating chili at the local pub."

"With the local constabulary," he added. "Relax. No one is paying us any attention. And if they are, they're more interested in who pays the bill—after all, their taxes pay my salary."

She smiled and relaxed enough to swallow spicy chili Trevor had chosen. They spoke of the joys and sorrows of tourism. They bantered about solutions to the rise in youth crime as if they were attendees at the Stratford religious symposium.

While they waited for Nell to bring dessert, a pudding ominously called Spotted Dick, Rose told Trevor of her rivalry with Joan. He listened without saying a word.

When she finished, he leaned forward.

"I'm not sure how to say this." He toyed with his pint. "I feel monstrously uncomfortable, in fact."

Her palms went wet. Her stomach tightened. She knew what he was going to say as if she were clairvoyant. She gripped the napkin on her lap.

"I should have spoken immediately, but—"

"Spit it out."

Trevor reached under the table and covered her hands. "I knew Joan rather better than I've let on."

"I take it that means you knew her as well as Vic did."

He nodded. A look came over his face, one that reminded her of the many she'd witnessed on naughty boys who were pinching someone during a school photo shoot.

Nell, decked out in a gothic array of black and purple, placed a bowl in front of Rose. The Spotted Dick turned out to be a warm, dense cake-like dessert studded with currents, surrounded by a pool of rich custard.

When they were alone again, Rose pulled her hands from under Trevor's with a nonchalance she did not feel.

They ate in silence, each spoonful of what would have delighted her a few hours before a chore to swallow.

"Please say something." Trevor folded his napkin and set it beside his bowl.

"I don't think there's much to say." She propped her elbows on the table. "I suppose I should be upset that Joan shared her favors with half the men of the Cotswolds. It may be what killed her, but something else is bothering me right now."

She took a deep breath. "You see, she wrote me dozens of e-mails, many of them beyond weird—rambling discourses on evil—but never, not even in one e-mail message did she say, 'Hey, Rose, I've met this incredible guy—or guys—and by-the-way, I'm sleeping with him—or them.'"

She leaned back in her chair and felt incredibly weary. "Were you all so unimportant? Or were the weird happenings here so much more significant than her love affairs? I have to find out."

"I'll tell Munson about Joan's e-mail. Write down her screen name, which provider she used, and some dates for me." He shoved his notebook toward her and watched her write out the information. He pocketed the notepad. "Now, let the police handle it."

"I think you already have." Rose threw her napkin onto the table. "If you don't mind, I'll let the taxpayers get this one."

She brushed by Nell who held the check in her hand. Outside, looming behind the contemporary library, appearing as if it had sprouted from the flat roof, was the medieval tower of the church.

An overwhelming need to pray sent her across the street, dodging motorists rounding the village tribute to the Wars of the Roses. With a fleeting thought that Vic's aunt was a Yorkist with all her white roses, she cut through one of the alleyways, found herself in a court overflowing with hanging baskets and heavy with the scent of kitchen herbs. The sharp contrast of the lush beauty with the ugliness of Joan's end sent her running from the court.

She took the long way around and finally stood before the church. No police blocked the entrance. No signs lingered of Joan's death.

The organ music drew her to what she needed—quiet prayer among the faithful, to kneel with those who still believed in goodness and reviled evil.

The huge carved door stood open an inch or two. Light from candles spilled out. She thought of Christmas Eve services, of passing the flame from candle to candle as was the habit in the one church in which she'd spent more than a few months before her mother's boredom had sent them elsewhere.

All Saints Church reeked of mold. For the first time she saw a huge iron contraption by the gift shop—a furnace to force hot air loaded with mold spores around the nave. What might it be like for asthmatics in the winter?

Rose stood at the entrance to the long nave. No choir sang, but the distant sound of footsteps told her they were exiting from some place behind the pulpit where Father Nigel stood.

Her mind said leave, but her feet carried her forward to a man who sat in the back row, as far from the preaching as possible. Her instincts told her *he* was just what she needed, maybe as much as the prayers.

"And the mighty shall fall," said Father Nigel from his pulpit though no one listened—or Rose supposed Vic wasn't listening. His eyes were closed.

She sat next to him and when he put out his hand, she automatically entwined her fingers in his. Somehow it felt natural. And calming. She felt no fear of him, or that she should stay away as Trevor had warned her. Nothing from Vic's touch communicated anything but comfort and peace.

They listened to the sermon on . . . Rose wasn't sure what it was on. Tiny hammers began to tap in her temples. The chili sat uneasily in her stomach.

Father Nigel looked out over the rows of seats, sweeping his gaze about as if hundreds filled the vast space. He never faltered in his delivery, never gave any indication he wasted his breath.

"No evil thing walks by night, in fog or fire; no stubborn ghost has hurtful power over any evil."

Rose remembered sitting with Joan in church on a summer day. Another minister's monotones burred on in the background. Rose could almost feel the heat again and smell the sweat mingled with talcum powder on their mother.

They'd been Protestants then, and Joan had been old enough to take communion, while Rose had not. Joan had crossed her eyes, stuck out her tongue, and shook the little communion cup in front of Rose's face. The wine had spilled down the front of Rose's white dress.

In her mind's eye, Rose saw those drops again, in slow motion this time, falling, one at a time.

Vic lifted her fingers and kissed them. Where their hands had rested were dark spots.

Not wine. *Blood.*

She opened her mouth to cry out, but no sound came. The individual spots spread, covered her lap. Pineapple and custard bubbled up in her throat.

"Submit to the present evil, lest a greater one befall you." Father Nigel intoned an amen.

Vic pulled Rose to her feet.

Rose wanted to scream there was blood on her skirt . . . no, just wine . . . Joan had spilled the communion wine.

Rose shook her head. No, that was twenty-five years ago.

"Blood, Vic." Her hands shook on the rumpled cloth.

"Sorry, Rose. I hit my head." He touched the back of his head and she saw the dried blood on his fingers.

She took a deep breath. "What happened?"

"Uh. I slipped. It's nothing. Let's go home."

"I want to pray." Her words came out way too loud, almost in a shout.

"Our favorite spot?"

They headed to the memorial for the British War Dead. Vic propped his elbows on the *prie-dieu*, and closed his eyes, resting his forehead on his folded hands. She watched the play of shadows on his cheeks.

"What did you think of the sermon?" he asked.

"Pretty vague."

"Not vague, just shoddy work. He always mangles his Milton," Vic whispered. "He can't be bothered to get it right. I used to nod off when I came with Alice . . . in Nigel's early days. Alice didn't much care for him, so she quit."

"You can't quit religion."

"You can quit a church."

"I guess. If this were a Catholic church, we could light candles for Joan," Rose said.

Vic pulled out a book of matches and set flame to the candelabra they'd used in the crypt. The bronze on the memorial gleamed. So many names. So many dead.

Joan dead as well, but without some tribute to mark her passing. Except maybe her book.

"Thank you," Rose said when he settled beside her again. The flames glistened as if seen through water. She tried and failed to make the words come—words that might cleanse her guilt.

Tears dripped through her fingers to drop on the smooth oak surface of the *prie-dieu* railing. "Trevor slept with Joan, too, but I suppose you knew that. Maybe you compared notes."

Vic put his arm around Rose's shoulders and drew her close, kissed her forehead.

"We're not monsters, we're just men."

But she saw on his face they probably *had* shared tales.

She shifted. "My knees hurt."

He pulled her against him. "Damned uncomfortable without the cushions."

"I'm so tired. My head's pounding," she said.

"Mine, too."

"Geez, Vic. I forgot about your head and you told me

what—five minutes ago? Maybe you should go to an emergency ward. Head injuries can be dangerous."

"It's nothing Nurse Rose can't cure." He lifted her face, kissed her. "I don't want to spend another night without you. Come back to the cottage?"

She watched his face. "I'm not sure."

Vic nodded. "Trev put you off me, did he?"

"No, but he told me you'd gone back to the club."

"I found the Fallen Angel."

"Who is it?" she whispered.

All around them, the darkness gathered.

The only lights were her candles for Joan. A shiver of cool air touched her neck.

"Tell me," she repeated.

"Donald."

"What do you want with him?" said a voice from behind her.

Rose almost fell off her kneeler as Father Nigel set his hand on her shoulder.

"What makes you think we want anything with him?" Vic stood up and propped his fists on his hips.

"You were talking about him," Father Nigel said, taking a step back from Vic's aggressive stance.

"It's a free country," Rose said.

The vicar's lips tightened into a narrow line. "We don't need any of your rudeness here, miss. I'm sorry for your loss, but it's no excuse for insolence."

"I am sorry," Rose said, suddenly contrite, embarrassed at the way she'd spoken to the man. Her head felt stuffed with cotton. She needed to leave or she'd vomit.

Vic, a head taller than Nigel, made no effort to be polite. He took a step forward. Nigel retreated again.

"We'd like to speak to Donald if he's about," Vic said. "And if he's not, tell him V. F. Drummond wants to see him tomorrow. Come along," he said to Rose, pulling her to her feet and after him down the aisle.

In the church yard, amid the higgly-piggly headstones, she called a halt by jerking her hand from Vic's.

"I can't believe you saw Donald at the club. He can't be—"

"As lost as the rest of us?" He shrugged. "Everyone's got a dark side. Believe me, I write this stuff. Donald sins are as banal as a bank cashier's."

"How did you know he was the Fallen Angel? And how do you know he was *Joan's* Fallen Angel?"

Vic lifted her chin. "You want it in a tidy package, but it isn't. At first, I thought it was Trevor. It was the hair. Then I got close. It was Donald. And I have it on good authority—authorities—that the man we know as our All Saints curate spends his time in Club 7734 playing at games in a white robe, calling himself the Fallen Angel. He must be the man who took Joan to the club. Why he'd expose himself to someone predatory like her . . . forgive me." He wrapped her into his embrace. "That was a bloody stupid thing to say."

She nodded, rubbing her nose on his shirt. "You stink."

"I know. I'm in the shit."

"No, you stink. Of cigarettes. Were you smoking?"

The stars overhead spun. She sagged against him.

"You're acting drunk, but I think it has nothing to do with the local ale."

Vic hauled her up the lane to his cottage. Once inside, he made her sit in the kitchen while he put the water on to boil.

"I'm feeling better, now. There's no need to set me back with tea." And she did feel better, her head clear. "No mold here, thank heaven. Why don't you drink the tea and I'll look at your head."

They exchanged places. He winced when she examined the damage to his scalp. "This is quite a goose egg."

She cleaned it and filled a cloth with ice.

"So, were you smoking?" She sat on his lap and held the make-shift ice bag against the back of his head.

He encircled her waist and nuzzled her throat. "I wasn't, but since I spent my afternoon at the club, I probably have it all over me. I should also smell of incense and some woman's perfume. They've got their own mold problem under the place, too. Part of the club is a disused rail station. Do you want more tea?"

"I don't need tea."

"What do you need, Rosie?"

His voice had gone low and soft. It sent a luscious shiver through her. "I think I need a touch of Spotted Dick."

He started then grinned. "I haven't any spots, but if you're hungry . . ."

They kissed. Slow, leisurely kisses. The ice pack fell to the floor.

"I can't be afraid of you, Vic. Trevor wants me to stay away, but I just can't," she said against his lips.

"Bloody Trevor," he murmured. "My bed or yours?"

"Yours."

They burrowed under Vic's duvet. She explored him from throat to hip, skimming her fingertips so lightly they raised goosebumps in their path. She teased his nipples with her tongue, stroked him hard, then sat back.

"May I take your picture?"

"What?" He opened his eyes.

"I want to photograph you—the way the light plays on your body." She danced her fingers over his skin. "You're beautiful."

"Flattery will get you everywhere." He captured her hand. He licked her fingers, then drew them down the scratch on his chest. The line gleamed silver in the moonlight.

"No pictures. And I told you why."

She forgot to argue as he slid into her without preamble or preparation. She moaned with each quick hard thrust of his body, tucked her head against his neck, and hung on.

Sensations of want flooded out all others. This is what she'd needed, this cathartic giving way. Giving up to something primal.

And healing.

"You have magic hands," she said when they lay panting on the mattress, the duvet on the floor with the pillows. "I'll miss them when I go."

He rolled to his side and gripped her chin. "Don't go. Finish the bloody book for Joan, then stay. And recover."

She shook him off, sat up, and wrapped her arms about her knees. "I don't know how to recover."

ALTHOUGH HE HAD SAID no, Rose got her digital camera when he fell asleep. He lay on the white sheet, one hand splayed on his belly, lightly snoring. The light from the bathroom door cast shadows on his ribs and stomach. She set up her tripod, barely breathing.

She felt wicked.

She shot him in black and white from shoulder to knee. She zeroed in on his scratch, but only for curiosity's sake and in case he wanted some kind of documentation of his "stigmata" for the future.

The other photographs she took were strictly for her pleasure.

When he shifted and turned onto his side, she wished she could capture the shadows on his face, the curve of his lips, the rough-smooth texture of the new beard growth on his cheeks.

Instead, she took her camera down to the sitting room and opened his laptop.

An hour later, Rose tucked the camera into her backpack next to Vic's bed. She climbed onto the mattress, bent over him, and drew her tongue along the line of his lips and the smile that formed as he woke.

His skin tasted a touch salty from their lovemaking.

"I took your picture," she said as she climbed astride his hips and settled on him, rocked to seat him deeply within her.

He moaned and gripped her hips. His voice went hoarse. "When?"

"While you were sleeping." She kissed his mouth to still his protest. "I think they might be my best work."

She curled her fingers about his throat. His pulse hammered wildly against her palm. "But I was thinking that no matter what I put into a picture, there are some things I can't capture."

"The scent of you." She ran her nose up the side of his throat.

He made a feral sound in his throat and closed his eyes, stilled beneath her.

"This moist heat where we're joined."

"Rose. Stop."

"And I can't capture the tastes." His throat worked beneath her lips. "The Vic-aroused taste."

He came with a hoarse groan.

She climbed off his hips and curled at his side.

"That was rather one-sided," he said, stroking her hair from her face. "Let me take care of you."

And she closed her eyes, imagined the feast for her camera lens as he moved down her body and settled between her thighs. Then she thought of nothing, just gave herself to the heat of his mouth, the stroke of his fingers.

29

ROSE UNGLUED HERSELF FROM Vic's hips. She stood by the window and watched a rabbit ravage his Aunt Alice's herbs, but hadn't the heart to do anything about it. When he'd finished his nibble, the bunny hopped past the topiary rabbit Vic had ruined. The limbs looked sad in the gray light, wilted, patchy with dead spots.

As the dawn returned color to the room, she took a long bath. Her body ached when she touched the washcloth between her thighs, the parts Vic seemed most fond of.

She sat up abruptly, water sloshing close to the rim. "Vic," she called. "Vic."

He appeared at the door, his hair standing on end, bedding creases on his chest and belly.

"Wow," she said softly.

He frowned. "Ignore it and it will go away. Now what's so damned important you have to wake me before noon?"

She forced her mind back to her theory. "Who's the best looking guy in Marleton?"

He scratched his belly. "For some reason I think I'm not in the running."

Rose climbed from the tub and snatched up a towel. "No, you're not. Come on, who's the best looking guy in Marleton?"

"Nell's William."

She wrapped the towel around her and pushed by him. "I don't mean who has the biggest biceps. Who's handsomest?"

"I give up. Who?"

"Donald!"

"If you like your men perfect enough to be an advert for plastic surgery. So what?" He yawned.

"So, I know Joan. She would be after the best looking guy in town. No offense. You might be filthy rich, and for that reason you'd definitely be on her list, but as to allure, fascination, desire—"

"Should I be insulted here?" He grinned.

"Take it as you wish."

"Okay, so Donald is fascinating and desirable and I'm pig ugly; we already know Joan went with him to the club. I'm thinking you woke me for nothing."

FATHER NIGEL DID NOT knock on the door of Stitches. He used a key and found Mrs. Bennett pressing the hem of Mrs. Edgar's mother-of-the-bride dress.

"Drummond wants to see Donald. We have to do something."

Mrs. Bennett sighed and put up her iron. Nigel could be so tedious, especially in the morning hours if he'd been up late. He took his duties seriously, but was no longer young.

"This turned out rather lovely, but I do wish Mrs. Edgar had not picked this particular shade of blue. It will make her look jaundiced. Unlike the same shade on Alice Drummond. Alice looked lovely in blue."

Mrs. Bennett clucked her tongue as she fitted a padded hanger into the dress. "Donald is such an asset. He draws them, he does."

"He's drawing unwanted attention, is what he's doing."

The blue silk went into a garment bag. "He's been at the heart of several wonderful conquests."

"He will bring us down." Father Nigel's voice rose to a hoarse squeak.

"There's no need for panic."

He mopped his brow with a handkerchief that looked limp and damp though it was not yet six of the morning.

She drew her own handkerchief, one she'd embroidered herself with a neat border of Monkshood, and dabbed at non-existent tears. "I suppose you must consult the others on his dismissal. I shall miss him. And who will take his place?"

"It would be premature to even consider a replacement."

"Perhaps Vickers Drummond might."

"Drummond." The name exploded from Nigel's lips.

"Don't dismiss him. He's very popular in the reading world. If he were at services, we'd have every horror fan for miles joining our congregation. And probably the ones who just like to sniff around money." She neatly folded her handkerchief. "I wonder if he can sing? We're desperately short of choir members."

"IT ANSWERS SO MANY questions." Rose dropped her towel on the end of Vic's bed, and scanned the room for her panties.

His heart went pit-a-pat. "Not dyed," he said.

"What?" She tipped her head and propped one fist on her hip.

And he loved her for the joyful sensations jolting through his groin. "I said, 'not dyed.' Your hair."

She touched her ponytail, wet on the end from the bath. "Why do you say that?"

"You've the same marvelous coppery glints in your maidenhair as I'm seeing in your topknot."

"Maidenhair?" Understanding flitted across her face and she donned a virgin pose, one hand across her pubic mound. "I don't know what to call it and bush seemed a touch coarse," he said, climbing back on the bed and draping the duvet over his overactive imagination.

"You are a part-time gardener." She plucked one of his jerseys from the chair and pulled it on. It skimmed her to mid-thigh. "Show's over. Now focus."

"My kingdom for a camera," he whispered when she crawled over him to sit an unfortunate yard away on the other side of the bed.

"Donald is absolutely gorgeous. Joan probably made a play for him, succeeded, they played their little games together and before long, she finds out he's a member of this Club 7734."

"Nothing new, mate. I'm awake for nothing." He stretched and dropped his arm behind her, encircled her bum, resting his head on her thigh. He nuzzled the warm, smooth skin there.

"Please stop that. I can't concentrate."

"Concentrate later." He ran his hand under his jersey to the lovely coppery down between her thighs.

She shimmied away, pulling the duvet over her legs. "What did Joan tell you about herself? It might be a clue as to what she told Donald. That might tell us how panicky he was."

Vic sighed, fell to his back, defeated, and stared at the pattern of shadows cast by the ivy on the ceiling. "Are you trying to say Donald pushed Joan down the crypt steps?"

"Maybe."

He heard the quiver in her voice and knew this was not idle speculation, but something she feared.

"It's not on, Rosie. He's possibly a bit sexually addicted. Might have a history of depression. But a murderer? No. I trust my instincts. He's a runner, not a pusher.

"Then Harry the Peeper."

"Maybe. Anyone else on your list?"

She shook her head.

"Me?"

"I eliminated you on completely specious data . . . feminine intuition."

"Trevor?"

"Are you sure it wasn't him in the club?"

"Yes. It was Donald. And I eliminate Trevor on purely specious evidence. Friendship. Thirty years worth."

They lay in silence. Vic hugged her close. "You need comfort, but I think you also need to assign guilt."

"Help me assign it."

"All right. You asked me what Joan talked about. The single most valuable thing I can remember is that she was a photojournalist."

"Exactly." Rose bounded to her knees like a wind-up toy. "Joan always said she was a photojournalist, except she wasn't really. Oh, she spent time with my dad when he did a reunion thing in Vietnam and helped him do a magazine piece on it later, but she also had to make money. She did coffee-table books."

He shrugged. "What does this have to do with our Donald?"

"Be patient. I'm not saying Joan's books weren't beautiful. She certainly won awards for them, and I know the potters she featured in her Pueblo book received tons of recognition. Galleries clamored for their pieces, but still . . . she craved the kind of recognition my dad once had. It was what *he* had always hoped for her."

Vic rolled to his side and tried another assault on the castle wall with no luck. Rose proved rather skilled at clutching a duvet and jersey simultaneously.

"Frankly, the Joan I knew was an unlikely pick for the kind of journalism that wins awards. Can't imagine her soiling her designer shoes, let alone her hands."

"Exactly. So imagine what luck it must have been to have "fallen" quite literally into a piece that might have made her famous."

"Not following."

"Only because you're thinking about sex, not the matter at hand. How much will your tabloids pay for juicy photos? What if Joan could deliver a piece *with* photos, an exposé for instance on Club 7734? A club with a la-de-da clientele and at least one priest partaking of the forbidden fruit? And think about the illegal drugs there, too."

And what of bound women?

"You think Joan took a camera in?" he asked.

"I don't know. Probably not. I'm assuming the idea of an exposé occurred to her on or after her first visit. But what if she wanted to go back and Donald refused to take her? What if she tried to blackmail him? What if he tried to shut her up?"

Vic rolled out of bed. "Get dressed, we're going to see Alden or Munson. We'll run your theory past whoever's home."

"We should find out if Joan had film in her purse."

Rose's eyes filled with tears. There was nothing Vic could say. She waved him off when he tried to embrace her, so instead, he left her alone. He took a quick bath, then pulled his jeans from the washing.

"Ah, Vic?" She knelt in the center of his bed. Her eyes were puffy, her skin blotchy.

He thought her beautiful. "What?"

"Can we go by the church before we see the police? I think I want to go to a service and it's nearly seven."

He dropped his jeans, opened the closet, and pulled out tan trousers.

"Don't you own underwear?"

"In London." He searched a chair for a clean jersey, didn't find one and snagged Rose around the waist as she tried to climb off the bed. He sniffed her from throat to waist. "Just checking to see if I can wear this again."

He was rewarded with a smile from her. The first of the day.

"You are hopeless," she said.

She pulled off the jersey and spent a wonderful long time helping him on with it. She sniffed him from shoulder to groin as he had her. "You smell wonderful and if we weren't short of time I'd be tempted to—"

"I'm quick," he said.

Her smile became a laugh.

"Thank you, Vic." She rose on tip-toe and kissed him.

He held her close. "I might not be able to part with you when . . . well, when."

30

JEALOUSY, THOUGHT TAMED, SNAPPED at Vic's heels when he found Trevor with PC Alden in Munson's office.

"Aren't you supposed to be priest-sitting?" Vic asked.

Trevor put his arm around Rose's shoulders. "I am, but I stopped off here first to let Munson know I'd found Rose temporary lodging. Nell at the Pig and Pie has a decent room over the pub. It's Rose's for as long as she needs it. Will you wait outside for a few minutes and I'll take you over?"

When Rose was gone, Vic saw color fill Trevor's cheeks. "Actually, Vic, I'm here this morning to come clean about Joan. I've added myself to the suspect list as well as the witness list."

"How bloody stupid." Vic turned to the police officers. "I can give you better suspects."

"Relax, Vic, I've already given them Rose's list. It's taken care of. Now, I'm off to the Pig and Pie."

Vic's jab of jealousy turned into an urge to leap the desk

and tear Trevor's liver out through his arse. "Rose is not going to Nell's."

Everyone stared at him.

"No need to shout," Trevor said.

"I wasn't shouting." His mobile phone buzzed in his pocket. He pulled it out and cut off the call with a stab of his thumb to hide his embarrassment.

What was wrong with him? He felt on a roller-coaster ride that had no end. Trevor had been his friend since he'd come to Alice's to live.

"If Trevor's on that bloody list, then I should be as well."

He didn't like the smile on Munson's face.

"Have you found Joan's car? Her luggage? What are you doing sitting on your arses?"

"Mr. Drummond, I think you should do what you do best, and we'll do what we do best." Munson gave PC Alden a nod, and the two of them left the office together with Trevor.

The phone buzzed again.

He flipped the phone open. "What?"

He held the receiver away from his ear as Oliver babbled and shrieked about some raid in London.

"Bloody hold on a moment; I can't follow what you're saying." Vic saw a copy of *The Times* on Munson's shabby couch. The phone to one ear, Vic flipped the folded paper open. The headline Oliver kept repeating, "MP caught in Hell," was more discreetly termed MP Gaff, in *The Times*.

"You need to read a better paper," Vic said when Oliver wound to a halt. Then his stomach clenched. "Yeah, it could have been me. Yes, I'll destroy the card. No, no one will know I got it from you."

He rang off. So, the club card had come directly from Oliver, not from a contact.

Vic read the article. It detailed the raid on a sex club the night before. Illegal drugs were netted along with a popular MP who had been found naked in a private room with a young man not of legal age. "So much for his career," Vic muttered.

He kept the paper and tailed Rose to the Pig and Pie. He

did not ask permission to climb the back stairs to the only room he knew could be termed "decent" by Trevor who was rather fastidious where it didn't matter.

Rose sat on the single bed in a pool of sunshine, a newspaper on her lap. Bloody Trevor was gone. Some of the wretched acid brew in Vic's gut flattened out as if he'd dropped an anti-acid tablet down his throat.

She held up the paper. "Nell gave me this."

Vic raised his *Times*. Rose patted the bed beside her. He sat down and she put her head on his shoulder. They swapped papers.

"Missed the lurid details, I see," he said when he'd read her tabloid. "MP was charged with gross indecency, using illicit drugs, pandering, soliciting, and others. Poor sod."

He folded the paper and dropped it on the floor.

"Vic, this might have been you."

"Too right."

"And when did you get a cell phone? I thought you didn't approve of them?"

"I keep one in my car, and I don't."

She'd chosen a black skirt and white top for church. He liked the way the soft cotton draped her breasts, molded her erect nipples.

She fussed with the papers, folding them and creasing the edges with great care. "Did you know PC Alden is jealous of Trevor?"

Weren't they all? "No, why?"

"I overheard Alden saying that with you in this case, it will get lots of attention. It might mean a speedier promotion if he does a good job on me—liaison-wise. But Trevor keeps popping in. Alden wants him warned off or something. Munson said Trevor will not interfere as he has too much experience and integrity to do anything that might jeopardize a later court case."

"Munson's right. And Alden's right. Trevor needs to take himself to Stratford and nail his arse in a chair somewhere."

Red touched Rose's cheeks.

She twisted a strand of hair around her finger. "So . . . I

never asked you . . . did you go back to the club for the fun of it?"

"No. I thought we were thick not to have questioned customers or showed Joan's picture about. Do you remember the chaps with the clever chains attached to their naughty bits?"

"Naughty bits?"

"I'm cleaning it up for you."

"Oh." She still didn't meet his eyes.

"They helped me find Donald. I was there for the facts, mate, not the sex."

She stood between his thighs. "I can't picture myself here."

The room was furnished with cast-offs—a single bed, an oak dresser. Extra chairs from the bar were neatly stacked along one wall. "I'll speak to Nell about cheering it up for you."

"That's not what I was hoping you'd say." She cupped his face, lifted it, and met his gaze.

"If you want to stay at Alice's cottage, you don't need an invitation. *Mi bed, su bed.*"

He turned his head to kiss her palm. She made a lovely, breathy sound in her throat. "I wanted to do harm to Trev this morning. For touching you. For this room."

"And you'd just been to church. Shame on you."

"I don't know what's wrong with me. The instant I see the two of you together, something inside me lets go. I'm usually rather slothful. Drumming up energy for anger is beyond me."

She pushed on his shoulders until he lay back. He tensed when she opened his trousers and slid her hand inside.

"You don't seem slothful now," she whispered. "You did say you could be quick about it, didn't you?"

Her hands were magic, her lips and tongue so hot on him he wanted to shout. He pulled the silky mass of her hair aside so he could watch. Then he closed his eyes, unable to restrain the roiling sensations that emanated from his groin, yet somehow were also inside his chest.

A vivid image came into his head. Rose at the club with her gown open down her back.

"Stop!" He held her off, panting.

She looked up, a question in her eyes. Her lips gleamed, her hand still moved in slow strokes. "What's wrong?" she whispered.

"Not now. That is. Nell will never let me hear the end of it . . . if she hears the end of it."

Color flooded Rose's face and she drew abruptly away. "Sure. Later. Okay."

She went to the dresser and pulled a brush from her bottomless rucksack.

He spared a fleeting moment of thought on why he felt a compulsive need to be honest with her at all times.

"Rose." He zipped up and went to her, put his hands on her hips. "I was not very truthful just now."

"Don't explain. You warned me you were a liar, so just forget it."

She caught up her hair in a wicked looking plastic clip.

"I closed my eyes and was back in the club. I saw blood on you. It put me off."

Their eyes met in the mirror. "Blood?" she asked.

"Running down your bare back." He illustrated by dragging his fingertip down her spine.

She pulled off the cotton shirt. The scratch on her back stood out as a livid stripe. He put his hands on her shoulders, drew off her bra straps.

"This looks raw," he said.

Her body quivered. He pulled off his jersey. His scratch also looked fresh.

He pressed their scratches together by wrapping his arms about her waist. Heat flared between them that had nothing to do with temperature or arousal.

It shook him. He tightened his arms.

"I'm a little scared, Vic."

He watched her face in the mirror as he cupped her breasts, rolled her swollen nipples between his fingertips. "I'll take care of you, mate. And I don't mean sexually, though I'm having a damned hard time keeping my hands off you."

His craving now stood in equal proportion to the need he'd had a few minutes before to pull away from her caress.

He lifted her skirt. When he hooked her knickers off her hips, she propped her hands on the dresser and pushed her bum back at him in blatant invitation.

It was unRosie, but also unrefusable.

The mirror banged the wall to his rhythm but he no longer gave a damn. They came together.

"Again," she said, drawing his hand down. She rode his fingers. The room filled with the musk-floral scent of her. It intoxicated him as no scenario in a sex club had.

He pulled the clip from her hair and used the silky mass to caress her back and shoulders.

A tiny drop of blood welled from her scratch, like a tab to pull a zip. Unable to control the urge, he followed the bright crimson with his tongue, followed it until he was on his knees.

She writhed against his hand, keened like a banshee when she came. He kissed the fever-hot skin at the base of her spine. His heart thudded so hard, he thought Nell in the bar might be able to hear it.

When his body returned to a semblance of normalcy, he stood up and stepped away. She hastily drew up the lacy knickers and down the demure black skirt. It bothered him she did not meet his eyes while she pulled on her bra and top.

"Have you thought about the fact that I could be called Vic the Vital? Where before I met you I was Vic the Vapid?"

Rose reclamped her hair. "Not getting it, Vic. What are you talking about?"

"I'm the laziest sod in Marleton, maybe all of the Cotswolds. I can barely wake up each day. I've not made love to a woman three times in twenty-four hours in years. I'm forty-fucking-one."

"Four times, but who's counting? And you're forty-two. Trevor said so." She began to straighten the bed, a bed they'd not used.

"I'm so passive, I don't even argue with myself. Now, I want to take on Trevor and anyone else who looks your way. What's going on?"

His chest itched. He rubbed it with his palm.

She drew on her rucksack, plucked his jersey from the floor. Finally, she looked at him. He saw no regret for the frantic joining and sighed with relief.

"Stop scratching," she said. "I don't know how many times an old guy like you should be able to get it up, but I figure its just the newness of this thing we have. And your jealousy of Trevor? I think it's kind of sweet."

31

ROSE TOOK A NAP. Tempting as it had been to join her, the purple shadows beneath her eyes told Vic she needed the sleep.

And there was Donald. If Nigel passed his message along, Donald should pay a call.

Vic searched his laptop for the pictures she'd taken during the night. He felt no guilt. She'd taken them without permission, he'd look at them without permission.

It took him almost an hour to find them.

He gave a shout of laughter.

She must have gotten up very early to have already completed her magic on his images. He had to admit the camera made him look damn good, and he could set to rest the fear his fans would be measuring his cock size on the Internet. A daisy sprouted from the juncture of his thighs.

He logged onto the Internet and visited her website, something he should have done the first day they'd met.

"What a wanker, I am," he whispered. Each photograph in

the Early Photography Gallery stunned him. It was artistry equal to Joan's and surpassing it as well, he thought. Rose concentrated on people and nature. And understood them.

Her photographs were sorted by category: wedding, baby, family, and something she called "wanderings."

He copied the ones he liked into a folder he named Rosie's Work, and the ones that made him uncomfortable in another he called Rosie from Planet X. It was the off-planet Rose he wanted to go up against Bloody-Fallen Angel-Donald.

When he heard her in the kitchen he brought up a headless portrait of himself.

"Rather good, that," he said when she set a mug of tea next to the laptop.

She patted his shoulder. "You're not pissed?"

"Pissed means drunk here. I am angry. You disobeyed me. But I've a feeling you're not much of a rule minder, are you?"

He swiveled about and pulled her close. "Your work is brilliant. You must win a few awards yourself."

Rose shot Vic a suspicious look. He was usually caustic, not complimentary.

"What is it you want? And don't patronize me and say sex. Just spit it out." She took a sip of the tea which she'd found wasn't bad if made with Alice Drummond's honey.

"I want you to go up to the church today and talk to Donald."

"Me? Why me?"

"I'm sober now and if I'd been last night, I'd have known that the last person Donald will talk to is me. You, he'll talk to. He'll not suspect anything."

"Suspect what?"

"Suspect us of detecting."

"Oh." She sipped her tea. "Better an information conduit than just another shag toy."

Vic shoved her off his lap. "Shag toy? Where'd you hear that?"

"At the club. Some guy on the dance floor offered me a thousand pounds to be his."

She smiled into her mug as Vic stared at her, his mouth open.

"A thousand pounds? And I'm getting it for free?"

"You should be flattered."

"I'm humbled." He kissed her hand. "Now take yourself off to the vicarage before I haul you upstairs."

"Don't you think Munson will be a more effective interrogator than you or I?"

Vic waved off her objections, spilling drops of tea across his desk. "It's not rocket science. I'm sure it's just common sense."

"Do you consider yourself a man of sense?"

"I have enough sense to know a man is more likely to talk to someone who has no power to hurt him before he'll talk to someone who can put him jail for lewd acts."

"His activities were likely all legal, Vic."

"Not in the UK."

"So, Donald will suffer a few bruises to his reputation."

"Then make use of that. Tell him you'll blacken his reputation, make it impossible for him to get even the lowest curacy in England if he doesn't come clean about Joan."

The tone of Vic's voice made Rose pause. "Come clean? You're one to talk."

He swiveled away from her and opened the file for his sequel to *Do You Believe in Evil*? "We're back to that are we?"

She wrapped her arms around her waist. "I guess I'll be back to that from time to time. It's not about you. It's about me and Joan."

"And not being able to fix things? Maybe fix isn't the correct word." He used his elbow to mop up the stray tea drops. "I know with Alice, there will always be this unresolved stuff. I owed her and thought I had a lifetime for payback."

She nodded. "Maybe that's it. Joan and I had unresolved stuff and now, it'll always be unresolved, but I can't confront Donald about anything. Or I don't think I can. Now, if you don't mind, I'm going to the Rose and Thistle to pack my things and take them to the pub. I might not use the room,

but I'd feel better if I have a base somewhere that's not sub-
sidized by someone who's filthy rich."

VIC FOUND HIMSELF AT odds with his computer the minute
Rose was off to pack. He'd not been able to dissuade her.

Neutral territory, she called it. Bloody inconvenient,
he'd said.

Now, his mind said, "Work, you lazy bastard," but his fingers kept opening the photo software and playing with the images from Rose's website. His printer chugged out the results.

He cut and pasted a pregnant woman's bare stomach onto
the thin stalk of a drooping orchid. But satisfaction eluded
him as his mind returned to Donald and Club 7734. And
shied away from reading through his manuscript.

He computer-painted his pregnant orchid crimson.

No matter what Rose said, she needed to confront Donald.

Vic pounded his forehead with his fist. "I'm the one who
needs to confront Donald. About Alice."

He printed off his orchid, stuck it to the mantle with
sticky tape, next to the portrait of Rose he'd also taken from
her website and crudely merged with an angel's body he'd
purloined from a greeting card company's website.

His photo-altering efforts draped the mantle, bookshelves, and window panes. If nothing else, they most graph-
ically showed him the artistry of Rose's work—and the
invisible work she did with her computer.

He tapped each photograph of Rose's he'd printed. Her
digital images of the church had an eerie quality missing
from Joan's. Some looked as if they'd been taken in medieval times, and he knew it was because she'd "danced" on
them as she called it.

One image drew him over and over. The one of him at the
pulpit. He looked as if he were demented, his flashlight beneath his chin. And the shadows cast behind him looked like
wings on the pillars. He knew it was just the shadows in the
folds of the saint's robes who suffered to hold aloft the ceiling, but still, it looked a bit like he had wings. Not angelic

ones at that, but more like the ones the latex demons in Club 7734 sported.

He skimmed his fingertips along the shadows. Maybe Rose could do her magic with the image and get rid of the specter of malevolence cast by the wing-like shadows. He might not be a saint, but he certainly wasn't evil.

As he shoved the photograph under a pile of papers, he had an errant thought, had Rose put the shadows in? Did she see him as evil? But she'd not seen the demons and the wings were uncannily like the leathery ones he remembered folded down their backs.

Vic went back to the computer, but his efforts at wing removal were painfully inadequate to satisfy him.

What had Joan said? Digital photography and image manipulation by computer was lying. If you did it really well, no one knew you were lying.

Joan had said one of the things that had drawn her to photojournalism was the idea that the camera never lied. Now, in the digital world, Joan had said, the camera lied all the time. What can you believe in anymore, she'd asked him.

Vic remembered saying photographers had been manipulating pictures in dark rooms since the dawn of time, and if not there, then in the staging of the subject. Hadn't the brilliant Sir Arthur Conan Doyle been duped by mock-up photographs that had convinced him of the existence of fairies?

But Joan did not debate the issue. She had her view and that was that. He imagined his Rose must have wanted to pull Joan's hair out by her dark roots on more than one occasion if she was as bloody argumentative to a sister as she was to a casual lover.

Luckily, Joan and he had segued into a heated debate over what constituted lying and never returned to photography, or he might have been tempted to tip her sherry into her lap.

As Vic roamed the sitting room, taping up Rose's magnificent images from her website, he wondered again at lies.

A sin of omission, rather than an out and out lie about his sexual relationship with Joan, was what he'd committed with Rose, but still, it had hurt her.

He paused before a pair of aging lovers. She'd posed the laughing couple with heads together and caught their every wrinkle in black and white. She'd also captured without a word, the immediate impression of lovers who had grown together, laughed together, perhaps at times, suffered together. She'd caught it all in the symmetry of their laugh lines, the near mirror image of their wrinkles.

Or had she? Had she moved a few lines? Touched an eyelid, a lip, with her artist's touch?

Vic put his nose to the photograph and tried to discern some enhancement. It was like his demon wings. If alterations were there, she'd done it with perfection.

Speaking of demons, where was the little devil, anyway?

Impatient for her return, he printed out what he could find on her digital camera.

He pasted up rose petals, white and red as they drifted along the river. It was York and Lancaster entwined as they disappeared under the old stone bridge.

Family portraits rubbed shoulders with views of Marleton in a row across the bookshelves. He enlarged a picture Rose had taken of his cottage window. The foggy image of a face appeared to be peering out.

Fact or illusion? He propped it next to the photo of him in the pulpit.

"Explain those," he said aloud.

His printer ran out of ink. Left without further avoidance techniques, he opened his manuscript and skimmed through a few chapters to get back in voice.

Icy fingers, familiar friends, crept up his spine and caressed his nape.

The priest tried to be calm. "You're a fool, Alice," he said to the old woman.

"And you're one, too." She climbed into a polished mahogany coffin and fussed with the skirt of her blue suit until it was arranged to her liking. She folded her hands. "Fools go to hell, you know."

The priest shut out her words by slamming her coffin lid and screwing it down.

Vic's hands shook. He cut the offending lines and deleted them, but when he restarted his computer and returned to the file, the words were still there.

Words not written in any sane moment he could remember. *Was he barking mad and just not aware of it?*

They were new words, but they proved just as tenacious as others he saw were finally gone. He burned the small clip to a CD.

He took the CD out to the garden. The rabbit topiary was blotchy with dead needles. He gripped it about the neck, jerked it from the pot, and dropped his CD in. Just one among many.

He could not go back to the house. What he needed was a beer. Maybe at the Pig and Pie.

As he jogged up the lane, he saw a familiar figure.

"Well, well," he said. "Look who's lying now."

Rose stood at the vicarage door, head down, eyes on her toes.

"Just in time for a tête-à-tête," Vic said and tucked himself into the shadows of the lytch gate.

Donald opened the door. After an initial start, he mustered what looked like a dutiful smile for the bereaved and ushered Rose in.

Vic's impulsive side told him to sprint the last fifty yards and slip through the narrow gap left when Donald had not quite shut the door. Prudence kept him under the lytch gate, battered by brash tourists, intent on viewing the ancient grave markers.

ROSE CLEARED HER THROAT and tightened her fingers on the strap of her bag. She forced out the words she'd rehearsed.

"First, I want to thank you for your kindness when . . . Joan was found."

Had this man killed Joan? Set his hands on her in anger and pushed her down the crypt steps?

Tears crowded at her eyes again. When would they go away? Why did they appear gone and then just crop-up again without warning?

Donald nodded and handed her a tissue from a box handy on Father Nigel's desk. "Are you sure you wouldn't rather see Nigel? He'll be back momentarily."

The action of extending his arm drew back his sleeve revealing faint scars on his inner wrists. She remembered Vic's suggestion Donald wrestled with inner demons. If he was responsible for Joan's death, Rose hoped he slept not one wink until he came clean.

"You were more than kind, but Father Nigel has not half your compassion." She had only her one interview over photography on which to base her opinion of the vicar, but her guess looked on target as Donald nodded.

"That's not what I came for," she said. "Or not completely, though I did want to thank you."

"How else may I help you?"

She had to have Donald repeat himself twice to understand him.

She opened her wallet and drew out the receipt with the scribbled Club 7734 on the back. "I think Joan went to this club at least once, maybe twice or more."

If it was possible for a man's skin to become transparent, then Donald's did. She saw every minute blue vein on his downcast eyelids. She saw red flow through the capillaries on the flare of his nostrils, but the rest of his face remained drained of color.

"And?" The one word sounded like a long sigh.

"And I thought as you've been to the club, you might have some idea why Joan went?"

Donald's gaze flitted from one corner of the vicarage office to another, lighting briefly on books. His fingertips fluttered just as lightly from pile to pile of church papers.

"You're mistaken." He stood up.

Rose remained in her seat. "Yeah. I figured Vic Drummond was nuts when he said he saw you there."

"Vic Drummond told you he saw me there?" This time, the man spoke so slowly, she could translate every word as they fell like BBs into a metal dish.

"Yes. I told him he was nuts." She swept her hands out in a "go figure" gesture. "I think he spends too much time with his computer."

Donald subsided into his seat. He composed his features along with the crease in his black trousers. "It's our belief that V.F. Drummond has taken over Vickers Drummond. The man dwells on evil. How can he not be tainted by such an association?"

"I don't really believe in evil, but let's forget Drummond for a few moments."

She propped her elbows on the edge of Donald's elegant mahogany desktop. She toyed with the receipt. His gaze zeroed in on the scrap of paper and, she hoped, all its implications.

"I'd rather know why you let Joan in after hours to take pictures of the church. I mean, Father Nigel had a fit when I asked him about it. Why was it okay for you to take Joan in, but not me?" She put a petulant whine into her voice. "Not to speak ill of my sister, I mean, I loved her, but she got all the breaks. If I'm going to finish her book, I'll need a few breaks, too."

Donald cleared his throat. He reached across the leather blotter and plucked the receipt from her hand. "You Americans are so impulsive."

He tucked the receipt under the edge of a paperweight crafted to resemble one of the misericords. Rose had seen the heavy object in the gift shop. The contorted figure meant to hold up a seat grimaced in some private agony.

"Sorry." She sat back and sighed. "I'd love to get in after dark."

When she leaned forward again, Donald fought a visible recoil. "Whatever she offered, Father, I'm offering double.

What do you need? A donation to the roof fund? New Lenten vestments? You name it."

His Adam's apple bobbed. Sweat glistened on Donald's brow. Gilding on ivory, Rose thought. Or a visible sign of guilt?

She mentally crossed her fingers that although Donald might not cop to the sex club, he might admit to a little after-hours photography.

Donald's voice turned silky. "If your sister wanted to visit the church after midnight, then she did so on her own. I would never disobey Father Nigel."

Without knowing for sure, Rose thought he'd just told her the time of Joan's photo excursion. After midnight.

"You should do more preaching," she said impulsively. "You'd fill the seats. I mean, you have so much more charisma than Father Nigel. I'll bet you do really do well with the younger generation."

The change of subject threw him. He stammered a thank you, his face flooding with all its missing color.

"That's not empty flattery to get you to help me out with the pictures, either."

A very cynical smile twisted his full, sculpted lips. "I rather imagine the opposite."

She waved off his words. "No. I'm not just saying it. I saw how the young female tourists followed you around the other day. All you'd have to do is hold a cup in your hand while you wander about the church and the women would fill it to the brim. You'd have a new roof like that." She snapped her fingers.

His color had returned to normal, but the smile still played on his lips.

"Come on, Father. Or may I call you Donald?"

"Ah, Donald will do."

"Donald will do. That's it. You will do it, won't you? Help me out?"

Although she tried for false tears, she found the ones that rolled down her cheeks were all too real. "I have to finish

Joan's book. It's going to be a tribute to her, you see. I'm begging you to help me finish it—in her memory."

Donald ran his tongue over his upper lip. In another red-blooded woman, the action might have sent her into a swoon, or at least caused a three on a wet-panty meter of four, but Rose found his mixture of religious hypocrisy and sexual profligacy left her cold.

"Shall we compromise?" Donald said. "I shall seek to change Nigel's mind, and you shall be patient."

"Okay. But I can't stay too much longer—"

"How much longer?"

32

"**WHAT DID HE SAY?**" Vic asked, leaping out from the lytch gate. Tires squealed as she almost fell into the path of a speeding motorist.

He steadied her with an arm about her waist.

"You'll be the death of me yet," she said, slapping his hands away. "He said he'd try to get Nigel to let me into the church."

"Damn it, Rose. *I* can get you into the church. You should have gripped him by the balls and asked him why a man of God is getting hoovered in a sex club."

"I did ask. Well, not quite in those words, and got nothing but his back up."

"Now what?"

"I'm not sure. Obviously, he isn't going to 'fess up' just because I've asked him. This really is a job for the police."

She blinked back tears. Vic slid his hand in hers and whatever confusion she felt at the moment disappeared. Any lingering tears dried when she set foot in the photograph festooned sitting room.

"Holy moly. You have my whole website up here."

He urged her into the desk chair. "Show me how you did them."

She looked over the photographs he plucked from mantle and bookshelves. "This is Mr. and Mrs. Dombrowsky. I didn't do anything except ask them to tell me about their life together. I took dozens of shots as they talked. Case closed." She shifted the others about. "This one was done with a filter. Simple stuff. This one . . . I just took tons of photos and picked one I liked."

He swept the pictures up and dumped them on the couch. "So, I was right."

"About what?"

"You're an artist. If you didn't stage all those," he tapped the pile of photos, "how did you do this?" He dropped the pulpit picture onto her lap.

She picked it up. "Do what?"

"The wings, mate, how'd you give me the bloody wings? And this?" He placed the enlargement of the cottage window on top of the pulpit shot. "How'd you put this griffin in the window?"

"DONALD, IF YOU'RE NOT busy, I thought we might have a word."

Donald looked up. Nigel was flanked by two congregation members.

Donald's limbs felt like a marionette's whose strings were tangled. "I've work to do."

"I'll take over," Nigel said. "Now hurry along."

"Aye," said Harry Watkins. "We'll have you back for evensong."

ROSE SPREAD A BLANKET on Vic's back lawn and watched him tend the flower beds. He named each plant and gave her more information than she really wanted. As he plucked weeds, watered pots, and ruined topiaries, she studied the photographs in her lap.

She could not deny the wavy image captured by her camera. Whatever trick of light and distortion of old glass had created the face, it was undeniably there.

"What's a griffin?" she asked and winced when he pruned too much from the paw of a tiny hedge work dog.

He sheathed his clippers in his back pocket and picked up a watering can. "Griffins are mythological beasts usually with front bits of an eagle, hind end of a lion. Sometimes the head has the ears of a lion."

"You mean a gargoyle."

"Not even close. Griffins represent protection. Strength, vigilance."

"It's you, Vic." She beckoned him near with the photo.

He abandoned his watering can, but wouldn't look at the picture. "You're barking."

"No, I'm not *barking*, I'm thinking somehow I captured the essence of you. A different essence than I got when I did the nude study."

Two spots of color bloomed on his cheeks. "The essence of me is a morass of laziness."

She shook her head. "You look out for me. You looked out for Alice."

"I'm no Hound of Zeus."

Rose mused on his words. "Maybe not. Officially. But how can we account for this? It explains everything." She set the two photos of him on the blanket, side-by-side. "Intelligence and strength combined," she said. "Somehow my camera saw something in you. A fighter for good against evil?"

He set his fists on his hips and roared with laughter. When he calmed down, he pulled out his clippers and shook them at her. "You had me there for a moment, but you went too far. I'm more likely to run from trouble than fight it."

He shook his head and went to the dying rabbit topiary.

"You can laugh all you like, Vic," she said softly. "But I didn't fake the photographs."

33

ROSE PLAYED WITH VIC'S "wings." She removed them with
ease, but preferred another version, the one in which she
made the wings distinct. Vic might deny it, but she thought
there was a protective quality to him.

The work on the All Saints Church photographs did not
go as well. Nothing pleased her.

Joan would not be pleased.

"I can't do this here," Rose said. "I'll have to go home."

"The pub'll be crowded with tourists," Vic said.

Rose frowned at him. "I didn't mean the Pig and Pie. I
meant home, home. I need better software if I'm going to do
this right. I have it on my studio computer."

Vic balanced her loupe against his eye as he lay on the
sofa. He looked like he was wearing a mutant monocle. "Just
pop over to Marleton Camera where you bought this."

"I can't. The software I need is beaucoup expensive."

"Phone, mate." He snapped his fingers.

She brought him the cordless phone from the kitchen. Although she shook her head violently, protested in mime and even soft whispers, Vic bought what she needed.

"Go get it. And don't make faces. I'm filthy rich." He closed his eyes and yawned. "Off with you, that's a good girl."

She took a deep breath. "I don't know how to thank you."

"When you get back, do something wicked."

AN HOUR LATER, ROSE manipulated a photograph on the computer screen. She loved the surge of creativity she felt, the return of confidence that she could finish Joan's book in a manner that would make Joan proud.

"Nice to be rich," she mused as she played around with a few features her older version of the software did not have.

"Vic. Look at this." She swiveled the desk chair around and nudged his foot. He lay flat on his back on the rug, contemplating the inside of his eyelids.

He dragged himself upright and draped himself over her shoulder. She tapped the screen.

He yawned. "Huh? Grubby old tapestry. Full of mold. I can smell it now."

"No. No. Look at the top edge." She scrabbled about in the pile of papers she'd printed off the Internet. "The Marleton tapestry used to have a name." She read from one page. "It was originally called the Road to Paradise, but in 1964, the BBC did a documentary on Flemish tapestries and referred to it as the Marleton Tapestry and it's been called that ever since. It's believed Rubens might have designed it."

"Come to the punch line." He looked longingly at the sofa. "So, where's the road?"

A look of alertness edged aside his somnolent look. "No road?"

"No road. And catch this. One of the photographs Joan hid in her red folder." Rose set a photograph on the desk. It was dated nineteen fifty-three.

"Behold the road," he said, plucking the picture up and examining it.

"Why cut off the top of the tapestry? I'm not seeing anything in my research that indicates anything other than its use here as a way of concealing the devastation of the fire that destroyed the north transept. And the wall it's hanging on is huge. Why cut it?"

"Frankly, I don't see what difference it makes. So someone cut it down. Maybe it was damaged or something. Ask Mrs. Bennett, down at Stitches. She'll know. She's been tending the tapestry for at least ten years, maybe longer."

Rose pulled the clip from her hair and shook it out. She examined the pile of photographs she needed to get through if there was even to be an attempt at a book. "Maybe later. Right now, I wish I knew what parts of the history were important to Joan. Was she emphasizing age? Subject matter? The artists?"

Rose dealt a row of altar screen photographs across the sofa. "And don't forget she hid that tapestry photograph."

He held up Joan's files. "If you really look at these folders, there's not much here. She was compulsive with her databases—addresses, dates, and so forth, but kept very little for reference when she returned home. These pamphlets are so general they're almost useless. The church documents are not much more than a chronology of purchase and so forth. Whatever books or printouts Joan used, they're missing."

Rose met Vic's eyes and knew they were thinking the same thoughts. Where was Joan's car? Her luggage?

Rose chewed the inside of her lip.

Vic put the files by her elbow and ruffled her hair. "Maybe Mary Garner can help you. After all, she did say Joan spent time on the library computers."

"Come with me?"

"I've my own research to do. And a few thousand words I should be writing."

"You mean you'll be napping."

He grinned and shoved her in the direction of the door.

Outside, the wind had picked up. Rose felt as if it were autumn, not mid-summer. She turned up the collar on her zippered sweatshirt and dodged the milling tourists. Despite the chill, the sun lay a golden sheen on the Cotswold stone—except for the library. The sun made it look as if the concrete had liver trouble.

At the library, she waited for Mrs. Watkins to finish an intense discussion with Mary Garner. The women were such a marvelous contrast, Rose's fingers itched to sneak out her camera. She mentally framed Mrs. Watkins in her seasonally inappropriate tweed suit and sensible walking shoes with Mary in her pink, frilly sundress and fashionable matching slingbacks.

Mrs. Watkins hissed and pointed at a placard in the library window like the Wicked Witch of the East casting a spell, while Mary just smiled with gracious ease, soothing the woman to the door.

When Mrs. Watkins stalked out, Mary indicated Rose should wait another moment by lifting a hot pink-tipped finger. She went to her counter and wrote a long note, sighing as she did so.

"What was her problem?" Rose asked. "Not that it's any of my business."

"She wants some of our fete proceeds to go to new choir robes. I think a roof far more important. Now, how may I help you?"

"I need to do some research," Rose said.

"Then you're in the perfect place." Mary ran her hand over her already perfect hair and almost wriggled with delight. "My middle name is 'Look it up' and hardly anyone wants to do much of that these days."

"Well, my idea of computer research is looking up the best price of a camera lens. And that's not exactly in the same league with the kind of research Joan did. Is there any way I can find out what sites she visited or used?"

An expression of pity filled Mary's face. "Let her rest in peace."

"I can't. I'm finishing her book."

"Why?"

"There's a small difficulty of the advance the church gave her."

Mary frowned. "You're not in funds, I imagine. Joan said you were . . . well, suffice to say, I know she wished she could have done more for you."

The implication that Joan was "in funds" while she, Rose, was not, saddened her. It spoke so eloquently of Joan's view of life compared to the reality of it.

Rose took a deep, steadying breath. "At first I had this idea for Joan's book, of using the computer to take each piece—altar screen or whatever, and make it appear to age from the artist's first conception to how it looks today. For instance, the banners in the church . . . well, it doesn't matter. But now," Rose had to squeeze her fingers into a tight fist to keep from tearing up. "But now, I think I want to do the book exactly as Joan meant to. And that means knowing what research was most important to her."

Mary nodded. "I understand. You want to honor her memory with this final book."

"Exactly."

A man Rose recognized as the tour guide from the church entered the library. Mary's attention instantly shifted to him. "Excuse me, but that's my Jack Carey. I want a word with him."

Mary sailed away, almost skipping.

"Too young for him," someone said.

Rose peeked behind a bookcase and saw Nell from the pub sitting on the floor bookended by a pair of blonde twin girls no older than three. The girls wore T-shirts with pigs gobbling pies.

"Mummy will be a minute," Nell said and handed the picture book she'd been reading to the girls. They clutched the book between them, and peered over it with huge blue eyes.

Nell played with a leather thong around her neck. "I couldn't help listening."

"I'm sorry we disturbed you."

"You weren't disturbing us." She smiled at the girls, the plethora of silver jewelry on her face glittering. "We can read anywhere, can't we?"

The twins bobbed their heads in agreement.

Rose composed the shot in her mind to capture the simple sweetness of the little faces looking at their mother from over the huge picture book. If framed properly, the dog on the front cover might look as if he were reading to them.

"Joan was here a lot."

"Did you talk to her?"

"She never noticed us," Nell said, with a gesture toward the girls who had reversed the book, the dog now standing on his head.

"She was always putting paper in the bin. She wore a track from the computer to there." Nell waved her arm.

"What bin?" Rose glanced around.

"The one for recycling." Nell settled back on the floor with her daughters. "She did a lot of printing and most of it she tossed. Over there." Nell pointed out a narrow nook fitted with a table and a tall cardboard bin about a foot square on a side and at least waist height.

"There's a recycling firm who takes the lot away about once a quarter, but they've not been here in an age, so you might find something of your sister's."

The bin was almost full. Rose's first impulse was to wait for Mary to end her conversation with Jack Carey, but the librarian was in mid-flirt and Rose hated to interrupt her. And then, there was Nell watching her with a hopeful expression on her face, the twins tumbling around her legs, book forgotten.

Rose pulled the first few inches of print-outs from the deep carton. She scanned a few sheets. They represented an amusing glimpse into the lives of the villagers. Someone was heading to Land's End, another was considering a career change. Rose skimmed a search for baldness cures as well as the personal e-mail of someone named fatgurl47 whose brother begged her for twenty quid.

Nell had settled the girls beside her and found them a new book. Several other children gathered at the barmaid's feet. The murmur of their voices and laughter lifted Rose's spirits. She was about to sneak off, hoping Nell would not be insulted, when she noticed a website address and date at the foot of a page.

Three days before. Every page had an address and date. Rose dug quickly through the bin, piling the nearby table with stacks of paper, looking for the Friday when Joan had last visited the Marleton library.

Rose mined the bin to the last few inches. There, she hit pay dirt. She put all the paper from that fateful Friday and every sheet under it on the table. She scooped the newer print-outs back into the carton for recycling.

She stared at the six inch stack of paper with no idea what to look for. Nell came up behind her with a chair.

"You'll ruin your back like that."

Rose realized she'd been stooped over the table. "Thank you, Nell. This was such a clever idea."

Nell shrugged, but Rose could tell the woman was pleased. She went back to her miniature fan club.

The high-backed chair cocooned Rose in the corner with the pile of paper. The world disappeared as she looked at each sheet, wondering if it had been placed there by Joan. She imagined her sister at one of the computer stations, printing information, but for some reason, discarding it.

Much of the paper with the right dates had nothing to do with Joan, but distributed throughout the final inches of paper were articles about tapestries, altar screens, and All Saints Church.

Rose's heart tapped uncomfortably in her chest as a single page caught her eye, one she'd almost discarded as not Joan's.

She forced herself to read the tiny print that filled the page. It was a discourse without paragraphs, capital letters, or headings. No white space eased the eye down the page.

As she read, her skin crawled. She hid the page under those on church art. Whatever momentary lift the little twins had brought to Rose's day disappeared.

Rose now knew how Joan had spent part of her last day of life. She'd spent it in the library, reading about evil.

* * *

VIC DID NOT REST. He wrote. Or tried to write. But his hands kept sweating, his fingers slipping off the keys.

He had new concerns unrelated to his physical discomforts. A private club housed in an abandoned underground station had somehow worked its way into his tale. It was not in the detailed outline he'd made for the book. Nor were the women tempting his protagonist, a stock broker whose newfound success allowed him to join the club—one that advertised all sexual fantasies satisfied.

The women who fascinated his main character were bound at the wrists, waiting to be auctioned off to the highest bidder for an evening's pleasure. A scenario way too similar to that of Club 7734 for Vic's taste.

Now, his stock broker who'd once been enthralled by the idea of owning a serial killer's ring, was high bidder at the auction.

Vic shut down his laptop and poured himself a drink, tasting the peat of the highlands as the whiskey flooded his mouth and washed away another taste—that of mold. If things didn't improve, he would never finish his book. He'd chuck it in.

No sequel to *Do You Believe in Evil?* would hit the shelves. Maybe Rose would help him dig a grave for his laptop, too, and he could be done with writing forever.

A HEADACHE CLAMPED ITS fingers on Rose's skull as she gathered up the pages she thought were Joan's. Nell and her girls were gone. Only a few older gentlemen remained, reading the newspapers.

Rose clipped together the pages she wanted to keep with hot pink paper clips from Mary's desk. Did Mary have clips to match all her perfect ensembles? While Rose mused on the matter she noticed Jack Carey slipping out of the library, his tie tucked into his back pocket.

Rose thanked Mary for the use of the library.

"I didn't do a thing."

"You're one of the few people to make me feel welcome."

Mary froze, hands poised over a cart of books needing shelving. "That's exactly what Joan said. 'Few people make me welcome.'"

Rose frowned. "She was unhappy here. Her e-mail messages reflected that."

"I can't imagine why she felt that way and told her so. After all, she had plenty of company. And once she joined the fete committee, well, they meet ad nauseam."

34

"JOAN AND THE FETE COMMITTEE? Not on." Vic shook his head as he took Rose's backpack, then led her toward the tantalizing aroma of coffee. She was impressed when she tasted it. It was stand-your-hair-on-end strong.

The man could be taught.

Lunch, however, was eggs and sausage, Vic-style, swimming in the butter and sausage drippings.

"Other than time commitments to her book, why wouldn't she help out? If it put her near Donald, I'd think she'd jump at the chance."

Rose held out her mug for more coffee in hopes the triple dose of caffeine might prevent some artery clogging. While they ate, Rose dug out the pages she'd purloined from the library recycling bin. Topmost was the diatribe on evil. Even touching the page filled her with distaste. She set it on the table.

"Why the frown?"

Rose stared at the page. "I swear I put this on the bottom." She shook off the idea and returned to that of Joan and the fete.

"What if we're wrong, Vic? What if Joan took those night pictures because she hid in a broom closet after a fete meeting? What if we're maligning Donald unjustly."

She watched Vic slather marmalade on his toast. He had strong hands.

Hands for pushing.

Rose felt dizzy. She gripped the pages and swallowed hard.

Vic has a key. He could have taken Joan into the church as easily as Donald.

The words reeled through her mind. She dropped the pages on the couch and threw open the front door. Immediately, the cool air swept the mugginess from her head.

"What?" she asked, aware Vic was speaking.

"I was saying that the fete committee meets in the library, not the church."

"Oh. Mary didn't mention that."

Rose watched myriad expressions flit across Vic's face. He stared at and through her, lost in his own thoughts. She shivered and felt guilty she'd had such a ridiculous notion about him pushing Joan.

They'd gone over and over the Vic and Joan ground. It was time to lay it to rest.

Rose buttered her toast and tried Alice's marmalade. "When this jar is done, there won't be any more."

Vic put some on his toast. "Does that idea depress you?"

"A little. There won't be any more books by Joan either."

Vic picked up the print-outs from the library and riffled the pages, allowing her a moment to collect herself. "At least she'll live on in restorations funded by her book."

If I finish the book and it sells well.

"This gives me the perfect opportunity to talk to Donald," Vic said. "I'll ask him how Joan *served* the fete committee, and while I'm at it, I'll ask him about his jaunts to Club 7734."

His tone had gone cold. And hard.

"Don't go," she said.

"Why not?" He frowned—no—glared at her.

"I'm not ready to confront Donald."

"You? You're not going. If you need something to do, see Mrs. Bennett and talk tapestries. I intend to talk to bloody Donald alone this time."

"Wait, the tapestry isn't important. And it doesn't matter what Joan did for the fete. Stay here, please?"

"What's the matter? You wanted me to talk to Donald before, why not now?" He dropped the pile of papers. "I've put off telling Donald what I think of him for long enough."

Rose grabbed his arm. "What's wrong with you?

He jerked his arm away. He cleared the table in silence, but the clatter of the crockery in the sink spoke eloquently of his mood.

She tried to think of something to delay the confrontation she was sure would result if Vic walked up to the church in his present mood. "Can you wait for a while? I'd like your help."

"Help?" He stood with one hand on the garden door.

She pointed to the stack of print-outs from the library. "We need to go through these papers."

Vic retreated from the door.

"I've put them in order by date. I think they're a pretty accurate picture of what Joan was doing . . . that Friday. What I need to know is what's missing."

"Missing?"

"Yeah. See." She spread out one of the groups she'd clipped together, shoving aside the page on evil with the tip of her finger. "Joan discarded seven sheets from this website on rood screens, but kept one. Page four of eight. I want to know what was on page four. We both know it's not in her files."

He blew out a long breath. "What you're saying is *you* want to know, but *I'll* be looking."

"If I promise you a wicked afternoon, would you?" She smiled.

He went to his laptop. "Nice delaying tactic, but when I'm finished here, I'm going after Donald. And nothing wicked will change my mind."

VIC STABBED EACH KEY as he entered the website address in question. Rose plucked the sheet of paper from the printer a few minutes later.

"Did you know that the Marleton altar screen was regilded four times?" Rose read from the page while handing him another website address to search.

He grunted and punched the keys. They worked that way for half an hour, him searching, her organizing.

"Did you know those huge candle sticks around the altar were a gift from a church in Australia?"

Vic swiveled away from his computer screen. "Did you know I'm bloody bored?"

She smiled.

His printer spit out another sheet. She retrieved it and read, "Griffins and gargoyles? Friends or fiends?"

"Are you asking me?" Vic tipped the chair causing it to creak and squeal as he stretched the old swiveling mechanism.

"Just reading what Joan saved." When she put the page with its partners, she realized there was a single sheet still lying on the desk—the stream of consciousness thesis on evil.

He glanced at the bottom of the page with its referenced url and then at her. "What's this about?"

"I don't know. It gives me the creeps. I'm not even sure if it has anything to do with Joan."

Vic brought the website up on the screen. She read over his shoulder.

"Bloody nut case whoever wrote this," he said.

"Do you think so?"

The printer clicked to life. "No one believes the devil walks among us as a real being."

She shivered. The room darkened for a moment.

"Are you sure?" she said softly.

He didn't answer.

The printer still held two pages from one of Vic's previous searches. She grabbed them. "More on tapestries." She read the bold-faced heading half-way down the page. "Repair of tapestries."

"Your sister was obsessed with tapestries."

"Want to know how to preserve a tapestry?" Rose asked.

"Thank you, no. Nothing but dust collectors, if you ask me." He killed his Internet connection and opened a file that looked to her as if it might be his book.

With relief, she saw he intended to write. Surely, that would keep him from fisticuffs or verbal assaults on Fallen Angels.

And her from thinking about raising devils—real or imagined.

She watched the printer chug through the pages.

Or thinking about men with keys.

She sat on the edge of a footstool, waiting for the pages on evil. The printer worked with sluggish inefficiency. It printed a few lines, stopped, printed, stopped, and then stuttered on. Twelve pages of solid type ended up on Vic's desk.

Rose slotted the one from the library on the bottom and wondered if Joan had accidentally discarded the final rant.

Touching the pages made her feel uncomfortable. The paper felt different. Rough. Scratchy. Maybe it was the solidity of the text . . . so much ink wasted on hatred.

Whoever published the piece hated everyone and everything. It was a tirade on organized religion, holier-than-thou clergy, and condemnation of anyone or any institution that dared think the Apocalypse was not upon them, that the evil in all of them *was* the Apocalypse.

An incipient headache, surely brought on by squinting through the tightly packed lines of print and the hateful invective of the author, made Rose set the pile aside.

For what reason had Joan printed this matter? Or had she? There was nothing here on church art. Had the presence of the word church and a few uses of the word "artful" captured it in a search? Had Joan then printed the article without reading it?

Had someone else entirely been interested in the nature of evil?

Rose put the sheets under the gargoyle and griffin pages, smoothing her hand over a graphic of a griffin guarding a castle in Wales. She cleansed her mind of the evil diatribe with thoughts that here, in Vic's cottage, one was safe from the ugly side of mankind.

Vic typed and she perused a dry database that listed tapestries designed by Rubens as well as those thought to be, though unconfirmed. Halfway down the latter list was All Saints Church's treasure. "Here's another reference to The Road to Paradise."

"I know the road to paradise," Vic said.

She met his eyes. He lifted his to the ceiling.

Her insides went haywire.

"Want to make the journey?" He put out his hand.

They only made it as far as the rug. She pulled him down on top of her. "Is the trip worth it?"

"If it isn't, lodge a complaint with the Automobile Association."

For long moments they lay entwined in each other's arms, kissing in a feast of tongues. She palmed him and slid her thigh between his.

He whispered her name and a few suggestions of wicked things he'd like her to do with her hand. Rose wondered if there was anything more inflaming than a man's words of need at a woman's ear as he grew aroused by her caress.

She drew up on her knees, planting them on either side of his hips. They dueled tongues while he opened her shirt and lifted her breasts from the cups of her bra.

His mouth was hot and hungry on her. She whispered her own desires, and he granted her wishes, stripping his pants past his knees while she hiked up her skirt.

She drew him one small step farther along the road to paradise by rubbing the silky crotch of her panties on his erection in a blatant invitation.

Every muscle in his body went taut when she drew aside her underwear and held him against her moist heat.

"We could head straight to paradise," she said against his lips, "or we could take a small detour."

"You're the tour director."

She licked him from his navel to ankle, discarding his khakis. His feet were sensitive. So were the insides of his thighs, the backs of his knees.

The scratch down the center of his chest looked faded and more like a scar than a new injury in the gray afternoon light. She teased her way up it to the hollow of his throat.

"No more detours," he growled.

She smiled and took him in, rode him slowly, unable to rush it, knowing she did not want a frantic coupling, knowing she wanted this to last and somehow erase the dark images that had filled her mind when she read hateful messages of evil.

Or when she thought of keys.

He put his hand between them, stroked her with rhythmic gentleness. She lost herself in the mystery of how one man's hands could conjure such a unique magic.

It was a journey of sensations from the taste of scotch and marmalade on his tongue, the scent of the rich earth on his clothes, to the furnace hot skin of his penis. She savored every step of the journey. How could she part with this man when the time came to go home? What torture would it be to lie in bed, thousands of miles away and remember his hands on her—remember the way his mouth felt on her breast?

And worse, remember the feel of his body inside hers.

She went molten hot from head to toe. Then, there was no more gentleness, no more languid strokes of tongues or fingers. His tongue stabbed into her mouth as he bucked his hips. She ground down on him, gasping, churning through a climax that followed only an instant after his.

She collapsed on him.

He locked his arms around her neck. "Do you believe in love?" he asked.

She didn't know how to answer. A few days before, her answer had been no. Now, so much had changed, a part of her wanted to say yes. Another part of her was afraid to let him see inside her. "Only in novels," she compromised.

He fisted his hand in her hair and drew her head back so they were nose to nose. "This isn't a bloody novel. This is two people who can't get enough of each other."

With a deft twist, she slipped from his grasp. She re-aligned her underwear, dropped her skirt. As she buttoned her blouse over a faint mark he'd sucked on her breast, she shook her head. "That's not love, Vic. It's just lust."

She sat at the computer. They'd not used a condom and her clothing felt wet.

But he wouldn't let it go. "I've been in lust and it lasts as long as the orgasm. Then it's thanks for the memories."

He swung the chair around so she had to face him. He'd put on his khakis, but not zipped them. She could not look away from the dark line of hair that arrowed down his belly, nor could she pretend it was just sleeping with him that kept her in his house.

"I've learned the hard way, Vic, that men don't like to talk about love. It scares them. And it scares me. Love implies commitment, longevity, tomorrows."

"Then let's just talk about moving you in here without any of those scary words. Tell Max you're on holiday. An extended holiday."

"I'm already here."

"Your belongings are down the pub. And if you wanted to get on a plane and go to Prince of Prussia, you could do so without a wave good-bye. I want your knickers in a drawer upstairs so I know I've got time."

"For what?"

"Wooing."

It was not what she'd expected him to say and she could not help smiling. She wriggled on the desk chair. "It's King of Prussia, and the spare knickers would come in handy."

"Damp where it matters, are you?"

She nodded. "When did we stop using condoms?"

He frowned. "I don't know and don't care. I want skin to skin with you, mate."

"You could be riddled with STDs."

"I'm clean as a whistle."

She sighed. "And I'm on the pill, so you don't need to worry about pregnancy."

"I'm not worried. I love kids." He lifted a strand of her hair. "A daughter with this coppery mop would suit me fine."

Fear ran through her like a knife, fear of the future, of waking up to nothing more substantial than memories. "You've had your family, Vic. You don't need more children."

"I grew up lonely, Rose. I used to tell Alice I wanted a dozen kids."

"Were you often alone, Vic?"

He smiled and looked into some distant past, she imagined, but he just as quickly shook it off. He gathered up the stack of pages by the printer and squared the edges with a sharp rap on the desktop.

"I had my mates, but when my father wanted something nicked, I was on my own."

His smile went flat. His eyes were no longer focused on her, but on something to her left.

She followed the direction of his gaze to his laptop. *His manuscript.* So much for holding his attention beyond the orgasm. What had it been? Three minutes?

A draft swirled cold air across her bare legs. "Would you rather be writing?" she asked.

"No."

His tone lacked conviction. In fact, it sounded generated by the computer next to her. "Vic? Vic?" She snapped her fingers in his face.

"Rose?"

"Where'd you go?"

He licked his lips. "I'm not sure. How long was I gone?"

"Only a second or two. You zoned out. I guess I wasn't as

fascinating as whatever you see there." She jerked her head toward his computer.

His voice hardened. "Nothing there fascinates me. And I didn't write it."

"You didn't?" She skimmed the words on the screen. "Characters climbing into coffins alive? Sounds like your kind of thing."

A nerve twitched beneath his right eye.

"Not mine. That is . . . I guess I'm the author, but I can't remember . . . writing it."

Rose looked the words over again.

The priest tried to be calm. "You're a fool, Alice," he said to the old woman.

"And you're one, too." She climbed into a polished mahogany coffin and fussed with the skirt of her blue suit until it was arranged to her liking. She folded her hands. "Fools go to hell, you know."

The priest shut out her words by slamming her coffin lid and screwing it down.

"You didn't write any of this? You've got four hundred and two pages here." She pointed to the bottom of the screen where such statistics could be found.

"Oh, I think I did about four hundred of them. Just this is by . . . someone else. I told you. I keep deleting this scene . . . and a few others. They keep coming back."

He poured them each a tumbler of whiskey and although she didn't particularly like it, she sipped it.

"This is silly. Let me try." She highlighted the words he'd sketched over. With a keystroke, she eliminated the words. "There. Done."

"Won't help. It'll be back." He picked up the printouts and began to read.

She read as well, caught by Vic's words. She saw immediately that the scene she'd deleted had nothing to do with the paragraphs before or after it. Fascinated, she scrolled to the start of his book and dove into the tale. As she read, she was conscious of pages fluttering to the desktop as Vic finished with them.

Then she noticed nothing, lost in Vic's imagination until he spun her away from the computer and jerked the laptop cord from the wall. He snatched her from the chair and in one stumbling motion, fell with her to the sofa.

She locked her hands on his chest, but he swept them aside. His kiss crushed her lips against her teeth.

He jerked her skirt up and gathered the wet crotch of her panties in his fist.

Do it. Do it. Fuck me. A voice in her head screamed for completion.

Wind rattled the window sash. The curtains snapped sharply against the sill. Cold air swirled across the hot, wet skin between her legs. And chilled the heat inside her.

"Whoa, Vic." She gripped his wrist, but he looked through her. He twisted her underwear, ready to tear it away.

With a thunderclap of awareness, she knew he was not in a haze of lust for her, but just in a haze.

"Vic. Vic. Stop." She bit his ear lobe. It inflamed rather than dampened his ardor. He moaned and bucked his hips against her. She kneed him in the thigh.

"Damn it." He rolled off her.

She tugged her skirt down. "What's wrong with you?

He scrubbed his palms over his face. "Did I hurt you?"

"No. Did I hurt you?"

Vic staggered to the kitchen, ran a glass of water, and drank it without stopping. When he returned to the sitting room his face was alert, but grim.

"Sorry, mate. I don't know what happened there." He rubbed his thigh. "One minute I was reading, the next—"

His labored breathing filled a sitting room that a few minutes earlier had howled with wind.

The floor was littered with the pages on evil. The black computer cord snaked through the mess. She plugged his computer in. She shifted the pages on evil with her toe. "You were reading this crap, weren't you?"

"Don't touch it," he said softly when she bent down to gather the sheets of paper together. "Let it sit. I feel like a character in my book, only it's not a ring I put on, it was that shit I read—"

"That did what? Made you crazy?"

"I felt like I was watching from over there." He jerked his thumb toward the front window. "Looking in the window, watching some chap force himself on you."

Rose ignored him when he warned her again about touching the pages. She gathered them up and tossed them into Alice's fireplace. She put a match to them and watched until every page was reduced to ashes.

When it was done, Vic touched her shoulder. "Would you do an experiment for me so you understand I'm not insane?" he asked.

She nodded.

"Open my manuscript and see what's on the last page."

She did as he asked and found the words she'd deleted there, underlined, the cursor blinking at the final period.

"Delete the whole damn file," Vic said.

"I hope you have it backed up somewhere."

"Oh, believe me, I have it backed up."

The words were still there after an hour of experimentation. And an hour after that as well. She deleted his book file again and again. She tried only small sections, before and after the passage that so offended him. She cut and pasted, moved sections, made new files, but still, when she shut down the computer and restarted, the words were there.

Vic sat on the sofa, propped his elbows on his knees, a mug of tea clasped between his palms.

His voice was low and hoarse. "She's trying to tell me something. It's all I can think of. She's got something to say, and I'm not able to hear it."

"Who, Vic?"

"Alice."

35

VIC HELD ONE OF Alice's umbrella's over Rose as she examined the rabbit topiary. For the first time in a long time, he smelled the damp earth, the rosemary nearby, maybe even the rain drops.

"Looks like a goner, to me," she said and took the umbrella.

"I suppose." He flicked a finger over the surface of the rabbit. Brown, brittle needles stuck to his wet finger.

Rose gasped when he pulled it from the pot. She reached in and dug around in the pile of CDs.

"What the hell?" She shuffled them like cards. "Nine?"

"Used to be ten, but I hammered one to death."

Alice's umbrella, a red confection with a ruffled edge, cast a gleam on Rose that bronzed her skin and turned her hair to molten copper. For a moment, he forgot about messages from the dead. Then he remembered how he'd handled her. He cast the topiary aside and shoved his hands deep into his pockets.

Rose's mouth twisted into a stiff smile. "This is a touch perverse. Why'd you save them?"

"I guess I wanted proof I wasn't crazy." He took a deep breath. The next bit was hard. Harder than telling her about the words. "When I'm working on those bits—trying to obliterate them—I'm gripped by this anger . . . and I feel like I'm looking in a window laughing at what a wanker I am to even try and get rid of them."

She put out a hand. He took a step out of reach.

"I know I'm a writer, but I'm lacking the proper words to tell you how much I want you . . . here. But after grabbing you maybe Trevor's right—you should stay at the pub."

"I'm not going to lie to you, Vic, you scared me. But another part of me wanted to grab you back. Something on the edges of my mind said, 'Stop.'" Her voice dropped to a whisper. "The inside part said. 'Fuck me.'"

The word was wrong on her lips. Like tasting beef when you were expecting lamb.

She propped the umbrella on her shoulder and looked up at the sky. Black clouds piled up over the village, but he realized it was the church tower she was looking at.

"Vic. It's time you talked to Donald."

"Earlier you weren't keen on the idea."

"You've got unfinished business with him. And if Alice is talking to you, who better to consult on messages from the dead—or on evil—than a priest?"

THEY WALKED UP THE footpath. Vic would not share her umbrella though the rain now came down in a steady downpour. He wore only a light windbreaker over his T-shirt. His hair was wet, his expression grim. Tension radiated from him, like heat from a stove.

No tourists vied for space on the footpath or took pictures of the church up ahead. She imagined them in the tea shop or the pub, or in Stitches buying souvenirs.

"Take a deep breath and remember you catch more flies with honey than vinegar," she said when they reached the church and the walkway to the rectory.

He smiled and reached out. He ran his fingertips along her

cheek to her lips. His fingers were cold and wet, but she would not have traded the short caress for a warmer one on a sunny day.

She watched him walk up the vicarage path to confront Donald, or maybe his own guilt.

And what was she going to do while he was about it? She bobbled the umbrella, pulling her camera out. She tried to capture how the rain painted the rough stone of the church with black streaks. Water poured from the gargoyle spouts. One, a particularly malevolent looking fellow, pissed the water instead.

The sky grew darker, the wind tugged on her umbrella, almost tearing it from her hand. She held the camera with only one hand, bracing against a bicycle rack and focusing on a raven that strutted about the churchyard heedless of the downpour.

She shifted the camera to the church—and almost dropped it. Through her viewfinder, the flying buttresses transformed the medieval building into a hulking spider.

The wind snatched at the umbrella, turning it into a bright red tulip. Rose sheltered her camera against her chest, put her back to the wind, and fought the umbrella down.

But she wanted that picture, wanted to capture the malevolent look of the architecture though the place was supposed to be a haven of comfort and good.

Rain sheeted across her path. She dashed for the lytch gate.

Two steps from shelter, she saw something bright white dangling from the center beam of the gate's peaked roof.

The umbrella slipped from her fingers. Rain pelted her shoulders, ran down her face.

The figure twisted toward her. The wind fluttered the blond hair, tugged at the skirt of the white robe.

Rose dropped her camera. She ran straight to the hanging man and gripped him about the knees.

And screamed.

36

V<small>IC LED</small> R<small>OSE TO</small> the church porch while the constables cut
Donald down. The pubs and shops had poured tourists the
instant the police cars had drawn up in front of the church—
the second time in one week.

Vic wanted Rose out of public scrutiny and both of them
gone when the press arrived. She huddled against his chest.
"I couldn't lift him. He was too heavy," she whispered.

"You couldn't have saved him; I think he'd been there a
while."

Vic stroked the ropes of wet hair off her face. His ears still
rang with Rose's screams. He'd never forget the sight of her
trying to support the young man, though one look at Donald's face and one knew the effort hopeless.

Could he have prevented Donald's death if he'd gone after
him earlier? Or was it just ego to think such a thing prevent-
able?

Two tourists, in bright yellow slickers, held an animated

discussion with two other figures in dark suits, whose faces were hidden by black umbrellas.

Shit. The press, he thought until the suits headed in their direction. It was Trevor and Munson.

"What the fuck went on here?" Trevor asked when he reached the porch. Munson winced.

"Rose found—" Vic said.

"She can speak for herself."

Rose quivered, but after a moment's hesitation, she pulled away. Trevor immediately put his arms about her. The urge to string the copper up to one of the iron lamps in the church porch made Vic shove his hands deep into his jacket pockets. It was better than succumbing to an urge he knew he'd later regret.

Munson jotted down Rose's halting account of finding Donald. "Harrison, take Ms. Early back to the pub. I've sent for Alden, miss. He'll stay with you."

"She's coming with me to Alice's." Vic grabbed Trevor's arm.

"I think she should go to hospital," Trevor said.

"I think I can make up my own mind," Rose said.

Trevor shoved his face into Vic's. "Every damn time you're around, something happens to her."

"You think I had something to do with this?" Vic placed his palms flat on Trevor's chest and shoved.

Trevor shoved back.

A haze of black dots danced at the periphery of Vic's vision. He shoved Trevor again.

Munson and Rose stepped between them. "Stop this," Munson said softly. "The press will have you on page one."

Trevor backed off.

Coward.

"Vic. Vic." Rose tugged at his forearms. "Listen to her."

He sucked air into his lungs. The lump on the back of his head throbbed, his mouth tasted like hot metal.

Munson pulled Rose behind a pillar of the church porch. "Think about what you're doing. Those reporters are headed here."

Vic saw a trio of men in rain gear dodging tourists, heading for the police cars. Rose's jacket had come open. Her blouse was so wet and sheer, he could see the lacy pattern on her bra. That Trevor could see it too sent another bolt of anger through him.

He jerked the edges of Rose's jacket closed. Then he took her hand. "We'll be at Alice's."

Before anyone could protest, he threw open the church door. She didn't fight him when he led her through the nave. *Away from Trevor.*

She began to slow. He tugged her along. "I need a weapon," he said.

"What for?"

As they passed the altar, Vic twisted a thick candle from one of the floor stands and threw it to the ground. He hefted the iron stand in his hands.

"What are you doing?"

"It's for Trevor." He brandished his trophy like a lance.

Rose's hair hung in lank ropes about her face and shoulders. Trevor had brought her to this. She'd probably get sick. Die. *Like Alice.*

The cold metal bit into his palms.

Rose backed away, into the tapestry. She moaned.

The sound sobered him. *Sickened him.*

Slowly, Vic set the iron holder in place. With his eyes locked on hers, he retrieved the candle, and gently replaced it.

When he approached her, she turned and fled. He ran her to ground at the north porch, her fingers fighting the ancient lock.

"I'm not going to touch you," he said.

"Go away."

He worked the lock and pushed the heavy door open.

She almost fell from the room. He followed her into the icy rain and remembered flinging her to the grass here when she'd been sick.

Now, it was he who was sick. Sick in the mind. Ill with something he could not touch or see. Or explain.

But he tried. "It's the church, Rose."

She looked above at the tower.

"I would never hurt you," he repeated.

She ran up the footpath to Alice's. Something inside him uncoiled. He almost shook with relief that she'd not run the other way—to the village.

The gate was locked. She huddled against the wall, shivering. He scaled the wall and dropped to the other side. He held his breath as he undid the latch.

Would she still be on the other side?

She was—and looked like a drowned rat. She pushed past him, but when they passed the topiary rabbit lying on its side, she knelt, heedless of the wet grass and stroked the rotting branches as if had once been alive.

She struggled to her feet, her knees muddy. "I think the evil killed it."

"Evil?"

Rain wet her cheeks. Or was it tears?

"Yes, Vic. There's evil in this place. I think it killed Alice. And Joan. Maybe even Donald. I think it killed this rabbit. And if we don't do something about it, I think you're next."

37

Munson and Alden climbed out of their gray Ford at half past seven. Trevor was only minutes behind them. The rain had stopped. Pools of water lay on the flagstones, reflecting the evening sun.

The brook seethed under the plank bridge. A row of reporters stood on the other side, hungry for fodder for the ten o'clock news. He'd been expecting them all. Police, press. Chums.

He composed himself. He jerked the door open before they knocked. "Couldn't wait one bloody day?"

"We need to see Ms. Early," Alden said.

Munson nodded. Trevor said nothing.

"She's sleeping."

Munson flattened her hand on the door and put one foot in the doorway. "We need to see her."

"They've been warned not to trespass," Alden said when a series of flashes went off behind them.

Vic stepped reluctantly aside. He locked the door and drew the curtains across the windows. "She really is sleeping."

"We'd like you to wake her." Munson kept her gaze on her competition. Alden remained at attention by the fire screen.

Vic left them and went up to Alice's room. Rose was not asleep—or in bed. She sat in a small chintz-covered slipper chair, wide awake.

"Who is it?" she asked.

Her hair had dried to a wild mane of curls. He wanted to bury his face in them, hide from the snake inside him. But he had promised not to touch her.

He held onto the door knob. "It's your FLO and Munson. And Trevor."

"Rose?" Trevor stood in the doorway with Munson and Alden on his heels.

Vic felt neither anger or surprise that they had followed him upstairs. He only felt weary. Without a word, he left them.

ROSE WORE ALICE DRUMMOND'S dressing gown. The soft cashmere smelled of lavender sachet and was embroidered at the lapels with tiny violets.

The room was crowded with the three police officers.

Trevor put out his hand. She linked her fingers with his and held on tightly.

Munson sat on Alice's bed. "Donald had a note in his pocket," she said without preamble.

Rose braced herself for what she saw on Trevor's face.

"Donald killed Joan," Trevor said gently.

Rose nodded. She bit her lip to stem the tears. She felt no surprise, only grief.

"If we hadn't the note, we would still have the vicar's confession," Munson added.

"Confession?" Rose said.

Trevor stroked his thumb across the back of her hand, but it was Munson who said, "Nigel says he saw Donald leave the church very late on the day we believe Joan died. Nigel didn't realize at the time that anything . . . that anything as ghastly as murder had been done. He just knew Donald was upset, running away and weeping." Munson and Trevor exchanged a glance.

Munson continued, "Donald came back later very drunk and passed out. Nigel blames himself for not going after Donald at the time—"

"If he had, Donald might have confessed at once," Trevor interrupted. "And some of your anguish would have been spared."

"Nigel is very sorry," Alden interjected.

Where was Vic? She wanted his hand, not Trevor's. She wanted to crawl into his arms and hide from the images in her head.

"How? I mean, why?"

"We don't know all of it," Munson said. "It's impossible for one man to lift that coffin lid, but in his letter, Donald takes all blame upon himself. He wrote that your sister was blackmailing him over the London club." Trevor released her hand and began to pace. "He felt desperate. Those were his words. Desperate. He shoved her in anger, Rose. He wrote that it was an accident, not deliberate."

"Not deliberate?" She felt like a stupid parrot repeating the words, but her mind could not wrap around the word blackmail.

Oh, Joan, why could you not be content with your life as it was? Embrace the project that would save historical treasures instead of reaching for a dream that had been more their father's than it could ever have been Joan's.

Alden patted her shoulder. "Donald asked that whoever found the letter should tell you how sorry he was. He asked your forgiveness."

Munson stood up. "He also detailed where he'd left Joan's car—a car disposal yard near Manchester. We requested local police search it, and they've reported nothing in the boot, I'm afraid. No materials for her book, no photographs, no luggage. Either Donald got rid of them or the car's been ransacked."

Rose wiped her eyes with the tips of the belt. "I'm sorry, I can't seem to stop crying."

"You can go home after the inquest," Munson said.

Rose nodded.

"I hope you won't," Trevor finished.

38

ROSE LEFT THE BEDROOM door open so she could hear the creak and squeal of Vic's desk chair. It comforted her. As long as she heard the sound she knew he was downstairs writing. Vic writing was a good thing. All was right in the world if Vic was writing.

No, nothing was right in the world.

He climbed the stairs at two. When he did not stop at her door, she realized she'd been lying there for hours waiting for him.

He'd promised not to touch her, and he'd carried it so far as to leave her completely alone.

She hated being alone, especially with her thoughts.

She hated the idea of Joan blackmailing Donald. She hated the sordidness of it all. Hated thinking of the newspaper stories, of having to explain it all to Joan's friends at home. How much more terrible it would be if her father were alive. Or if her mother were able to understand.

She donned the cashmere dressing gown and tip-toed

along the landing. The light Vic had left on in bathroom cast a triangle of light across his still form.

Was he awake? She opened the dressing gown and let it slither off her shoulders. His sharp intake of breath answered her question.

She lifted the corner of the duvet and climbed into the narrow bed. They faced each other and she knew he would not touch her first.

"I kept thinking of keys," she said, softly. "Thinking about you and your key, thinking maybe you let Joan into the church."

He shook his head.

"I'm so ashamed of even suspecting you." Knots jammed up in her throat. "I need you, Vic."

But he shook his head and shifted a few inches away, so no part of their bodies touched.

"What's wrong with us?" she asked.

"Maybe something evil."

"But I'm a good person, Vic."

"The best."

"You're good, too."

She gripped the duvet with two hands. If she didn't, she'd be grabbing him, and she sensed he did not want her touch. Not yet.

"You said I was next."

"Maybe I was a bit crazy right then."

"And maybe you're a fool for being here now."

She examined his face. "When we're like this . . . I don't feel any fear. In the church . . . I was terrified." She leaned over and kissed his mouth. He didn't kiss back. "It wasn't you," she said softly. "You didn't even look like yourself."

"If Trevor knew you were here—"

"He does. I called him with my cell phone, and said I wasn't going to the pub tonight. I blamed the reporters."

"And what he said was unfit to print?"

"No. He reminded me that Alden is still mine twenty-four hours a day if I need him."

"Bloody Trevor's in love with you."

"Maybe." She shifted an inch closer. He moved a corresponding distance away.

"And maybe we should have Alden here to protect you. From me."

"I think evil killed Joan," she said.

He didn't reply.

"She had evil thoughts, Vic. That's what she said in her e-mail messages. Look how important that idea was. She reads your book when she hates commercial fiction, then re-reads it. She marks it up and writes, 'I believe,' at the end."

Vic rubbed his arm and she saw the gooseflesh there.

"I'd forgotten. That bloody book is haunting me," he said.

"It's the only way I can reconcile my sister and blackmail."

"I didn't know her well enough to see anything out of the ordinary in her behavior, but I know myself. The urges I've had to smash Trevor aren't part of my normal psyche. I've never even raised a hand to one of my sons."

He held out one of his hands and flexed his fingers. "I remember the sensation when I held the candle holder. My fingers felt bloody arthritic. I couldn't get them to obey."

Rose took his hand in hers. She massaged his fingers, stroked the valleys between his knuckles, pressed her lips to his palm.

"Are you sure about this, matc?" he whispered.

She rubbed her cheek against his hand. "I'm not sure about anything. I need time, that's all."

"I need time, too," he said. "I need to prove I didn't lie where it matters. And that I'm not mad."

She tucked her body into the hollows of his.

"Promise you'll call bloody Trevor if I get out of hand."

"If you promise to think about what I said. About evil. About Joan."

39

Vic clipped away the broken canes on the rose bushes ravaged by the heavy rains that began on the day of Joan's inquest and ended two days later with the adjournment of Donald's.

Rose plucked the CDs from the flower pot and dropped them one by one into a bin liner. Vic wasn't sorry to see them go. He handed her a sheaf of broken blooms, and she put them in a vase on the patio table.

"I still can't believe Donald's dead," she said, fussing over her arrangement.

"I wonder why he chose to hang himself in broad daylight when anyone might have seen and stopped him." He sheathed his clippers in his back pocket. "*I* might have stopped him if I'd gone up in time."

She buried her face in the petals. When she looked up, there were tears in her eyes. "You can't think that way."

"Yes, I can. I've been shredding Donald's reputation all over the village for going to the pub when he might have saved Alice, and now, I've gone and done the same damned thing. He was drinking, I was fucking."

She flinched.

Black clouds filled the sky with an ominous memory of the sordidness of Donald's death.

"*I* held you back. I hate confrontations." She clutched the vase close to her chest, a barrier between them.

"I love them." He jerked the ties closed on the bin liner. "Donald might be nursing a broken nose today, not lying in the morgue if only—"

"Stop, Vic. Please, stop. Any delay belongs on my head, not yours."

"We're bloody stupid, both trying to take each other's blame."

He hooked her around the neck and pulled her close.

"Maybe no one's to blame. You didn't have an appointment with him, and you didn't introduce him to that club, either. Maybe it's egotistical of us to think we have any power over life and death in this world."

"Just touching you is healing," he said against her hair. "You're all that is good."

"Will anything happen to Nigel? He looked pretty bad at the inquest. Not saying anything once he knew Joan was dead." She slipped from his embrace.

"Nothing will happen to Nigel."

"He should share the blame with us. If he'd gone to the police, Donald would be alive."

"Maybe Donald preferred heaven to the hell of prison."

"That's if he asked God's forgiveness before he died. Asking mine won't get him anywhere."

She lifted a sprig of lavender to her nose.

"Can you forgive him?" Vic asked.

"He was a troubled man; you said so yourself. And to live with guilt . . . well, we both know how destructive guilt is. But as Munson said, it's all over now. I can go home."

He encircled her waist, but she would not lie easy against him. He needed time and he knew only one way to get it. "You're not going anywhere. You have a book to finish."

* * *

THE FETE COMMITTEE SAT around the library's conference table. Mrs. Watkins served the tea and Mrs. Edgar passed around her delectable raspberry pastries.

Mrs. Bennett waved off both. "We can't let this latest disaster cancel the fete. Now, we must have someone to replace Donald. Any suggestions?" She tapped her pen when no one spoke.

"Nell's William? He does a wonderful Guy Fawkes celebration each year."

"Nell gossips."

The committee nodded in unison.

Mrs. Watkins cleared her throat. "What of Vickers Drummond?"

Mrs. Edgar snickered. The other ladies shushed her.

"Enough out of you," Mrs. Watkins said, glaring across the table. "Donald drew the young ones. Drummond has that same appeal. Think of all his fans. Wouldn't they come to our fete if he were there? We might get a few new church members as well if he attended services."

"He never attends," Mary Garner said.

"But if he helped at the fete," Mrs. Watkins said, "we might be able to draw him into the fold, so to speak, when it's over."

"His sort only writes cheques," Mrs. Edgar snapped.

"I think Mrs. Watkins has a wonderful idea." Mrs. Bennett smiled around the table. "I, for one, suggest we ask Drummond to head our fete committee. Mary, will you invite him?"

Mary sighed. "I already know his answer."

VIC'S CLOWN CAR WAS filled to the brim with boxes and bags.

"I see the press is down by half today."

"You haven't heard," Rose said, grabbing a few bags. "A gang of teenagers have been arrested for disrupting the symposium on Youth Crime in Stratford."

"Disrupting? How?" Vic hefted a box and carried it into the cottage.

"It seems they burgled the hotel rooms. Nary a clergyman was spared. Several of them were servers at All Saints by the way."

"Trevor should be thankful he's on special leave over Joan or his arse would be in a sling."

Vic got back into his car and accelerated down the road, leaving behind a cloud of black smoke, as he headed to the garage he hired. He returned as she set up a combination scanner, copier, fax machine on his desk.

"This is rather expensive, and excessive, isn't it?" She eyed a shopping bag of ink cartridges. Dozens.

"I don't like to shop, so when I do, I tend to be a bit frantic."

"Thank you," she said, her throat tight, her eyes filling up again with the same damned tears that had plagued her since Joan's death.

"You have a book to finish and you can't do it without the proper equipment. Can you work one of these buggers?" He slapped the scanner. "Personally, I'm heading down the pub for a spot of sustenance . . . and to find out what's being said about Donald's inquest. Are you coming?"

"No, I want to play with the new toys."

Rose watched Vic jog along the footpath, foiling the remaining reporters who waited out front. He ran with long, easy strides. How he could be running and still look lazy was beyond her.

When he disappeared from view, she got down to work. The scanner proved handy for working with Joan's contact sheets. Rose enlarged the small images to eight by ten, and because Vic was filthy rich, she printed each one so she did not have to look them over with the loupe.

The work drove away dark thoughts and mental images so she could concentrate on the paper ones. Over the past two days, she had mapped out Joan's book. When Rose envisioned the finished product, it was no longer a giant book the size of Vermont with nothing but blank pages. It had shrunk to the size of Joan's other books, and if Rose imagined turning the pages, she saw the altar screens, the glass windows, the gargoyles, the threadbare banners that would people the pages.

She knew her frantic industry was an avoidance technique, but she was glad to have the work.

When Vic appeared, he enveloped her in a fog of beer fumes.

"I need sun, mate, or I'll be sucking someone's neck, probably yours."

"You're out of luck. I think it's going to rain again."

"We need a substitute. Put on your yellow dress?"

As she pulled the soft cotton on, feeling wicked, remembering Vic's fantasy, the sun came out. The Cotswold stone steamed.

They dragged the patio furniture to the center of the emerald green lawn, along with Vic's laptop, his printer, and the new scanner. She found she needed the sun as much as he did. The warmth and sweet scent of the roses rendered the image of Donald, garbed as an angel, his body twisting in the wind, surreal.

Vic fired off text for Joan's book as if he wrote non-fiction every day, and if occasionally his hands stilled on the keyboard, and a frown marred his brow, she didn't remark on it. She knew he was checking his manuscript file and finding it unchanged.

Some ghosts had not been put to rest with Donald's death.

Vic read a snippet of text aloud for her.

"You have an agile tongue." His face went scarlet and she laughed aloud, startling them both.

He touched her cheek. "Are you better?"

"I will be after Joan's cremation. That's all that's left."

"And the book."

"Of course. The book."

She leaned back and let the sun warm her face. She was better—somehow cleansed.

He set a photograph on her lap, managing a stroke of her thigh at the same time. She smiled, but ignored the invitation.

"The tapestry, loomed in Flanders—" he said.

"Vic," someone called from the footpath. Mary Garner peeked around the back gate. "Am I intruding?"

"No," Vic said, hopping to his feet and swooping down on her, swinging her around as he had in the library.

"This man is hopeless." Mary straightened her sage green linen dress. "What are you doing?"

Rose noted the slightly darker shoes and matching bag that hung on the librarian's arm and felt like she was wearing a yellow dust rag, since she'd not ironed the dress after washing it out in Vic's bathroom sink.

"We're finishing Joan's book," Vic said.

"Of course. I must be thick." Mary paged through a few of the folders, looking at the photographs, sometimes reading the text Vic had written. Last, she picked up the photo from Rose's lap and said softly, "It's going to be lovely."

She rooted in her purse and brought out a hankie embroidered with tiny purple flowers which she dabbed under her eyes. "Forgive me."

"What brings you here?" Vic asked, setting out a third chair.

"I've been sent as an emissary from the church."

Rose watched Vic's face stiffen.

"We, that is, the fete committee, would like you to take on the task of chairperson," Mary said.

"Not bloody likely."

"At least listen, Vic," Mary said. "You won't have to do a thing. Just let us use your name, be there, maybe shake a few hands—"

"I said no."

"Why not?" Rose frowned at his icy tone.

"I'm allergic to mobs."

Mary stood up. "Well, I tried. Thank you for hearing me out."

"You hardly tried at all," Rose said and drew a sharp glare from Vic.

Mary sank to the edge of her seat. "Please, Vic. With Donald's death, many think we should put the whole thing off, but the library needs the funds from the book stall now.

And we've the fund to start the bells up again. Two chaps from London are willing to train ringers. And there's the roof, too."

"I'll get my cheque book."

"That's what the committee said, 'He won't help. He'll only write a cheque.'" Mary sighed.

"Is there a way Vic can be sheltered from the crowds?"

He made a growling sound in his throat.

Mary smiled. "Yes. We only need him on hand to help Father Nigel open, then we can set out one hour for him to appear again and sign books. After that, we can whisk him away to London, or wherever, so he won't be bothered." Mary directed her remarks to Rose.

"Sounds reasonable," Rose said.

"To whom?" Vic snarled.

"Everyone in their right mind. If the fete's going to take place, you might as well be part of it. Didn't your aunt start this fete business?" Rose asked. "Maybe she'd have wanted you to help."

"The paparazzi is here already," Mary reminded him.

She held her breath and exhaled sharply when Vic promised to think about it.

"That's it. I'll think about it. And don't nag me."

ROSE TAPED THE PHOTOGRAPHS up around the sitting room as Vic had done. They'd almost been electrocuted when, as Mary shut the garden gate, the sky turned black. It had been moments after hauling all the equipment and papers inside that the sky had opened up again.

Now, rain sluiced down the window panes, gushed under the tiny plank bridge, and drove the reporters to the pubs.

The Marleton tapestry did need its own double-page spread, Rose decided. She rearranged a few of the photographs. Nothing pleased her.

Vic was sleeping in the bathtub she assumed, since he'd gone to clean up and not returned.

She went to Joan's folders and pulled out a picture of the

tapestry dated 1953. It showed the fine detail of the road along the top of the tapestry. But the image was tiny, and the body of the tapestry was partially concealed by a pair of clergymen who stood before it, smiling at the camera. The scanner enlarged, clarified, and enhanced the image. She used a photo software program to cut the men from the picture. Last, she took one of the newer photographs she'd taken in black and white and cut out the center. She then merged the two and prepared to hide the effort.

She chose a knight's shield with its simple geometric heraldic device as a starting point. She tapped the keys to enlarge the image.

"What the heck?"

She picked out a soldier, enlarged him as well. With a muffled curse, she printed off the merged images, the originals, and two enlargements she made for the hell of it. She jerked all the tapestry photos off the mantle and bookshelves, put the newspaper photo on top, and took the stairs two at a time.

The sight of Vic arrested her progress into the bathroom. He lay in the tub, feet hanging over the end by the taps, a washcloth demurely draping his private parts.

An overwhelming desire to toss the photos on the floor and jump his bones made her sigh.

"In or out. You're causing draft."

His words snapped her out of her reverie. She shut the door, hooked a small vanity stool close to the tub, and sat down.

"You have to see this." She held the newspaper photo she'd enhanced out of the reach of any water he splashed.

"Kind of foggy in the center."

"I cut some men out. Probably the vicar and his curate. She put that photo on the bottom and held up another. "Then I took my photograph and merged the two."

Next, she flapped her merged picture, enlarged so only a yard or two of the tapestry's fabric could be seen.

"Hold the damned thing still, you're making me dizzy." He squinted. "And?"

"Can't you see it? The pieces don't match." Her heart began to beat and it had nothing to do with the fact that his washcloth had floated away on the mini-waves he'd caused as he moved.

"So, they don't match?"

"So, the All Saints tapestry's a fake."

"A fake?" He smiled. "Looks pretty damned old and authentic to me."

"Look." She traced her points of comparison. "If it was the same tapestry, these lines would match. I've done this dozens of time. I know my stuff. To quote you, I'm brilliant.

"These soldiers and shields, peasants and so on, will never match up because it's not the same tapestry. That explains why there's no road on The Road to Paradise. It hasn't been lopped off, it was never put in the fake."

Vic spread the washcloth over his face and slid lower in the water. "I'll call Trevor in the morning. Maybe he knows someone in art fraud."

She scooted from the bath and spread out the pictures on the bed.

"Don't tease me and leave me," he called.

"Tease you? How was I teasing you?" She rearranged the photos.

"Come here and I'll show you."

A frisson of desire sent her to his side, the tapestry forgotten. "How was I teasing you?"

"Just your presence. Join me?"

She pulled off her yellow dress. His smile broadened when she took up the soap and began to massage his feet. His penis did a periscope imitation.

"See. Teasing. Now jump in here."

Rose soaped her hands again and ran them up and down the insides of his calves. "I will if you'll help Mary out with the fete."

He grinned. "Well done. I'll help Mary if you promise this will be the loveliest bath of my entire forty years."

She slipped out of her underwear and perched on the end of the tub. The water lapped her calves. The warmth mirrored her inner heat, moist and heavy in her groin. She shifted her knees apart and smiled. "Forty-two, but who's counting?"

ROSE RESTED HER HEAD on the edge of the tub and considered Vic in the bright light of the bathroom. With his eyes closed, she could not conjure the fear or anxiety from the church. Here, if she ignored the mark on his chest, he was just a man.

She nudged him with a toe. "Let's stay in this tub forever."

He opened one eye and smiled. "Your bum will wrinkle."

"It's already wrinkled. What time is it?"

"Just gone midnight."

"I should take more pictures of the tapestry."

"With or without permission?"

"Your larcenous nature is rubbing off on me." She spoke with studied nonchalance. "I think we should use your key."

"Now?"

"Yes. I want to get into the church again. Without anyone knowing."

He drew her hair aside and kissed her throat. "I've corrupted you."

"It's the church that's corrupt. It's all about the church."

"What if I grab a candle stand?"

His body radiated tension, his thigh muscle taut against her hip.

"You won't. We're not going in unarmed."

"You watch too much bloody television."

"I don't mean with guns, silly. I mean we're forewarned. And forewarned is forearmed. I'm not going to let the church get to you or make me sick. I have a plan."

ROSE SWEPT SHADOWS ASIDE with her flashlight beam, illuminating saints, casting sinners into darkness. Vic remained in the far aisle, his beam of light tracing the floor.

She experimented. She walked slowly down the nave and dropped bright pink paper clips at each stone where her perceptions changed. One clip for the beginning of a headache. One for the tango in her stomach. Two for a nearly uncontrollable wave of fear that brought goosebumps to her arms and a shake to her hands.

Vic did his own experiment. He remained in the far aisle, concentrating on Alice and her extreme goodness. It was what they'd agreed. He gave Rose a thumbs-up when he reached the bell tower stairs.

That meant he felt no urge to smash something—or someone.

Rose knew she could endure the illness, wasn't sure about the dizziness and fear, so she chanted a mantra given her when her mother decided the only way to happiness was through hours of meditation.

Usually, that meant her mother slept for several hours uninterrupted by childish demands, but until Rose had caught on, she'd dutifully said her mantra. She repeated it now.

She checked her camera settings. Vic set up her tripod and ranks of candles by the tapestry. She did not speak to him as promised, letting him repeat his own mantra, the litany of times Alice had either bailed him out of trouble or forestalled it.

As she waited for the camera to do its time-exposure magic, she listened. Wood creaked, wind moaned around the tower. The scent of old incense and mold was stronger here where the drafts did not stir.

When the photographs were all taken, Vic switched on his flashlight. The beam picked out a silver thread on the tapestry. It drew her. She traced the sparking line as it formed the edge of a knight's gauntlet. The cloth felt clammy, the mold-scent heavier. She lifted the edge of the tapestry and examined the back. Every breath filled her head with the stench of damp, decaying cloth.

She broke their agreed upon silence. "I don't think this is a fake."

Vic collapsed her tripod. "Why?" he asked tersely.

"The cloth, the stitching. Give me a boost up? I want to examine the top edge."

He looped his fingers. As she set her foot on his palms, the church spun. With a gasp, she staggered away, tripped on her backpack, and but for Vic's support, would have fallen on her face.

"Steady, mate."

She pushed him off and took long, deep breaths. Vic waited patiently for her to recover. A sound, like the scrape of a match, came from over by the gift shop. Vic doused his light.

They listened. She said her mantra and hoped Vic said his.

Nothing stirred. The church was not completely dark with so many tall windows, but her eyes ached at the effort to interpret the shadows. The church was not silent either though whatever had startled them was not repeated.

The building breathed. Wind pushed against the tower like air sighing in and out of lungs. Ivy scratched on stones. Timbers creaked overhead. All were sounds one ignored unless listening sharply as they did, their own breath held until expelled in long sighs. She flicked the switch on her flashlight.

Vic linked his fingers, offering her another try.

She did not tell him her dizziness had morphed to nausea when she stepped onto his hands. Quickly, before she was overcome, she plucked at the header that attached the tapestry to the wall.

"Down," she said and stumbled away as he eased her to her feet. "Definitely cut down. I'd bet money this is the real deal."

She grabbed her backpack, the tripod, and headed down the central aisle of the nave, sweeping the floor with her flashlight beam, looking for the pink paper clips.

"Here's where it starts," she whispered at the first clip she'd dropped on the floor, even with the last row of seats.

Vic squatted by her, his light trained on the innocuous pink clip.

Overhead, the gauzy banners fluttered as if someone had opened a window.

"Trevor would be angry if he knew we were here," Rose said. "But I want to tell him how the church makes me feel." She picked up her backpack.

"Trevor!" He spat the name.

"Vic?" She tried to take his hand. He jerked away.

"I'd like to see him stabbed . . . one of the lances . . . through him." The tendons stood out in high relief on his throat.

Rose kept her flashlight beam on his face. "Think good thoughts. Remember? Think *only* good thoughts, damn it."

The flashlight dropped from his fingertips. It bounced on its rubber casing and rolled away. "Drive it through . . . no."

He caught the flashlight and it captured his face, casting demonic shadows on him as it had when he'd pantomimed at the pulpit.

She could smell the acrid scent of his sweat. It beaded on his upper lip, but his lips looked dry enough to crack. "Snap out of it, Vic. Don't let it get to you."

Her own stomach roiled as if she stood on a ship's deck. Her head pounded.

The sighing wind coalesced into the shuffle of sandals.

In the south aisle.

Whispered prayers filled the cavernous space, grew louder, echoed off the stone pillars.

"Rose. We . . . have . . . to . . . leave."

The cacophony of murmurs coalesced into the audible chant of monks. The scent of incense floated around her.

The dark nave flared bright as clouds revealed the moon.

And she saw them.

A score of monks, each bearing a single candle, filing down the aisle. As they drew level, warmth flooded over her as if she had stepped before a roaring fire.

They were good. They were nothing to fear. She knew without being told that they were the men who had built the place, who had worshipped here centuries ago.

Did they walk to protest the deaths of Joan and Donald? Or to protest something else, something more malevolent?

Fear washed all peace away.

"Do you see them?" Vic asked.

"They're not really there," she shouted, hauling on Vic's hand.

A frantic need to leave the church clutched at her.

He could take care of himself.

She threw off his hand and ran straight to the bank of doors.

They were locked.

"Rose?" Vic called.

He paced the monks down the nave, swinging his torch from side to side. Searching. For what?

A victim?

She doused her light. Her head echoed with chanting.

She fumbled along the row of doors, trying each, but her mind worked more clearly here. The only door unlocked, the only way to safety was through the north porch. Her heart hammered. Saliva flooded her mouth.

"Where are you?"

She hunkered down in the shadows of the furnace. He called her name again, his voice penetrating the prayers of the dead monks.

She slipped down the south aisle, tearing through the vaporous monks. At the bell tower stairs, she looked back. Vic worked his way between a row of chairs on an interception path with her.

She remembered stroking her hands over the hard muscles of his body. She could almost feel the strength of his hands on her.

The beam of his torch swung in erratic paths, flashing along the rows of seats.

He whispered her name.

He's hunting me.

Fear tightened her belly. She groped for the bell tower door, eased it open.

Cold, fresh air washed over her face as she glanced up into pitch blackness. Shivering less from cold than fear, she closed the door. Behind the solid wood, she heard nothing but whispered prayers and gliding sandals.

They can't hurt me.

Rose ran up the twisting stairs. The rough rope handhold was wet. With a jolt, she realized it was simply sweat that slicked the thick hemp. She switched on her flashlight, concealing the beam with the palm of her hand, letting only a trickle of light through her fingers.

She swallowed down nausea less often the higher she went, but no matter how many rounds of the steps she did, the chanting remained clear. "They can't hurt me," she whispered.

"Rose," Vic called from the foot of the steps.

She shoved her flashlight into her jacket and froze. Her heart beat so hard, she thought he might hear it.

"Where are you? What the hell are you doing?" His shoes scraped on the stone stair. "Are you up there?"

She sank to a step, hid her face on her knees, and prayed he would go away.

The door below shut with a thud.

He's not fooling me. He's down there, waiting. If I move, he'll hear me. He'll know I'm here.

She suddenly needed to pee.

When she stood, her knees cracked. It sounded like rifle shots in the narrow stair. But only silence filled the tower if one could ignore the monks at prayer.

She clung to the rope handle and pulled herself up, one step at a time. When she reached the top, the door to the ringing chamber was locked. Panic clawed at her composure. She crept a few rounds back down into the utter darkness.

She heard the sound of breathing.

Above her.

Fear poured saliva into her mouth, drove sweat from every pore.

The hair on her nape rose. She threw herself down the steps, bouncing off the walls, skinning her palms on the rough stone.

A few steps from the bottom a glimmer of light showed in a narrow stripe on the floor.

Vic? She held her breath, eyes trying to pierce the darkness.

A hand touched her shoulder.

She screamed, turned and smashed her flashlight over the

fingers clamped on her jacket. Guttural howls filled the chamber as she beat at the black shadow.

Animal howls.

The scent of hot metal filled the tiny space. She screamed again.

The door flew open. She ran through it, crashing into Vic. He flung her aside.

A huge figure, a black outline in the welter of shadows grappled with Vic in the tower stairs. She lifted her flashlight. Red eyes gleamed back at her.

Moments later, Vic came through the doorway, tossed as if he weighed nothing. She crashed to the hard flagstone floor beneath him.

Something—the man or beast—trampled across them. Cold air rushed in its wake and brought with it the scent of rotting and mold.

Vic swore and rolled away. She vomited. He wrapped his arms around her, wiping her mouth with his palm.

"We have to get the hell out of here," he said, his words echoing in the cavernous nave.

The church was silent. No chanting, no whispered prayers filled the space.

A quarter hour before, Rose had run from Vic, but whatever she had feared, it was gone.

He led her down the nave. "Where's your stuff?"

"Behind the baptismal font."

He nodded. "Don't move."

She dogged his footsteps as he circled the font, searching for her backpack and tripod.

"You don't listen well, do you?" He stubbed his toes on her tripod and swore. He jerked his head in the direction of the north porch and jogged through the church.

Outside, she took a deep, shuddering breath. "What the hell happened in there?" she asked.

"Talk later. We'll take the long way about."

He forged a path across the grassy meadow and took a road she'd never been on, circling around the end of his row of cottages, crossing a plank bridge much like the one at his house, and headed home. He unlocked the cottage door and flung it open.

"In," he commanded.

The little cottage felt like a safe haven. None of what she'd seen could be true here.

He switched on the desk lamp. Blood streaked his T-shirt. Long scratches ran from his elbows down his forearms, criss-crossed the back of his hands.

"What was it, Vic?"

"Nothing human, Rose. But I've met him before."

VIC SAT ON THE edge of the iron bathtub and pulled off his T-shirt. Rose soaked a flannel and washed his wounds.

He shook her off when she tried to paint the cuts with antiseptic. "I'll live."

He gathered the bloody shreds of his shirt and stuffed them into the waste bin in his bedroom.

She stood warily by the door.

"I wasn't hunting you," he said. "I did as we planned. When I started to think about smashing Trevor's face, I concentrated on Alice. I tallied all the good deeds she'd done for me. It was working and not working, so I thought of Ian and Phillip and how it felt to hold them at the baptismal font. Trev's Ian's godfather. That worked. Then you were running."

"Did you hear the chanting?"

"There has to be something hallucinogenic to the mold in there. Joan thought she saw a gargoyle and we saw monks."

"Or ghosts and clawed beasts exist."

She stroked her fingers through his hair.

He groaned. "You ran from me," he said against her breast.

"I thought you were stalking me."

"I was searching not stalking. I was moving with stealth, trying not to make any more noise than necessary."

"I don't think it's mold that's affecting us. I think there's something evil in All Saints Church."

"I feel as if I've had all of Alice's sherry and washed it down with a bottle of whiskey."

"You won't admit there's evil in the church, will you?"

"Not anymore. I think the mold might act like those hallucinogenic mushrooms from the hippie era. It would explain the monks."

"But not the thing that attacked us."

"I can explain that without resorting to hallucinations. It was just someone dressed up in a demon costume."

"A costume?"

"I know what attacked me. It was one of the demon characters from Donald's club. Who from Marleton might have gone to the club with him?"

"Think of how he jeopardized his position with Joan. It stretches credibility that there would be two people he'd risk everything for. Come on, Vic. You write about evil. You believe in it."

Vic's scratches throbbed and burned. "Do I? Look, Rose, I spent a night at a sex club watching men and women dressed as that thing was dressed, dancing and drinking and swapping spit."

"Its eyes were red."

"Him. It was definitely a chap. Father Nigel was Donald's mentor, but he's too old and I can't see him at a sex club. He's dry as a stick. Harry Watkins? Donald and he shared a few pints at the local, but if it was Harry, he's been working out."

"Not Harry. He has quite a beer belly."

"Nell's William, then. The man was that strong and he and Donald were mates."

Rose took Vic's hands and turned them to display the long claw marks on his forearms. "These weren't made by a costume."

She stroked her hand down his chest. "When they fade, they'll be just like this one."

"I saw a demon in that stairwell, Rosie, just like the ones at the club."

"We can't go back to the church."

"That might sound practical, but it isn't logical. Whatever's going on in the church needs to stop."

Rose dogged his footsteps downstairs. Vic put on the kettle for tea. His arms itched as if ants ran inside the wounds. "I'm no knight in shining armor, but I'm not letting Will, or anyone else, get the better of me."

"Trevor will know what to do."

Trevor will think I'm barking mad. Or he'll arrest me, Vic thought.

When the kettle boiled he made them tea and smiled that Rose took it and drank it without her usual sneer.

She curled in the desk chair and played with his laptop. "The thing in your book has red eyes—and claws."

He slammed the lid on the laptop and whipped the chair around. "If I believed in the shit I write I'd be bonkers."

Her arms were fever warm when she looped them around his neck, her lips soft.

He scooped her into his arms and carried her up the stairs. Blood hammered in his veins; his eyes hurt. He wanted to stop on the stairs and have her. The force of his need shook him. He set her on her feet at the threshold of Alice's bedroom. "This might not be a good idea."

"Why not? I thought you said I shouldn't be afraid of you?"

A static charge leaped across the room. If he touched her, he thought sparks would ignite their skin.

"You tell me when, and I'll come to you," Rose said.

"When."

She hurled herself into his arms.

Rose tore at his zip, got his jeans to his knees and slipped to her own. He arched and bucked against her mouth as she dragged her teeth up and down his shaft.

"Not yet," he growled and pulled from her grip.

He shoved her blouse and bra up, then stripped her from the waist down, his head filled with the frantic thought he'd come before he was inside.

The hall dipped and swayed.

She climbed his body. They stumbled to the wall.

"Stop messing around. Put it in there."

He obliged. She heaved on him each time he thrust into her.

She came without a sound though her mouth was open in a scream. He followed in a powerful rush.

They slid down the wall and collapsed in a tangle of limbs on the carpet.

ROSE WAS COLD AND stiff when she woke up. She wore nothing from the waist down. Vic had his jeans about his knees.

"Oh, my God," she said. "Vic. Vic." She shook his shoulder.

He moaned and struggled off her. He hopped and tripped and banged into the doorjamb, trying to haul his pants up. He caught something important in his zipper, she assumed, when he yelped.

"What the hell happened there?" she asked. She sat on Alice's bed and tried to pull her bra down from up in her armpits, gave it up and jerked her top off, undid the bra, and readjusted everything.

"We've been drugged."

"Drugged?" She felt her head. "My tongue tastes like I licked your ashtray.

"I feel like I ate my ashtray."

He gave up on the jeans, took them off, balled them and tossed them onto the bed beside her. "You're not the kind to have sex up against the wall unless you were drunk—or something."

It was the "or something" that depressed her. Or was it the idea she was not bold enough to make love standing up. "Joan might have earned a few skid marks on her back from making love standing up, but you're right, I'm not so . . . bold," she muttered.

"What did you say about skid marks?" He stood framed in the doorway. Large, naked, wonderful.

"Oh, nothing. Let's just say, I'll be able to remember this for awhile."

"Bugger that." He went into the bathroom and switched on the light.

She sighed. He was rather impressive, even if his six-pack was not quite as distinct as it should be if he wanted to be in one of her favorite romance novels. She forgave him because he had a rather marvelous rear view to compensate. He was tantalizing as he bent over the sink, digging about in the medicine cabinet.

When he returned, he had a large dollop of something white in his palm. "Shirt off," he said.

Without thought, she pulled off her top and bra. He massaged the cream into her back.

"That stinks," she said. "What on earth is it?"

"Alice had arthritis."

"And now I'm going to smell like a locker room for hours."

She thought he was far too involved in his massage to care.

"This will keep Trev at arm's length while you tell him everything," he said.

"Changed your mind?"

"Yes."

"Tell him everything? How we feel in the church? How it lingers and makes us angry . . . or randy?"

"Not everything. Only I went into the church tonight, understand? Only me."

40

THEY MET TREVOR AT The King's Head pub where they sat among the tourists, drank their pints of ale, and talked about events that sounded fantastic in such a mundane atmosphere.

"Yes, I think you're crazy." Trevor glanced around him. "I don't believe in evil, other than the common or garden variety that makes people hurt one another. This other kind? Not on."

"How do you explain what happened? How do you explain Vic's anger when he's in the church?" Rose asked.

"I can't." Trevor shifted his chair a few more inches away from her.

Rose reflected that the arthritis balm was doing its job to Vic's satisfaction. "Then why not approach this with an open mind?"

"Because Vic's a horror novelist and you're far too close to *him*. Maybe there *is* mold in the church and he's allergic. And I don't know any men who'd complain they're getting it up too often."

Rose watched color fill Vic's cheeks.

"I'm usually rather peaceful, Trev. You know that."

"But when we were lads, you thought nothing of stealing what wasn't glued down or fighting when someone insulted you." Trevor leaned forward and dropped his voice. "You broke into a church. That's burglary."

Vic shrugged. "I used a key."

"It's still burglary. Did you take anything? Do any damage? You've put me in an awkward position, telling me this story."

Rose gripped Vic's knee under the table. A storm brewed between the two men. "He didn't mean to, he really didn't, and he didn't do any damage." As long as barfing on the floor wasn't damage. "Or take anything. You have to admit, it's all really strange. Look at Vic's arms."

Vic shoved the sleeves of his sweater to his elbows.

"He wasn't attacked by an overactive imagination," she said.

Trevor examined the marks. "I admit these look grim, but they could be caused by thorns on rose bushes."

Vic snorted and jerked his sleeves down. "I wasn't rolling in the flower beds."

"Come on, Trevor, you have to believe him."

"Maybe Vic's been writing horror for so long, he's lost touch with reality." Trevor pulled out his wallet and tossed a few bills on the table.

"That's shit and you know it," Vic said.

"I know only what I can see, hear, smell, taste, and touch."

"You've seen Vic's arms. That should be enough evidence."

"It's not."

"Then see for yourself," she said.

"And be suspended from the force? You are insane. I want the two of you to listen carefully. If you believe what you've told me, that someone has altered the tapestry, then go to Father Nigel, but be prepared for a less tolerant reaction." Trevor gestured toward the busy street, the crowded shops. "Surely, if what you're saying is true, the whole village would be sick by now, or it'd be on the front page of the tabloids, 'Mysterious Church Mold Is Better Than Viagra.' "

Rose watched Trevor stalk away. "I think we lost him when you told him how many times you've been making love every day. Not so tactful."

Vic grinned and Rose figured he'd enjoyed every minute of *that* revelation.

Vic ordered them another pint. "Trevor was correct. We put him in a tight spot."

"He's wrong about one thing," Rose said.

"What's that?"

"The whole town wouldn't be sick, just those who attend All Saints Church."

Vic nodded. "What do you think of Mrs. Watkins?"

"Miserable."

"Harry?"

"A perv."

"Mrs. Edgar?"

"I like her."

"She cheats the local merchants, or so Alice said."

"Wow."

"Fiona Sayer?"

"The woman in the gift shop? Don't know her, why?"

"She's a nasty piece of work, and her son, one of the servers, sells drugs. Or so Alice said."

"Or so Alice said." Rose repeated softly. She drained her pint. "And they all attend All Saints Church or work there."

"They're in the church every day, mate."

"I'm worried about Mary. She dates that Jack Carey guy, the tour guide."

"Mary goes to All Saints as well."

MARY GARNER BLUSHED. "WELL, I'm really not as regular as I should be. I often get migraines on the weekends, so I might miss now and then. And Father Nigel does wander a bit in his sermons."

"Thank you," Vic said. He took Rose's hand and steered her from the library and toward Edgar's Tea Shop. "Maybe her migraines are a good thing; they keep her out of trouble, but I wonder what she sees in Jack Carey. He's twice her age."

"He's very attractive. And maybe he's making love to her four times a day." Rose smiled as two flags of color appeared on Vic's cheeks.

Vic chatted with the ladies in Edgar's Tea Shop while she downed scones and clotted cream. She hoped they'd get along with the two pints of ale already sloshing about in her stomach.

Vic held hands, kissed a few fingers, teased and smiled his way around the room. Female tourists watched him. Male tourists frowned.

When he settled at the table, Mrs. Edgar brought him a pot of tea and a plate of tiny sandwiches, crusts cut off. They were shaped like the marks on playing cards. Rose recognized salmon, water cress, tomato and chives.

He inhaled the sandwiches before she could snag even one.

"Not much to help us here. Mrs. Bredon, the woman with the unfortunate purple dress, said there are so few in the congregation now, there's some speculation the church might close.

"I don't think they'd close it to tourists. But they could make the church redundant. It's done all the time. According to Mrs. Bredon, there've been thirty closures this year."

"Wow. What would happen to the members of the congregation?"

"They'd just be absorbed into the next parish."

"I wonder if they'd take the treasures with them? That altar screen is from the thirteenth century."

Vic ate one of her scones. "It would probably kill old Mrs. Bennett if they moved the tapestry."

"Speaking of tapestries. Joan's article said most tapestries are taken down for repair."

He shrugged. "Each hour, I find what happened to us harder to believe."

"Me, too." She touched her temples. "Maybe it was just a nightmare."

He pushed the sleeves of his sweater up. "These are real." With a glance at Mrs. Edgar, serving a nearby table, he jerked them back down.

A man and woman entered the tea shop. Harry Watkins and his mother. Although there was a table next to Vic and Rose unoccupied, they chose to wait.

"Come on," Vic said, emptying his cup. "Let's visit Mrs. Bennett and ask her if she has migraines."

Rose followed Vic to Stitches. Mrs. Bennett's shiny red bike was propped under the shop window. They opened the door and heard a small brass bell ring somewhere in the back.

Mrs. Bennett came into the shop front a broad smile on her face. "Good morning, Vicker."

By dropping the s on Vic's name, it sounded as if the woman was addressing a member of the clergy. Rose hid a smile. The only thing holy about Vic were his sweaters.

"And how are you, Miss Early?"

"You know my name?" Rose asked.

"I believe everyone in the village knows who you are by now."

"Oh. Of course." Rose wandered about, looking at pillow tops featuring thatched cottages, silk scarves, and tea cozies to cover her confusion. Vic leaned on the glass-topped counter and schmoozed with the old woman. Rose picked up an embroidered handkerchief just like the one Mary Garner had used. "Did you do this?" she asked Mrs. Bennett.

"I do all the work you see here. Nothing from Asia in here, luv."

Vic took the handkerchief but not Rose's money. Instead he flipped a credit card on the counter. "You've worked on the tapestry since 1974?" he said. "Has it ever come down?"

"No need," Mrs. Bennett said to Vic as she wrapped the embroidered hanky in tissue paper before putting it in a plastic bag like the ones Rose got from the supermarket.

"Wasn't it once larger?" Vic perched a tea cozy on a rag doll.

Mrs. Bennett nodded. "It was larger, but water got to it when the roof leaked. We had to salvage what we could. A true tragedy." She replaced the tea cozy with its brothers. "I believe that was the start of our fetes. Your Auntie Alice came up with the idea."

Vic took a scarf and looped it about the neck of a mannequin who wore a bright orange sweater and knitted tam.

"You're our new chairman, are you not?" Mrs. Bennett asked.

Rose smiled. Mrs. Bennett's fingers opened and closed in a slow rhythm, and Rose imagined the woman itched to undo the scarf, a purple flowered confection, but feared annoying the filthy rich chairperson of the badly needed fete.

"If the fete doesn't raise the expected money, what will happen to the parish? It's not in funds, is it?" he asked.

Mrs. Bennett snatched a bouquet of threads from Vic's hands. She gently placed them back on the counter. "Nothing would happen if you filled the void."

She touched her forehead.

"Do you get headaches?" Rose asked. "You're working with old textiles all the time, aren't you?"

"I've never been sick a day in my life." Mrs. Bennett preened a bit. "Father Nigel and I were just saying how well we all are. Why, I don't think one of us has missed a service in the last ten years."

"Who's us?" asked Vic as he tucked a pink doily into the neckline of his orange and purple design.

Mrs. Bennett closed her eyes for a moment as if in prayer then smiled. "Why those that matter, young man. The choir director. Nigel. The volunteers. And the young ones. The servers. Once we get them, they remain true. Not like in some parishes where the young just run wild, or worse, don't attend at all."

She did an end run around Vic when he reached for some embroidered silk evening purses. She sighed happily when he put his hands in his pockets. "And then the young go off to other parishes when they're old enough to work. We miss them, but a few remain and help train the new ones."

Vic picked up Rose's purchase. "Weren't a few All Saints servers in the shit over in Stratford?"

"Young man, I'll have none of that language here. If a few of our boys ran into difficulty, I'm sure it will soon be resolved. Nigel is looking into the matter."

They left Mrs. Bennett to rearrange her stock.

"Who's the choir director?" Rose asked.

"Mrs. Watkins."

"Choir practice must be a real treat. Do you always behave so badly when you shop?"

"No, but she was thinking about my disarrangements, not her words. Did you notice she only got huffy when I mentioned the servers."

"And?" She waited on the corner and for the punch line.

"What if we've discovered the reason for the rise in youth crime?"

"Mold in the church?"

"Or just the church. They serve, they steal, they spread out and take their shit to other parishes. I'm thinking my sons are lucky they were never servers. I'm also thinking they should stay with their mother until . . ."

"Until what?"

"Just until."

They walked to the center of the stone bridge and looked up the river to a bend, where the church sat in dominion over the village.

41

"YOU WANT ME TO do what?" Vic stared at the stack of photographs Rose had dropped in his lap.

Just enlarge them to the sizes noted on the back. Anyone with an opposable thumb can do it."

He grunted. The pressure was enormous after that remark. Pressure of the worst kind. The task took concentration without intelligence. And concentration was nearly impossible.

She'd bathed away his Trevor repellant and teased him with a new dress she'd bought while he questioned a final parishioner in a shop known for its London fashion, but Marleton low prices. The proprietor, a woman who admitted to infrequent visits to church, had asthma.

Rose's dress was long, flowing, and black. He wanted to rub his hands over her hips as she bent over her work.

He wanted to ease the hem up and himself in.

"What's this flower?" Rose held up the handkerchief he'd purchased for her at Stitches.

"Looks like Monkshood, but it can't be. Why would you embroider a handkerchief with a flower known for misanthropy?"

"Maybe because it's pretty?" She shoved it into the bag with a look of distaste.

"Monkshood is not pretty. A violet's pretty. So's a rose."

"Am I?" She said it lightly.

"You are so lovely, it makes my head ache."

He watched color rush into her cheeks. There was an innocence to her still. What a pleasure to find a woman who still reacted to a simple compliment

"I'll bet you say that to all the girls."

"Only the ones who drive me mad. Oh, shit." He'd forgotten to preview the photo before printing it and wasted another sheet of their dwindling supply of paper.

His concentration had gone to hell in a hand cart. Her new dress draped her lush breasts. It clung to her thigh. His cock twitched.

Her face went white. Paper white.

He bolted from the chair and caught her. She slumped into his arms, the pages in her hand cascading to the rug. He eased her to the couch, then ran for a glass of water.

"I know what Joan saw." Her lips quivered.

"What?" He combed her hair back and lifted her face.

"Did you ever do hidden pictures?"

He shook his head. "No, but my sons have. Look at the leaves in the tree and find the outline of an arrow. Sure."

She reached past him and plucked a page from the rug. It was a mock-up for the book. She'd pasted on a few photos of the Marleton tapestry, and outlined boxes for text.

"Look at this image," she touched the one she'd glued at the top of the page. "And then look at this one." She slid her fingertip to a picture that was centered. One she'd taken the previous night. The "Night of the Beast" she called it.

"Now," she whispered. "Think hidden picture."

Vic went down on his haunches and looked at the pictures. At first, they just looked like the same tapestry. A jumble of crusading knights, rearing horses, banners, and cowering peasants.

Then he saw it. One knight, looking devout in the first photo, looked sly in the second.

A priest who had hands up as if to bless a soldier off to a holy crusade now had pointed black nails.

The powerful sense of deja vu he'd felt in the club returned full force. He tapped the photo. "I saw this. In the club. Bound women being sold off to someone. I must have looked at this tapestry a thousand times through the years, filed this image away, but not really paid it any attention. This is a microcosm of the scene in the club."

"Where you were hit over the head?"

The woman in the tapestry had nipples showing in the second photo, none in the first. And instead of rope around her hands, in the first picture, she had corded trimming on her gloves. She was praying for the crusaders in the first, straining in anguish at their going, perhaps had a husband or son among the horsemen. But in the second picture, it appeared she was being led off by a rope. A rope that was a vine in the first photo.

Vic put the page on the floor. He drew Rose into his arms, but she pushed him off.

"What sick mind—"

"Maybe Mrs. Bennett's? What are the dates of this picture?" Vic asked. "And are there any others?"

"Several." Rose went to the desk and rooted about. She laid out a row of photos along the couch, shuffling until they were in a time sequence that pleased her.

The changes were done over many years, the most obvious the removal of the top foot of the tapestry. Although the fruit and flower border had been reattached, the road to paradise was gone.

"Not much hope of paradise to be found here, is there?"

Rose shivered. "With just a few shadows, the crusaders have gone from determined to malevolent. Look how that soldier is pushing his lance through that peasant's chest."

In 1953, the lance and the peasant were merely of close

proximity. Today, the lance's tip had elongated to pierce the peasant's smock.

Vic pulled Rose into his arms. "That's the lance I wanted to snatch off the tapestry—and drive through Trevor."

"We're looking at a process that took over thirty years."

"The tapestry's been in Mrs. Bennett's charge since 1974."

Vic took down one of his books and removed a letter he'd saved from Alice.

He read aloud. "They've resurrected the fete this year. Why not come down as I'm thinking of chairing it again—that's if Nigel promises to see there's enough tea. And I've things to show you that you might want to use in a book sometime."

"Do you think she meant the tapestry?"

"She hadn't been in the church for years, went over to Stratford after Nigel took over. If she started attending services again, she might have noticed the differences."

"And then?" Rose's skin was so pale, he thought she might faint again.

"And then she makes a to-do about it, and Mrs. Bennett gets upset. And . . . and what?"

"I don't know. Mrs. Bennett gets in trouble for turning the tapestry into a vision of hopelessness? What might it cost to restore it? Thousands of pounds, I imagine. In the United States, that's probably a felony."

"And what has this to do with Joan?" He knew by Rose's pale cheeks, it was not the issue of a national treasure despoiled that made her look so sickly.

"Joan loved hidden pictures as a kid. She'd spend hours doing them. And every time she looked at clouds, we'd have to find the ship or whatever it was she saw. Don't you see? Joan must have noticed the changes. If you hadn't distracted me with sex, *I'd* have noticed when I couldn't merge the old and new photos."

"Maybe she told Donald," Vic said.

"And where does it go from there? Even if she'd confronted Mrs. Bennett, what does it matter?"

"And we know why Donald killed Joan." Vic regretted the coldness of the words, but thought Rose didn't need dancing around the heart of the matter.

He clicked open his manuscript file. He did not need to search out the words that haunted him. No, the first set were front-and-center on the screen . . . unbidden.

"Vic," the old woman whispered.
She stood tall and thin in a blue silk suit, her eyes as red as those in the packet, as red as burning coals in a death-pale face. Her fingers, now rotting at the fingertips, pointed at the cigarette pack.
"They will kill you. They killed me"

Rose touched his hand. "I told you I thought you might be next. Maybe that's what your aunt thought, too."

"Why would anyone be after me? I'm worthless alive, let alone dead."

"Maybe Alice thought you'd eventually notice the tapestry. Maybe she told someone you had. Or would."

"I'd never notice a tapestry."

"Still. She's warning you, isn't she? You said you didn't understand what she's saying. Open your mind if not your eyes." Rose clung to his hand. "Don't go back in the church, Vic. Under any circumstances."

"I have to. I'm now on the fete committee. I've work to do."

"Vic, your aunt, my sister, they were all on the fete committee. Back out of it."

"That's cowardice."

"I don't care." She squeezed his fingers so hard the bones ground against one another. "I care about you. Quit for me."

How long had it been since someone had cared this much what he did? He linked his fingers with Rose's to ease the pressure on his hands. "I've never backed away from anything."

Rose jerked her hands from his. "That's what got everyone killed in the OK Corral."

He burst into laughter. "This isn't the wild west. It's a boring church fete. I'll be safe, mate. Mary has roped me into counting money in the gift shop. At one, I'll sign books on the lawn, right next to the bric-a-brac table. I've nothing to fear there but ugly china."

"But if it rains, you'll be in the church."

"In the gift shop again, not the sanctuary. It will be fans in one door, fans out through the other. Maybe everyone will pay the pound to take the church tour on their way out."

"Don't do it. Cancel out. Plead a broken wrist or something. Go to London."

Vic squeezed her fingers. "I'm not begging off. If they— whoever they are—want to come and get me, they can find me in the gift shop."

42

VIC TOOK ROSE TO the Pig and Pie for supper. He stuffed her with fish and chips and the local ale while he tried to convince her they had nothing to fear.

"We've uncovered an old woman who's been messing about with a tapestry," Vic said, "and we're so spooked, we're trying to make it into a supernatural event." He patted his pockets for cigarettes.

Nell handed Vic a pint of beer and Rose a double espresso.

When Nell was gone, Rose put her hand on Vic's arm. "And the thing that attacked us in the bell tower?"

He didn't answer. She looked around the crowded pub. The discussion seemed fantastic in such an ordinary place. "I think we should tell someone everything. As angry as I am with him, I think perhaps it should be Father Nigel. It's his church, after all."

Vic nodded. "He has a lot to answer for. And he needs a book of quotations."

"Most people wouldn't know it." Rose said, happy for the change of topic. "Were you studying the classics while stealing cars?"

He grinned. "No, but Alice dosed me with them at every meal." He drained his glass. "I have an idea. The fete is three days away—"

"Maybe they'll cancel it because of Donald's death."

"Chat at the bar says not."

"So, we have three days to . . . do what?"

"Make use of your skills as a photographer, work up a presentation for Nigel that will convince him the tapestry has been altered."

"When do you want to present it?"

"The day of the fete. While you help out at the tea table, I'll put him on the spot. If we're not happy with his response, we'll go up the ladder to the archdeacon. We'll show him our progress on Joan's book, so he can soothe the publisher, and while we're at it, we'll spring the desecration of a national treasure on him."

"Tea table? What tea table?"

"If I'm to suffer, you must suffer. And wear that yellow dress."

43

ON THE MORNING OF the fete, Rose put on the black dress, tied her hair back with a black ribbon, and slid her feet into the black sandals she'd bought in a stupid attempt to be more like the fashionable Mary. The ensemble was funereal, but she thought bright yellow might be inappropriate so soon after Joan's death.

How would Nigel receive the photographic essay on the tapestry? It represented hours of work on the computer, enlarging sections, showing comparisons of each alteration through the years. She was proud of it. Vic was proud of it. And her.

Nothing, however, bolstered Rose's confidence or stilled the small voice inside that said Vic should be in his car, heading for London.

The church fete was held on the lawns of the church and vicarage. Pony rides took place in the meadow behind.

She was the proverbial fish out of water as she reported to

the tea tent. The other volunteers examined her openly. She felt as if she had three signs on her back: *Murdered Woman's Sister, Found Father Donald*, and *Sleeping with Filthy Rich Local Author*.

Mrs. Edgar dished out instructions as she arranged plates of cookies and pastries. "You'll be just fine, dear. Shoo the flies and nothing's free. Don't let that Vic Drummond charm you out of a cake. He's to pay just like everyone else." It was said with an indulgent smile, and Rose figured Vic had charmed a number of cakes from Mrs. Edgar in his time.

"We've such luck to get so many lovely new tents. Of course your Vic paid for the lot. And it does look like rain, so we'll be glad of them, I imagine."

Your Vic.

Rose wanted to smile. But how much of Vic was hers? Maybe his right toe. The one that showed through a hole in his sneaker. He was a free spirit. Unfettered.

Their short time together had been a roller coaster of sorrow and joy. She would try to only remember the joy.

Joan's cremation would take place in five days. Then she'd take her sister's ashes home whether the book was finished or not. Vic might pretend otherwise, but Rose knew she could work on the book just as well in her studio. Once there, her time with Vic would be just an interlude fraught with emotion.

They'd probably trade e-mail for a brief period. The mail would grow sporadic. Then cease.

Her pleasure in the summer day faded. Never had she become so enamored of a man so quickly.

Parting with him would be like ripping out her heart.

But she'd go with dignity when the time came. She would tell him how much she cared for him . . . or she might not.

She followed the formidable Mrs. Edgar around the long tables of baked goods. She shook off her melancholy. It was a beautiful day, with none of the oppressive humidity that ruined many summer days in King of Prussia.

As the morning wore on, Rose realized the church fete

was not much different than any country fair. She filled cookie plates and saw that sugar filled sugar bowls, and cream was in the creamers.

She was overdressed. Almost all of the fete-goers were in shorts and T-shirts. Mary Garner floated around the book stall, casual in white. Her T-shirt read, "Ask Me Anything, I'm a Librarian."

Even the venerable souls, Mrs. Edgar, Mrs. Bennett, and Mrs. Watkins, wore shorts, their skin so white Rose knew this might be the one and only event of the summer to take them out of their twin-sets. Rose took a surreptitious photograph of Mrs. Bennett as she crossed the church lawn, but could not reconcile the wrinkled old woman in her baggy plaid shorts with someone who would deliberately desecrate a church treasure.

Rose kept one eye on the tea tables and one on the lookout for Vic. It appeared he was remaining true to his word. He was staying in the church. Had he presented their evidence yet? The vicar had opened the fete, but Rose hadn't seen him anywhere after that.

PC Alden joined her behind the tea table.

"You're still my FLO aren't you?" Rose asked.

"As long as you need me," he said. He wore civilian garb, T-shirt and shorts, but had a cell phone and pager clipped to his belt.

"I hope DI Harrison is back on duty."

"Not yet, miss."

"Why not? We both know he didn't kill Joan. Why isn't he back at work?"

Two small children came running up to the table and begged Alden for the money to ride the ponies. He doled out the cash. When they'd dashed off, he answered her with a question. "The investigation into your sister's death is ongoing."

Rose poured tea for a young woman. Discussion of murder and suicide was macabre surrounded by sweet treats and laughing families. "Why? Donald pushed my sister down the steps and hung himself over it. I'm taking her ashes home in less than a week."

Alden pulled out a folding chair. "Sit down, please."

She perched on the edge of the seat.

"Donald didn't hang himself. He was dead before he was strung up. It was neatly done, almost missed by the pathologist."

44

Rose escaped the tea table, promising Alden she'd be back in a few minutes. In less than a quarter hour, Vic would begin signing books and she might have no opportunity to tell him about Donald until the fete closed.

Tourists had been lining up all morning at Mary's book stall. If they made a donation to the library, they received a complimentary copy of Vic's book along with a ticket. Their ticket entitled them to meet Vic and get his autograph. That way, Mary had explained, everyone would have their individual moment to speak to Vic without waiting in a queue. Vic had muttered something profane when it became obvious he would be signing books all afternoon.

Rose passed the face painting and game stalls. She saw Nell and her girls at the pony rides. The barmaid scanned the sky with an anxious look.

Clouds piled up in the east—clouds with black edges and heavy gray bottoms.

The rain came down in torrents just as Rose reached the

church porch. Gloom encroached from the corners. Rain sluiced down the tall windows. Wet stone smells added to the potpourri of old cloth, dust, and mold. She slipped between umbrellas shaken by sheltering fete-goers.

Vic stood in the church doorway, hands on hips, watching the sky. He wore clean khakis and a white polo shirt despite the deep, ugly scratches on his arms.

An oscillating fan whipped side to side at high speed. Vic's mold cure, the fan purloined from the Marleton library.

Mrs. Edgar was spreading a festive flowered tablecloth where Vic would sign books.

"How's the fete doing?" Rose asked them both, unable to discuss Donald. She felt deflated.

"Oh, we're making money hand over fist," Vic said, smiling. It was more leer than a smile.

Rose realized the fan blew the black dress against her body. When Mrs. Edgar bustled away to fetch umbrellas for autograph seekers, Rose stood on tip-toe and whispered in Vic's ear. "Alden just told me the most incredible news."

"He's shagging Munson?"

"No. Trevor's still on special leave—"

"Why?"

"Because Donald didn't hang himself. I suppose that casts doubt on the note."

"Did Alden say that?" Vic rubbed his palm over his forearm as if his scratches itched.

"No. He just said Donald didn't kill himself."

"As soon as we're finished here, we'll give Trevor a ring." She folded her arms around her waist. "I've been worrying about you all day."

He gave her a perfunctory squeeze. "Thanks, but it wasn't necessary. I have a secret weapon."

"Really?"

"Holy water." He wagged his eyebrows.

"Where did you get that?"

He glanced through the door to make sure no one could hear them. Tourists clustered in the nave, seeking shelter by paying the pound to view the church.

"I pinched it."

"What? From the baptismal font?"

He shook his head. "It's from St. Michael's in the next village. I stole it during the seven thirty prayer service this morning. I've some for you, too."

She refrained from saying she'd always thought holy water was there for the taking, but if it pleased Vic to think he stole it, she wouldn't burst his bubble.

He took her hand and folded her fingers around a small medicine vial. When she peeked at it, she read, "Vitamin C."

She slipped the vial into her pocket. "You said you were going out for scones."

"You got your scone." He tucked a strand of hair behind her ear.

"Is holy water still holy if you steal it?"

"Must be. I feel great. No headaches. No anger. No desire to jab candle spikes in Trevor's back."

"Have you spoken to Nigel yet?"

He absently scratched his forearm. "Only about pennies and pounds. He's proved rather elusive this morning."

"Maybe we should wait until this matter of Donald is resolved."

"Good thinking, Miss Early," Vic said, bowing to Mrs. Edgar who burst into the shop with the first autograph-seekers.

Gushing horror fans seemed out of place in a church, but anything for the native son, Rose figured. Or anything for money.

"It's bucketing down," Mrs. Edgar said to Rose. "You'll ruin that dress if you try to get back to the tea tent. Why not stay right here? You could take Mr. Drummond's tickets." The tea shop maven leaned close to Rose's ear. "And keep these women from stealing extra books from under his nose. That oblivious, he is."

Rose did not think Vic oblivious to much, but assured Mrs. Edgar she would guard every book and make sure every person who entered had a ticket to do so.

Three hours later, despite the continued downpour, fans

were still being ferried from the many stall tents to the gift shop by fete volunteers armed with huge umbrellas.

Rose felt a touch of awe that Vic still had a smile and kind word for everyone. He never forgot to thank them for their donation to the library, either. She could not be so relaxed. The image of Donald hanging in the lytch gate intruded.

Her stomach knotted watching the horror fans exit the shop and queue up for one of Jack Carey's tours. Even now as she took a moment to peek into the church, she saw a group clustered before the tapestry, listening as Carey detailed its history.

A sudden shout from outside made everyone freeze.

"What's going on?" Vic paused in mid-signature.

"I'll find out."

A crowd had gathered on the porch by the huge doors. A woman cried for help. Rose wriggled through a cluster of agitated people. She curled her fingers tightly about the small vial of holy water.

She gasped when she saw a man lying in the center of the on-lookers.

It was Archdeacon Keeling. His face was gray, his lips almost blue. Mrs. Sayer shouted over the agitated group into a cell phone.

The fete-goers stood in a ring, gaping, doing nothing. Rose shoved through them and dropped to her knees. "Stand back," she ordered. At the same time, she loosened the priest's collar.

She touched his throat. His pulse was strong, his breathing regular though he looked frail and ancient. She drew the vial of holy water from her pocket and folded Keeling's cold, thin fingers about it.

An ambulance's siren throbbed on the air. The crowd gave a collective sigh.

Archdeacon Keeling was carried off without opening his eyes or saying a word. Nor did the small skirmish in the nave cause much of a blip in the attendance around Vic's autographing table.

Only Rose knew that the archdeacon's cold hand had

warmed within moments of touching the holy water, or that a headache had begun a vicious hammer in Rose's skull as she returned to Vic's side. Nor would she tell anyone except him that a roiling acid now burned in her throat and stomach.

45

FATHER NIGEL REAPPEARED TO CLOSE the fete long after the scheduled six o'clock closing, Vic still had ten fans left in his line. Although Vic tried to capture Nigel's attention, the priest hustled past the shop to the lawn, and without benefit of the microphone which would be foolhardy with the puddles surrounding the tents, he said a few weak thank-yous and ended the fete.

"Damn," Rose whispered. Nigel had struck off for the village. Rose exchanged a look of frustration with Vic. He returned to his signing.

Rose could bear the suspense no longer. Not a word had reached them on the archdeacon's condition. With a thought that Vic's bad habits were rubbing off on her, she pilfered one of the church umbrellas. She jotted a note to Vic that she was taking the pages on the tapestry back to the cottage. It wasn't a complete lie. She did stop at the cottage to gather a bouquet for the archdeacon, but she didn't leave the tapestry piece there. Instead, she stuffed it into her backpack along with the original photographs.

She penned Vic another note, one sure to tic him off. She fetched her car from the parking lot of the Pig and Pie and drove to Stratford Medical Center.

She found the archdeacon's private room, but remained outside for a few minutes, gathering her fortitude.

Would he think they were crazy?

The archdeacon lay against a pile of pillows, reading a small red leather book. His face lit up when he saw her.

Suddenly, tears flooded Rose's eyes. A torrent of emotions, held in check even with Vic, rushed through her. She took the archdeacon's hand. The flowers scattered across the blankets.

"There, there. Now, why don't you tell me what the difficulty is?"

She dumped the contents of her backpack on the bed. The story of Joan, Donald, the church, and the tapestry tumbled from her lips, without order or coherence.

"No, I don't think you're crazy," the archdeacon said softly. He patted the edge of the bed. "I've been thinking some of the same thoughts myself." He indicated his book. "And reading about them. I was lucky enough to prevail on the chaplain here to locate this book. I haven't read it since my seminary days." He plucked one of the white roses from the bedding and breathed in its sweet fragrance. "I feared my memory of its contents might be unreliable. It was not."

"What was it you remembered reading?"

"That evil is among us, ever vigilant, seeking ways to undermine the good."

"So, you believe in evil?"

Rose gasped, turned, and saw Vic standing in the doorway.

"Come in, young man. I was wondering where you'd gotten to."

"I was abandoned at a book signing." He walked warily around Rose, pausing a moment to examine the scattered tapestry pages and photographs that lay in a jumble among the flowers on the archdeacon's bedding.

Vic leaned against the windowsill and crossed his arms over his chest. "Everything Rose told you is true."

"You needn't fear I doubt her. I've first-hand evidence to guide me, son. Although I'm here overnight for observation, I did not have a heart attack. Strong as an ox," he said, touching his chest.

"How did you feel the last time you were in All Saints?" Vic asked.

"I've not visited All Saints before. I'm only recently appointed to the diocese. I'm specially charged to oversee the church redundancy committee. Joan's book was an idea I had to raise funds and stave off some closures." He sighed and indicated his book. "I've been reading about evil for several hours now."

"Uplifting." Vic said.

"Not very. I was just telling Miss Early I think it was pure evil that struck me down. I touched the doors to All Saints and was assailed with the most powerful sensation of bleak despair. I had no chest pain, just overwhelming waves of utter emptiness—until Miss Early came to my aid." He patted Rose's hand.

"We're not quite as afflicted as you were," Vic said.

"And I think I can explain that as well."

Rose met Vic's eyes. She shivered. How would he take the archdeacon's theories?

"I think everyone is affected by their surroundings. As to the church, I believe that effect is in direct proportion to how good we are. The more of good within the person, the more extreme the effect." The archdeacon's cheeks flushed red. "I'm not bragging." He stroked the small volume. "According to one of our church's early philosophers, the more one lives in goodness, the greater the putrefaction of evil will confound."

"So, Rose must be a pretty good person." Vic smiled at her, but the smile did not reach his tired eyes.

"You felt sick, too," she said, gathering the neglected flowers and stuffing them into a pitcher on the archdeacon's bedside table.

"A bit." Vic shook his head. "But I want to join the ranks, too. And what of the beastie we met in the bell tower?"

The archdeacon struggled to sit more upright. "I think you called forth a demon."

The word demon sounded surreal in the modern, antiseptic atmosphere of the hospital.

"I fear for you, son. You sway between feeling unwell and active aggression. Yet, the holy water worked for you. I believe you are one of those whom we would deem agnostic. You're unsure. And so I caution you, do not go into the church again."

"Easily done." Vic pushed off the window sill. "And our Rose?"

"She, too, should stay away."

Rose said, "I'm sorry, but we can't just leave things as they are. I believe my sister's death and probably Father Donald's are intimately entwined with All Saints Church."

"I'll see to it," Vic said. "You're out."

The archdeacon nodded and shut his book. He closed his eyes for a brief moment. When he opened them, he had an expression of grief on his face.

A shower of dread cascaded through Rose's body.

"I agree something must be done. In good conscience, I must warn both of you to stay away from the church. But I also fear it is both of you who must do it."

"Do it? Do what?" Rose could not make her voice rise above a whisper. Vic rounded the bed and slid his arm about her shoulders. "What is it you want us to do?"

"Take down the tapestry. And destroy it."

46

"ROSE. YOU'RE DRIVING ME barmy." Vic kicked off his shoes and tried unsuccessfully to snag Rose around the waist as she paced back and forth in front of the couch.

"I can't sit. I also can't believe the archdeacon wants us to destroy the tapestry."

"He explained himself rather well, I thought."

"I had hopes the poor man was ill. Perhaps barking, as you would say."

"The hospital corroborated the fact he didn't have a heart attack."

"And why they would give *you* that personal information, I don't know."

Her indignation covered her fear, he thought. "I promised them a new gizmo for the radiology department in exchange for some indiscreet gossip."

She propped her hands on her hips. Her linen dress was a mass of wrinkles. Her hair was half out of its black tie. She had never looked so alluring. His blood pounded in his head and his lap with equal force.

He also knew his thoughts of Rose blocked other, less palatable introspection.

Especially the idea that he was on the edge.

He imagined himself sitting on the rim of a bowl of acid-spewing, writhing snakes. If he fell in, he'd be devoured.

The rim of the bowl felt slippery.

"Vic? Vic? Are you listening?"

"Sure. Uh. What were you saying?"

"I wanted to know if you are going to make good on the promise to the hospital?"

"Sure. I'm—"

"I know. Filthy rich. Okay." She jerked the ribbon out of her hair and flung it over the arm of Alice's reading chair. "Please listen."

He sighed and wished she'd alight somewhere. Her pacing stoked his libido. Every stride drew the fabric of her dress against her thighs and hips.

"There's nothing more to say, mate. The archdeacon believes the evil resides in the tapestry, and likely in Mrs. Bennett who's been altering the damned thing. Apt word that . . . damned."

"But to take it down. Destroy it. Why not just dime on Mrs. Bennett? And with Trevor in our pocket—"

"He better not be in your pockets."

She did not smile.

"Rosie, the tapestry is destroyed already. It's been corrupted, the images made malignant."

She stood stock still before him. "And what if the archdeacon is right and some demonic thing tries to stop us? I don't *want* to believe in evil."

"No one does."

They had come full circle since their first meeting. Since her first question.

The idea drove all lustful thoughts from his head. "What's truly sobering is that you and the archdeacon sickened in direct proportion to your goodness." He shifted uncomfortably. "You're good, mate. I'm not."

She perched on his lap. Her body was pliant and warm against his.

"You are *not* bad. I would feel it, and I wouldn't be here. Nor would the archdeacon say I should stick by you."

"That's a bit of a gray area. He didn't say stick to me like this—your bum on my lap. He said stick by me when I take down the tapestry."

"You're just so . . . look, if I was to describe you in photographic terms, you're definitely not black or white. You're all the shades of gray. You don't think twice about stealing holy water, but you're the soul of kindness in other ways, were the soul of kindness to your aunt. And you're a good father, I'm sure."

He grunted. "Don't poll my kids until they're twenty-five. They've no perspective now. I've stopped their spending money twice this summer."

"Stop joking, Vic. Focus. I have to believe the good in you is the stronger side. I have to."

"What if you're wrong?"

Her arms tightened around his neck. "I'm not."

His throat felt thick. Only one other person had spoken so passionately of him. That had been years ago when he'd been in the shit with the headmaster over the theft of a bicycle. Alice had been dead wrong in her vehement defense of him then. He'd been guilty as sin.

What if Rose was wrong in her belief in him now?

He was suddenly grateful his sons were with their mother. If things turned out badly they, at least, were safe.

"Supposing there's nothing more than a mold problem?" he asked.

"Then Trevor would be right and all the parishioners would be sick. They're not." Rose tucked her head on his shoulder. "The archdeacon thinks the reason they're not is that they've been going to the church for so long . . . they've become evil themselves. It's the parishioners the archdeacon cares about. Who knows what they're up to in their daily lives?"

He thought of the young who served. The thieving servers. "What about tourists? You're the only one I know was sickened by the place."

"Archdeacon Keeling thinks many visitors might be bothered by the church depending on their—"

"Level of goodness?"

She nodded. "If I hadn't knocked over chairs, I would have gone outside, sat in the fresh air somewhere, and when I felt better, headed home. I don't think I'd have mentioned feeling sick to anyone. I'd just put it down to jet lag. As to parishioners, I think it might be like slowly acclimating yourself to allergens or something. After a while you're not sneezing."

"Like listening to Nigel bugger up his quotations. After a few weeks, you don't notice. Or maybe don't care."

Rose sat bolt upright. "What if he isn't 'buggering up' the quotations. What if it's deliberate? He could be adding to the slide to the evil side by . . . I'm not sure by what . . . maybe corrupted words."

"That might explain why he never uses Biblical quotes."

"Have we ever really prayed in the church? I remember thinking I wanted to, but I when I look back on it, something usually prevented me. Hard kneelers, headaches. The archdeacon believes the tours work against the holy nature of the place, too. He's argued against them, but unsuccessfully because the churches need the fees for their maintenance."

"Must be like sand paper, rubbing off the good bits."

"We'll never know how many good people enter the church, feel sick and just leave without taking the tour. Or how many parishioners like your aunt quit before it got them."

" 'Got them' implies an entity." Vic wrapped his arms loosely around Rose's waist. He sensed a tension in her that might send her back to pacing. "I think I'll use it in my next book."

She leaped out of his lap—and his embrace. "You already used it!"

She spun in a circle as if she'd won an award.

"How?"

"Objects owned by the evil one pass their evil on. It's just like your ring premise. Think about it. If the tapestry is evil, couldn't worshipping before it every day, or even once a week, over many years corrupt you?"

"Alice died of a heart attack, but the autopsy showed no sign of heart disease. Was she struck down like the archdeacon just for entering the church after years away?"

"But she died in the garden," Rose said softly.

Vic ignored her. "I think Alice was so sickened by the evil in All Saints, she only made it as far as the garden before collapsing." He met Rose's eyes. "And if someone good like you, mate, had put a simple bottle of holy water into her hand, would she still be alive?"

"It's hard to believe sitting here. But as the archdeacon pointed out, there's only one thing in the church that's changed over the last thirty years—Mrs. Bennett's tapestry.

Vic needed a smoke, but there were no packets behind his laptop. "Then I suppose we'd better get some rest. Wc've a tapestry to destroy."

47

Rose considered the sky, still filled with dim light. It was not enough light to read by, but enough to delay tapestry-trashing. Any other time, she'd be glad of the late evening sun, especially after the day's deluge. But now, she just wanted time to fly. She wanted the night over.

She wanted dawn to break. Maybe through the little glass window in Alice's bathroom, maybe on Vic, asleep in the tub.

Because if Vic was asleep in the tub at dawn, he would have survived the night.

She changed to black jeans and T-shirt.

"We have a few hours yet," Vic said from the doorway.

"Should we make some sort of plan? Make a list of tools to take? I don't think it will be any easy job taking that tapestry down. It must weigh a ton."

"The tools are taken care of."

"Good. Do you have a second vial of holy water? If not, we should divide yours."

"The holy water's already divided. If you think we need

more, I can run by St. Michael's. In which case, we should go now."

Rose watched his eyes flick toward the bed. "I think we should—"

"I agree," Vic said, sweeping her into his arms. "Let's go to bed instead."

He tossed her onto her back in the middle of the mattress. She squealed when he grabbed her foot and tugged off her shoe.

"That's not what I had in mind." She tried to twist from his grasp, but he wrapped his fingers around her ankle and she was as imprisoned as she might be in a steel manacle.

"I'm not playing games, Rose. If there really is such a thing as evil, and if the tapestry is somehow a purveyor of that evil, we might not get it down without consequences."

The long scratches stood out on his forearms. Many of his fans had mentioned them. He'd simply smiled and said he'd had a run-in with a gargoyle. It had drawn a laugh each time he'd said it and turned all other questions aside.

Her mind reeled with unasked questions. "You mean that creature-thing might be waiting for us."

"Or, good as you are, you might suffer the same fate as the archdeacon . . . or Alice. Holy water or no holy water."

A thick knot of fear filled Rose's throat. She relaxed against Vic's grip. He instantly freed her.

She held out her arms in invitation. "Make love to me," she whispered. "Just in case."

His kiss began gently, but escalated to fierce within a heartbeat. She shoved his polo shirt up and over his head. Her fingers shook as she removed her T-shirt and unclasped her bra. In a slow, languid caress, she shifted her breasts across his chest, lifted her nipples to his, arousing herself and him.

He groaned in the back of his throat—a feral growl. Her insides quivered. The sound reminded her of the beast in all men and of the creature in the bell tower stairs. Her heart thudded uncomfortably against her ribs.

But when he placed his palm over her heart, all fear subsided. Nothing that felt this wonderful could be evil. This was the good Vic. He came out of the shadows in moments like these.

"Touch me, Vic," she said. "Touch me."

He made short work of her clothing, and his fingers were warm where she needed them. He instinctively knew where to caress, when to ease off, where to put his mouth and his tongue.

"Make me come," she said, hands locked in his hair.

She rode the quick, heart-stopping orgasm in silence, until he moved up and plunged into her.

"I'm not parting with you, mate." He said the words between gasps. One word for each thrust.

It was rough. And it was perfect.

"I'm keeping you," he said.

His words intoxicated her as much as his touch.

His muscles went rigid. She no longer knew where his flesh and hers were separate. She moved with him, each glide of his body exquisite torture, a breath-taking meld of hot and wet flesh against equally hot, smooth flesh.

He slicked his fingers in the primordial soup between their thighs and brought his fingertips to her mouth.

With agonizing slowness, he rubbed his fingertips on her lips.

She licked them, tried to capture his fingers between her teeth. When she finally did, she sucked at the taste of their bodies. With each draw of her mouth, his body heaved into her.

He thrust his hands into her hair, pulled her head back, sealed his mouth on hers and poured his essence into her. Each jerk of his body drew a growl of pleasure from him.

Or was it from her? She no longer knew.

She lay exhausted beneath him, his thigh snugged between hers, her head tucked against his shoulder. Her skin was wet and warm where they touched.

"Don't get up," she said. "I don't want to go. Not yet."

He kissed her brow. "You're not going anywhere. Not tonight. I want to go into the church with the idea I've something to come out for."

"Don't talk that way."

"Why not? If I'm not proved good or worthy enough—"

"Stop it. You're scaring me."

"Not meaning to, mate."

"I don't care what the archdeacon says. You've the griffin spirit. We'll go together. And you'll protect me." She climbed onto her knees, straddled his body.

For a brief moment he stared at her and said nothing.

"You have to promise you'll protect me. Say you believe, Vic, say it."

He pulled her down. "If that's what you believe, then I believe it, too."

48

"WHERE ARE YOU GOING?" Rose asked.

Vic forced a smile, ruffled her hair, and tossed the duvet over her bare bum. "I want to write for a while. We've a few hours to kill."

He went to the sitting room, put on the desk lamp, and opened his laptop. My kingdom for a cigarette, he thought, clicking on his manuscript.

Miraculously, no unwanted words taunted him. Only words by V.F. Drummond appeared on the screen.

Without hesitation, he began to type. A few minutes later, sweat slicked his skin, prickled in the hair at his nape. No matter how he tried, he could not get his fingers to cooperate. They tripped over keys, refused to strike where he wanted. Pain lanced up his arms, threading through the scored skin. The lump on the back of his head pulsed in time to his heartbeat.

He gave up fighting it. His fingers relaxed, found the keys, found a rhythm.

When next he leaned back, his screen was filled with words.

He read them. Reread them. And knew what the scratches meant. Knew that sometime during the night, a demonic being would drag a claw down Rose's spine, crippling her. Probably killing her.

Vic wasn't sure of her death because according to the computer screen, he was lying on his back, staring at the rib vaulting, his chest ripped open in one long line, blood and gore all about on the flagstone grave markers.

Strange he should see the church ceiling so well, for he was definitely dead.

49

OUTSIDE THE SKY WENT FROM stark black to dazzling white. Rose jumped from the bed and threw up the window sash. Thunder cracked. A second jagged bolt of lightning lit up the garden for an instant as if it were broad daylight.

The curtains snapped and whipped around her.

Vic came into the bedroom, stood behind her, and cupped her breasts. A static charge filled the room, lifted her hair. She felt the thunder as if it were inside her.

He wrapped one arm around her shoulder and put his hand between her thighs.

She tongued the scratch marks on his forearm, followed the veins, and suckled the pulse at his wrist.

Rain washed in the window, drenched her breasts and face.

She was hot and cold. Water ran down her chest, her belly, into her pubic hair, dripped down her inner thighs.

Or was it something else? Whatever remained within her? His seed? Her desire? Or was it just the rain?

Each stroke of his fingers was luscious torture.

Another bolt of lightning filled the heavens. It silhouetted the church tower against a deep purple sky. And deep within her, the orgasm began as a quiver and spread through her like the thunder rumbling in the wake of lightning.

He soothed her and kissed the side of her neck. She felt weak, boneless.

"Bloody wild out there," he said. "By the way, I love you."

Nature lit the sky as if in celebration of his words.

"Vic—"

"Look." He pointed. A dim, floating light moved in the church's bell tower, illuminating each window in slow succession. "Looks like someone's taking an unofficial tour. Maybe the fucking demon."

"I'm scared, Vic."

"Bloody hell, so am I."

The light went out.

Vic released her. The wind was ice cold. He draped Alice's cashmere dressing gown over her shoulders, and she clutched it close, buried her nose in the fabric, breathed in the calming scent of lavender to compose herself and say the right words to go with his. But when she lifted her head, it was something charred, almost sulfurous, she smelled on the wind.

A dull thud broke the moment. "What's that?" she asked.

"It's the door. Get your knickers on."

"The door?" She dashed around the room, snatching up clothing and ran into the bathroom. Aware of male voices below, she hastily washed and dressed and slipped downstairs.

Trevor Harrison stood in the sitting room, hands deep in the pockets of his shorts. He looked as if he'd been yanked out of bed.

"Why are you here?" she asked Trevor, but she looked at Vic who wouldn't meet her eyes.

"Vic asked me to stop in and keep an eye on you while he runs up to London."

"Don't do this, Vic," Rose said softly. She knew instinctively that Vic hadn't told Trevor why he'd summoned him in the middle of the night. But she knew why.

Vic was taking the tapestry down alone.

TREVOR SAT ACROSS FROM her in the kitchen. "Stop messing about and tell me where Vic's really gone."

She bit her lip and looked at the door. How could she get past Trevor? He was a rather large object between her and the church.

He clamped a hand over her wrist. "You're not going anywhere."

He must have read her mind. "I might not approve of whatever it is Vic's doing, but he impressed on me the need to keep you here. So here it is, understand?"

On the window sill, nestled between pots of African violets sat a small medicine vial. Vitamin E it read. It was half filled with water. She pictured Vic setting it there as he went out the garden door. Casually, she went to the window and pulled a dead leaves off the plants. And tucked the vial into her pocket.

Trevor put his hands on her arms, above the elbow. "What did you just put in your pocket?"

Rose wilted like the plant she was grooming. "It's holy water."

Trevor laughed. "Now, what the hell do you need holy water for?"

50

VIC HUMMED A LITTLE tune to keep himself company. He ignored the monks behind him, chanting as they filled the choir stalls. The only thing bothering him were the ranks of candles lit about the altar as if some service might begin at any moment.

It would not do to have a coven of demons arrive for a service while he was destroying the tapestry.

He stood on a short ladder he'd pulled from a maintenance cupboard in the basement, happy for his intimate knowledge of the church from years of hanging about while Alice worked. As for tools, he snapped open the only one he needed.

A wicked sharp knife taken from Ian. Bad for young chaps. Great for slashing through ancient fabric.

Dust filled the air as he cut through the tapestry and its lining where it met the wall anchors. Touching the material was like handling stinging nettles. The scratches on his arms burned.

He resisted the urge to leap off the ladder and walk away. Somehow, the monks chanting in ethereal unison behind him kept him at the task. The archdeacon thought they walked in protest of the desecration of this holy place they'd built centuries ago, that they appeared in hopes someone good might heed their pleas.

"That means the person who sees them is good." Vic said aloud. He grimaced at the thought he had justified seeing ghosts as a good thing.

With half of the tapestry's length cut from its wall anchors, its sheer weight tore it from the rest. It cascaded to the floor in a cloud of dust. The sound was enough to wake the dead. He laughed out loud then coughed as he sucked the miasma of mold and dust into his lungs.

A collective moan sounded from the choir stalls behind him.

They're on your side, Vic reminded himself as he climbed off the ladder.

The spot where the tapestry had hung was stained with moist-looking streaks of mold.

He contemplated the tapestry stretched on the floor. How the hell was he going to shift the damned thing?

"Bloody archdeacon must think he's arch-bloody-bishop."

Vic stifled the angry thought, took out the vial of holy water, and rolled it between his palms. It stilled the leap of anger. The burning of the scratches on his arms abated from a ten to a five. Several welled with beads of blood.

He tucked the vial into his pocket and swallowed down bile that flashed up the back of his throat. He found himself staring at the monks. And the candle sticks.

Was Trevor trying it on with Rose now while the cat was away?

51

"LOOK, IT STARTED WITH something Vic wrote." Rose opened Vic's laptop. She felt infinitely weary trying to convince Trevor that Vic was stealing a church tapestry with an archdeacon's blessing. "If you won't believe me, at least believe that Vic believes."

Trevor read Vic's manuscript over her shoulder.

"That's what I call bloody scary," he said.

"It's new," she whispered. The arteries and veins to her heart felt constricted, blood no longer flowing to her head.

"If I'm reading this correctly—"

"Vic's dead," she said.

She now knew why Vic had brought in Trevor. Vic believed what he'd read on his computer screen. A flash of pain ran down the scar on her back.

"We have to go." She spun out of the desk chair and out of Trevor's reach.

"I promised Vic I'd keep you here."

"Then you better have a gun. Nothing less will stop me."

THE TAPESTRY PROVED IMPOSSIBLE to shift.

What a bloody nuisance.

It had taken him over a quarter hour to roll the damned thing up and drag one end so it pointed toward the nave. Strands of black sticky mold clung to his hands. He wiped his hands down his jeans and remembered a wheeled cart in the gift shop, one Mrs. Edgar had used for hauling the tea things about.

ROSE RAN UP THE footpath toward the church, Trevor splashed through puddles only a few paces behind her. No rain fell now, but overhead, flashes of lightning and cracks of thunder alternated with moments of utter, deadly black silence.

THE TEA CART WAS missing from the shop. Ripping off a string of oaths, Vic went in search of the damned thing. He found it in the basement, loaded with receipts and dozens of rolls of coins from the fete.

Vic automatically stuffed rolls in his pockets. He weighed one in his hand. What the hell was he doing pinching a few coins when he was richer than Croesus?

Why not take them? Who else deserved them?

Vic felt himself tittering on the rim of the bowl. The snakes in the bowl called to him, their hiss muffling the soft chant of the monks in the sanctuary.

He called to mind their tonsured heads bowed in prayer. He didn't understand their Latin, but he did understand their message. It cut through the desire to leap in with the snakes.

* * *

ROSE FOUND THE NORTH porch door unlocked. On tiptoe, she led Trevor to the center of the nave.

Trevor stumbled against her as she came up short. The choir stalls were filled with monks. She could see the ancient carvings on the wood behind them. Candles ringed the altar.

"Bloody hell," Trevor said, a tremor in his voice.

"Can you see them?"

He gripped her arm so hard, she knew she'd be bruised tomorrow.

"See them? I can bloody well hear them."

She smiled grimly. "Then you're good and it will be okay."

"Okay? I'm insane—" His words were cut off in a wave of coughs. Hacking coughs.

A huge rectangle of naked stone marked where the tapestry used to hang. The space was mottled with mold. Black, slimy-looking mold.

"He got it down," Trevor said. He coughed again. Sweat beaded his upper lip.

They went to the rolled tapestry, pointing like a compass needle to the west end doors. She put out her foot to nudge the tapestry with her toe, but at the last moment, she refrained. What evil could it still work?

A scraping sound drew their attention across the church. The bell tower door gaped open. In the black mawl of the stairs, a dim glow appeared, then faded away as if someone climbed the steps.

"Where the hell is Vic?"

"In the bell tower," Rose said.

I'M IN HELL.

Vic humped the heavy cart up the basement steps. At each step, either the cart creaked or the wheels squealed.

"Loud enough to wake the dead," he said. He swallowed an urge to laugh aloud as he eased himself and the cart through the door to the sanctuary.

He felt quite drunk. The cart thumped over the grave-stones embedded in the floor. "Are we keeping our heads?" he asked Saint Stephen on his way past the pillars supporting the great arched ceiling.

A small sound, like footsteps, made him pause.

The bell tower door was open.

52

Trevor settled his flashlight's beam on the man in the center of the ringing chamber. Father Nigel flung up a hand.

Rose took in the white hooded robe that mocked the real ones. She could not resist saying, "Do you always hold services so late at night?"

The vicar shrank from the light. "What do you want?"

"We're looking for Vic Drummond," Trevor said.

"Drummond? What would he be doing here?" Nigel sounded genuinely puzzled.

"He came about the tapestry. Where is he?"

Rose wished Trevor had not mentioned the tapestry. A sly look appeared and then disappeared from the priest's face. "The tapestry?"

"Where's Drummond?"

Nigel recoiled from Trevor's harsh tone. He licked his lips.

"Where the hell is he?" Trevor repeated.

Nigel set his candle down. "This way." He opened a door. "You'll need your torch."

Rose plucked at Trevor's shirt. "Wait. Why would he be in the attic?"

Nigel gave a ponderous sigh. "Because the real tapestry's in there. The one below is a fake."

Light showed at the western end of the cavernous space over the nave—bobbing toward them. Trevor flashed his beam along the ancient catwalk before stepping inside.

"Vic?" He headed quickly toward the light. A few yards in, the light went out.

Rose climbed his heels. "Wait, Trevor. The tapestry downstairs isn't a fake."

But Trevor ignored her and continued on. "Vic?" he shouted again.

Something metal clanged behind her. She half-turned and was shoved aside. Nigel hefted a sharp metal object like a knight's lance. A tent pole.

She screamed as Nigel drove it into Trevor's back.

53

Vic heard a high pitched scream. He dashed past the choir stalls and threw himself into the bell tower. He rebounded off the narrow stone walls as he took the steps three at a time.

The ringing room was empty except for a candle on a table. The door to the attic stood open. He approached cautiously, heart racing. He climbed up the one step onto the gangway. Rose stood a few yards away, her back to him, facing Nigel. The priest wielded a metal tent pole as if he were Little John jousting Robin Hood.

"What's going on here?" Vic called, trying to sound calm.

"H-he killed Trevor," Rose said, her voice hoarse.

Vic saw his friend sprawled face down, one arm dangling over the wooden planks. His torch lay pointing toward the roof, lodged where the vaulting met the outer wall.

Anger and grief swirled through Vic. He wanted to throttle Nigel. No mercy. Just a slow, painful choking.

But Rose stood between him and Nigel.

Nigel raised his makeshift weapon. The tip looked black and wet in the light of Vic's torch.

"If you come any closer, I'll run it through her, too."

Fear for Rose nailed Vic in place. He set his torch on the gangway, lighting the man's feet and Trevor's prone body. "Put the pole down," Vic said. "Plead madness, man. You've killed a DI."

"I'm not afraid of the police."

"You should be." Vic jerked Rose back just as Nigel thrust out with the pole.

Nigel jabbed again. Vic lunged for the pole, gripped the end, but his hands slipped off the bloody end.

Nigel howled and charged him. Vic knocked the pole from Nigel's hand and took the man down. He grabbed him by the back of his robe, hauling him along to the attic door and threw him on his hands and knees in the ringing room.

Vic stared at the man in disgust for only a moment before following Rose back to where Trevor lay. He stepped over the tent pole and knelt down.

She pressed her fingers against Trevor's throat. Vic trained his torch on a black splotch the size of a dinner plate that stained his friend's back. "He's alive. What are we going to do?"

"Call 999." He leaned over Trevor and touched his cheek. Still warm. But his breathing was labored. Vic ran his hands over Trevor's pockets but couldn't find his mobile. Then he spotted it on the sloping roof, out of reach, near the torch.

"I'll go," Rose said.

"I don't want you near Nigel. Stay here."

A long arm snaked around Rose's neck and jerked her back into the shadows.

54

VIC WATCHED ROSE CLAW at the arm around her neck. The hand showing from the billowing sleeve of its white, hooded robe was leathery, desiccated, the nails long and sharp.

Vic aimed his torch at the thing's face, blinding Rose as well.

"Let her go," he said softly.

The thing's whole body shook in negation of the order. It dragged Rose backward along the gangway and over Trevor as if he didn't exist.

Rose moaned.

Vic drew out his knife. He flicked it open and lunged. His blade sliced into the back of the demon's clawed hand.

The creature tossed Rose behind itself.

Then threw back its head and howled. Its hood slid from its head. Her head.

Could he kill a female? The thought cost him valuable

seconds. The thing reached out and snatched the tent pole off the gangway. With a quick whip of the pole, the demon cracked him on the wrist. His knife flew from his hand and skittered away on the ceiling below.

Black gouts of blood poured from the demon's wound. She lifted her hand, licked at the welling blood, and laughed.

She turned and stalked after Rose who scrabbled away on her hands and knees.

Vic looked around for a weapon, envisioning Rose with the tent pole protruding from her chest. He ran back to the ringing chamber and dragged a rusty pole from the mounded tents.

He stepped lightly onto the gangway. The creature's white robe gleamed in the dim light from Trevor's torch. The gangway quivered with every step he took, but the creature ignored him.

"Damn you," Vic shouted. The demon whipped around, Rose forgotten.

They met in a clash of poles. The reverberation stung his palms. Any thought that the being's strength was related to its size disappeared as the thing rained a frenzy of blows on his pole.

One of the ceiling supports popped. Several more followed in a gun-fire rapid series of clangs. The gangway swayed, throwing them off-balance.

The demonic creature slashed his legs, taking them out from under him. Their poles clanged together as they spun out into the shadows.

The creature lifted its head and snarled. At Rose. Rose coming to help him.

"No," he shouted.

Rose hesitated then turned away.

He remembered the words on his computer. Remembered the clawed hand that ripped Rose's spine.

He roared with anguish and grabbed for the demon's robe. He caught the loose fabric in his fist and hung on. The demon dragged him along, straining against the fabric, clawing at Rose's retreating figure. The back of Rose's T-shirt parted. Her skin gleamed white in the dark space.

Vic flung himself backward and took the demon with him.

55

ROSE SOBBED AND DRAGGED herself upright by the gangway railing. It quivered and shook as Vic and the demon wrestled each other.

She had no weapon. Nothing.

Another metal support separated from the ceiling. Every step pitched the gangway like the deck of a ship.

The thing tossed Vic over the rail as if he weighed nothing. He landed on a protruding boss. And lay still.

The demon turned on her. It lifted its clawed hand and licked at the blood that dripped from its long fingers.

Rose backed away, one step at a time, the creature mirroring her every move on the trembling gangway until Rose felt the cold stone wall against her bare back.

Trevor's torch lit the side of the creature's face. Its expression shifted. The priestly robe clung to a shape that was human . . . but not. Rose recognized the creature within and cried out.

The light from the ringing chamber door silhouetted the

being as it shifted, altered, showed its face and then meta-
morphosed back to its demonic form.

And the light threw a nimbus around Vic as he hauled
himself to his feet. He half crawled, half walked up the
vaulted ceiling toward the gangway.

Hope filled her. He had the griffin spirit. He'd save her.
But he needed time. There was no one, nothing between the
demon and her now. It reached out and stroked her hair. The
scent of rotting filled Rose's nostrils.

Vic scaled the railing. It swung and the creature looked
back. But he looked harmless, blood spreading around the
fingers he held to his side.

He headed toward them, limping slowly, so slowly she
knew he would never reach her in time.

The demonic creature grabbed her throat and shook her,
thumping her head against the wall. Rose clawed at the
hands, scrabbled for a purchase on the leathery flesh and
kicked hard.

There was a sudden clang of metal on metal. A slap like
stone on grass. Her captor howled and released her.

Rose gasped for air as the thing whipped around.

And forgot her.

Vic stood a fair distance away. The thing charged him.

He lifted his arm as if pitching a ball.

The demon went down with an unearthly howl, a clawed
hand to her head. Vic hung on the railing. The demon rolled
to her feet and hissed.

He remained in place, one arm wrapped around a support rod.

Rose leaped onto the thing's back and pummeled its head.
It shrieked and swung in a circle. And threw her off.

Vic lifted his arm again in a slow lazy sweep. Whatever he
threw hit the demon with a sickly smack. It staggered and
went over the side.

Rose ran to Vic and threw her arms around him. "Hurry,
it's all going to fall."

More supports popped like rivets on a ship's plates.

She watched in horror as a crack appeared around the

creature's body where it lay spread-eagle on the sloping nave below.

The crack starred out like rays of the sun.

"Say a prayer," Vic whispered.

And she did.

With a terrible groan, the ceiling beneath gave way.

56

TREVOR CRIED OUT IN pain as Rose and Vic lifted him to his feet. "We have to get out of here. This is all coming down," Rose said.

The gangway swung violently as pieces of the ceiling broke around the gaping hole and crashed to the stone floor below in billowing clouds of plaster and splintered wood.

Rose helped Vic support Trevor through the ringing chamber and down the bell tower steps.

At the foot, the floor was strewn with ancient timbers and chunks of plaster. Amidst it all lay a human form, though the pool of blood surrounded a head not quite that of a woman.

All was now still. But not silent.

In the sanctuary, the monks still chanted their prayers, the candles still illuminated the gilded altar screen and the weeping mold on the tapestry wall.

"Let me go." Trevor pulled from Vic's grip. "I can walk."

They went cautiously to the edge of the aisle where the broken body laid.

"What is it?" Trevor asked.

"Mary Garner. But not Mary," Rose whispered.

The look Trevor shot her made her realize he'd been unconscious through most of it. She shuddered when he patted along the thing's garments and plucked something white from the robes.

A handkerchief with tiny flowers embroidered at the hem.

Vic put his arm around Rose's shoulder. His squeeze told her to be silent. "You'll have to ask the archdeacon for its official name."

She did not believe people could be so evil they turned into demons. Her sanity required she believe there might be demons masquerading as humans.

"The question is, what will we do with it?" Vic said.

"We?" Trevor put out a hand so Vic could help him up. His face was pale and the hand Vic clasped shook.

"Where's Nigel?" She would never again use the appellation of Father for the man.

"Long gone, I imagine. Certainly he's not fetching the police. Nor are we. They're already here."

Trevor took the arm Vic offered him. "Let me think."

"Don't take too long. We've an evil tapestry to shift before dawn."

MRS. BENNETT GAZED OUT of the bow window of Stitches at the empty street. It was her favorite time of night. Or had she not better say day?

She admired the outline of her lovely church tower. She frowned. It was not the dawn peeking through the tower windows, but a light.

Where none should be.

"You'll be the death of me, Nigel. What a pest you are."

TREVOR DID LITTLE MORE than get in the way as they took the demon to Lady Agnes's crypt.

Trevor collapsed onto a stone step and winced. "I shall simply say it's my blood. If they don't believe I fell through the hole, the hell with them. Shit, I'm dizzy."

"DNA?" Vic asked.

"Why should they test the blood? I'm at least a pint down. Worse comes to worse, we confess and let the pathologists decide what that thing was."

Rose checked Trevor's pulse while Vic waited with the cart and its gruesome burden. "His heart's still beating."

"So he's malingering?" Vic said.

Rose started at his tone. "No, he's almost unconscious. What's with you? He's helped when he should be in the emergency ward."

"I'm not malingering," Trevor retorted. "Just gathering my strength for the lies I'll have to tell. Your archdeacon will have to come up with some story that covers Nigel. I'm out on that one."

They put their shoulders to the coffin lid, but it barely moved.

"May I help?"

They stared up at the man who stood on the crypt steps. Blood stained his hands. Tear tracks marked his face.

"Why not?" Vic straightened. "You've shifted Lady Agnes before, haven't you?"

"For her." The words were whispered.

"Then get over here and be useful," Trevor said.

Nigel scrabbled sideways to avoid Vic. Vic's body radiated an anger so tangible, Rose feared he might toss the man in with Mary when the time came.

And wasn't sure it would be wrong. Had the man killed Donald? Was he even a man?

The four of them put their shoulders to Lady Agnes's coffin lid. It took all of their combined strength to shift the slab of stone. Rose wondered who else had helped when Joan had been laid to rest.

When the deed was done, and Rose helped Vic hump the cart up the steps, she imagined they'd moved the lid only because so much adrenalin ran in their veins. It was like those stories you read where someone lifted a car in an accident and saved a victim pinned underneath.

Nigel sank to the floor beneath the clingy strands of mold and wept. Vic grabbed him by the collar of his hooded robe and dragged him to the choir stalls and flung him among the ghostly monks. Nigel sprawled there on his knees, weeping. "Can't see them can you, you bloody bastard."

"Vic! Leave him. We have a job to do." Rose indicated the tapestry. "Dawn's only a few minutes away."

They looked up at the windows that now showed clearly against the dark stone. Vic abandoned Nigel and with not much less violence, hauled Trevor to where she stood.

"Anticlimactic, this is," Trevor said. Vic lifted one end of the tapestry, and with Trevor and Rose's help, heaved it onto the waiting cart. "Feels positively light compared to Lady Agnes's lid."

They half pushed, half dragged, the tapestry down the nave, one eye on the gaping black hole overhead.

"I should have taken Nigel back up there and thrown him through that damned hole."

"Vic. Stop it."

"Yeah, shut up." Trevor's voice sounded distant. Rose wondered how long it would be before he collapsed.

They shifted rows of chairs to make a path past the roof wreckage. Nigel's wails formed an eerie counterpoint to the rhythmic chant of the monks and the thump of the cart as it passed over the gravestones of the dead.

"You disobeyed me," Vic said to Rose when they got through the door and onto the porch.

"What did you throw at her?"

"Rolls of coins. I pinched them from the fete. I'm quite good at cricket." He put his arm around her neck and pressed his mouth to her brow.

The sudden contrast of mood reminded her they were not yet shed of their burden.

They eased Trevor down onto a porch step. The entire

back of his T-shirt was wet with blood. He needed a hospital. Soon.

"Vic, come quick." Rose waved him back to the church doors.

No chants filled the stone edifice. No ghostly figures sat in the choir stalls. None filed down the aisles. All was silent. Still.

"The monks are gone," he said.

"So's Nigel."

57

They unrolled the tapestry on the church lawn. The viscous mold on the back stuck to Vic's hands. He scrubbed them on the wet grass as they started to sting.

Vic had wanted to get the tapestry as far away from All Saints as possible, to the meadow, but the cart sank into the soft grass and finally, would move not one inch farther. And they were too exhausted to do more.

Trevor slumped over a marble bench. Even in the pre-dawn dark, Trevor was as white as paper.

Vic reached into his pocket. "Bloody hell." He pulled out his vial of holy water. It was cracked.

And empty.

"The archdeacon said if the damned thing was . . . well, damned, the holy water would destroy it. Now what?"

"Oh, my God. I completely forgot about the holy water. I still have mine." She held up the Vitamin E vial.

He had left it for her. *Just in case.*

He looked from her little vial and his to the huge expanse of tapestry.

"Now I understand why you were so angry in there. You were unprotected." She tried to hand off her vial.

He couldn't have her unprotected.

"Hang on to it. I'll just make a call on the baptismal font."

But when he cranked the ornate hood up, the font was scaly from water long evaporated.

He returned empty-handed.

"It's okay," she said. "Put it to good use." She pressed the small Vitamin E bottle into his palm.

He smiled and kissed her forehead, then gently outlined the great ugly bruise on her cheek. "Pray this will be enough."

58

Vic SPRINKLED THE TAPESTRY with a few drops of holy water. Rose cried out when the fabric sizzled as if touched with acid.

The holy water ate away at the ancient threads, crept along the warp and weft of evil.

The smoky tendrils met a knight's lance and ignited. Another section burst into flame—the rope that had once been cording on a lady's glove.

A shriek rent the air. Mrs. Bennett ran up the lane. She halted a few feet away. Horror bloomed on her face as realization struck. Her life's work was being consumed.

Slowly, she turned on him. Her lips quivered. "You'll die. You'll roast in hell and eat the rotting flesh of your mother," she screamed.

As she hurled her threats, the wind rose. It beat in the branches, hammered against their bodies, whipped the embers to race along the paths of evil stitched over thirty years.

Mrs. Bennett stomped on flames, hurling curses at his head.

"She'll burn," Rose said.

"It's her choice," Vic said.

Rose dodged the paths of the flames and grabbed Mrs. Bennett's arm.

Any thought the seamstress was a weak old woman vaporized along with the flames she stamped out. She clamped her hands on Rose's wrists and shook her like a rag doll. "Put it out. Put it out or I swear by the power I serve, you will burn with me."

Rose's face contorted with pain as Mrs. Bennett twisted her arms until she knelt. Vic put one foot on the tapestry.

Mrs. Bennett pointed at him. "Stay back."

He lunged for her, but couldn't move a muscle. An invisible wall stood between him and the woman he loved.

Flames crept toward her.

He was frozen, every muscle paralyzed.

Not good enough. Not good enough to fight it.

"Isn't it me you want?" he shouted. The creeping flames climbed the voluptuous lilies, leaping from pistil to stamen. He stood with one foot in their path and could do nothing.

"You!" Mrs. Bennett spat. "You could have ruled with us. You made your choice." She bent to Rose, her wrinkled face contorted with malevolent fury. "Put it out."

"Let her go," Vic shouted. "She can't do it. Only I can do it. I swear it. Just let her go."

For a moment he thought Mrs. Bennett did not hear him. A flame licked at his shoe. The seamstress turned and with a smile, flung Rose away as if she were a sack of flour. Rose stumbled off the tapestry onto the blessed flame-free grass.

Vic took a step. And another. The flames leaped to the final flower. He stood in a ring of fire. And so did Mrs. Bennett.

In the distance, he heard shouting. Screams.

Within the circle of hatred and evil, he felt only calm.

"Did you kill Alice?" he asked.

"I struck her down as surely as I'll strike you if you don't stop it." Mrs. Bennett spun and turned as the flames raced along the tapestry. "Stop it. Stop it," she chanted.

"I am stopping it. Now." He held up the small vial of holy water.

He swept out his hand and watched a stream of water, a stream so thin it looked like a silver thread, arch through the air and entwine her.

59

THE TAPESTRY WAS A mass of flames. Inhuman screams rent the air. Sirens, shouting, moans filled Rose's ears. Her moans.

"Vic." A terrible pain clutched her middle.

She fell to her knees.

The conflagration gleamed through her tears, but she couldn't look away. Couldn't blot out the sounds of something demonic returning to the fire.

And Vic. She moaned.

A dark form burst from the inferno. He walked straight toward her, silhouetted by smoke and flame. She leaped to her feet and threw herself into his arms, swatted the cinders that glowed in his clothing and hair.

Vic took it for a moment before he wrapped her up. She buried her face against his chest. She had to hear his heart beat to believe he was alive.

Police, fire, rescue vehicles drew up, but she remained where she was, in the safe circle of Vic's arms.

Wind lifted scraps of wool and silk and danced them overhead. Burning embers gilded their edges.

And as they drifted away, a pang of fear twisted her gut. Where would they alight?

60

ROSE FOLLOWED THE FLAGSTONE path to the back of Vic's cottage and found him in the garden. He wore his grubby jeans, but had not put a T-shirt over his bandages and burn dressings. For a long moment, she basked in the pleasure of watching him move. She pulled her camera from her backpack and focused on the stretch of his muscles, the line of his profile.

"Ruining the topiaries, again?" she asked.

"Doing my best. Did you get your plane ticket?"

"Yes. I'm taking Joan's ashes home tonight."

"Are you sure you want to do this alone?"

"I'm sure."

"But you'll be back next week, won't you?"

"I promise." She took another picture for her private collection. A head and shoulders shot this time. She'd put it next to the black and white. "Nell heard the diocese has found a benefactor willing to finance the repair of the nave ceiling."

"Yeah. I think he'll probably repair the transept as well. Put in a few memorial windows."

"Do you think Trevor will be all right?" He and Vic had gone straight to the hospital, but Trevor had remained.

"Physically, yes. And Keeling will help him through this—and us. But as long as the constabulary thinks this was a book publicity stunt gone wrong, we'll be in the shit. Thank God for lawyers."

"No, just thank God. And PC Alden is still my FLO until they close Donald's case, so we have one ally. Now, turn into the sun a bit more, will you?"

He sheathed his clippers in his back pocket. She took another series of photographs, zeroing in on his chest, recording his injuries. She needed proof and it lay in the stitches, the burns, the singed eyebrow, the patch of hair missing over his left ear.

And in what was no longer there for the camera to record.

When she finished, she held the camera to her chest. "We saw what we saw, didn't we?"

"Stop fretting. Keeling's sure Mrs. Bennett used her tapestry to slowly turn the congregation to the dark side. They sat in full view of it for years."

"I think that was why Joan died. She saw what no one else did."

"Alice as well."

"We can't completely blame Nigel and Donald. They preached beside it every day."

Vic looked up at the square tower of the church. "Blame's a bit hard to set aside."

"What happened to Nigel?"

"I think the monks are . . . re-educating him."

"He did help us in the end."

"He tried to kill Trevor. It's just luck that pole missed vital organs."

She put her camera away. "I'm just glad the tapestry's gone."

He smoothed her hair from her face. "Promise me that when you marry me, there will be no tapestries in our house."

"Not one." She frowned. "What about the . . . things in London?"

"The archdeacon's on it. You'll have to trust him. There's no one better."

She kissed Vic between bruises. His skin was sun warm and she thought her world would be empty without him until she returned.

"I love you. You risked your life for Trevor. And for me." A flood of emotion filled her. "In the end, you turned out not to be such a bad guy."

"And you're not bad for a Yank."

"How do we explain this?" She put her hand over his heart. The skin beneath her palm was smooth and unblemished. They had mental wounds that might not heal so well, but the scratches Vic had called stigmata had disappeared.

"I don't try."

He traced the edge of her cheek. She felt the touch somewhere deep inside her.

"I've forty-one stitches to show for my efforts."

"Are you sure there aren't forty-two?"

He wrapped his arm around her waist. "You could count them."

"Only if you promise we can lie here in the sun, on the grass, while we do it."

"I knew you wore this lovely yellow dress for a purpose. I'll fetch a daisy."

He plucked a large Gerbera daisy from a basket of flowers on the patio table, a "get well" token from the regulars at the Pig and Pie. She settled on the grass and arranged her hem a scant inch from where she knew Vic would want to plant the flower.

He stretched out at her side, his grin a touch lop-sided from the swelling along his jaw line. He stroked the daisy up her thigh.

"So, Rosie, do you believe now?"

"In love? Absolutely."

Warprize

by Elizabeth Vaughan
0-765-35264-8 $6.99 ($7.99 CAN)

"Xylara, the Warlord has named his terms for peace." Xymund did not turn. He made his announcement as he stood looking out the window. His hands tightened around one another. I looked over at General Warren, who grimaced, and looked down at the floor.

"That is good to hear, Your Majesty." I swallowed, sensing a problem. "Are they acceptable?"

Xymund still did not turn. "I and my nobles are to swear fealty to him. The kingdom will remain under my control and the taxes and tithes that are to be paid are reasonable. All prisoners and wounded, if there are any, will be exchanged." There was a bitterness in his tone. Maybe because they had more of our men then we had of theirs. Xymund continued. "But he has claimed tribute."

My brother's gaze remained fixed on the horizon. My fears for a peace grew. If the Warlord claimed something of Xymund's, his pride would forbid acceptance of the terms.

"What does he claim?" I took a step toward Xymund. Still, he did not turn. I looked around, but no one would meet my eyes.

At last, General Warren drew a breath. "You," he cleared his throat. "He claims you as tribute."

. . . coming from Tor Romance in June 2005

The Dare

by Susan Kearney
0-765-35192-7 $6.99 ($7.99 CAN)

Inhaling the scent of his tangy breath, Dora savored the fact that Zical was coming to her in his own rough-hewn fashion. Ah, this was one of the reasons she'd so much wanted to be human, to experience the senses that fed the emotions that—

His lips caressed hers. He took his time, and the warmth of his mouth raked hers, heat slipping and sliding into her core, raising her temperature until a fever raged and erotic shivers trembled down her spine.

She parted her lips, welcoming his tongue and the taste of full-bodied masculine heat. Until now she hadn't understood how she could feel fire and ice together, in the same moment. She hadn't believed that every last sizzling cell in her body could be electrified by such a kiss, or how that energy could wrap her in a sensual cocoon of crisp and tangy desire. She hadn't understood that one kiss would make her want so much more.

Kissing Zical was like all the stars in the universe shining on her at once. Dora glowed from the inside out with a happy, uncontainable thrill that she would never forget. She wound her hands around his head, threaded her fingers into his thick dark hair, pressed her chest against his and reveled in the richly-textured sensations of humanity.

She, who had spent her life in a parched desert of circuitry, was drowning in lustrous, gleaming, torrid . . . life.

. . . coming in July 2005 from Tor Romance

Moon's Web

by Cathy Clamp & C. T. Adams
0-765-34914-0 $6.99 ($7.99 CAN)

Sue came out of the kitchen, favoring the leg that the little were-brat had bitten. I wanted to reach for her and bury my face in her shoulder-length auburn hair. She used to have honey-blonde curls, but we'd both made a change to match our new identities. I can't seem to remember my life before I met her, but we've only known each other four months.

I stared at her. Sue isn't gorgeous, but she's pretty. Her heart-shaped face compliments a well curved body. She'd dropped some weight after a recent coma, when we could only feed her through tubes. She was looking damn good anyway, and I let my eyes reflect the thought. She caught me watching and blushed. I still think it's cute when she does that.

I breathed in her scent as she walked toward me. Rain-kissed plants and warm rich earth from a forest in summer mingled with the baked cinnamon smell of love. I would never get enough of her scent.

"Sue, let me see your leg." The words cut through the cloud of her scent. Bobby's voice was the sharp command of a cop. Of course, Bobby *is* a cop. He's part of Wolven, the law enforcement branch of the Sazi. Call him double-o python. All agents of the organization have a license to kill. They're the nastiest of the nasty of each of the Sazi species. It's their duty to *permanently* remove from the gene pool any were-animal who breaks felony human laws or any of the big Sazi laws. Can't have a shape shifter locked up in jail during a full moon. The humans would find out we exist.

That is the ultimate rule of the Sazi: Keep our existence secret from the humans.

. . . coming in August 2005 from Tor Romance